EDCO
HISTORY
REVISE WISE

GW00646508

LEAVING CERTIFICATE ORDINARY AND HIGHER LEVEL

M.E. Collins

Edco
The Educational Company of Ireland

Contents

Notes for Later Modern Ireland: Topic 2, Movements for Political and Social Reform can be downloaded from www.edco.ie/LCHistory

Introduction

This book will be a great aid to you as you revise for the history examination. The chapters are laid out in bullet point form which is an easy way to recall vital information. In this book, you will also find a Study Plan which will help you to plan your work coming up to the examination.

How to use your Study Plan

It is very important to organise regular revision to make sure you do not leave it all to the last minute. By using the study plan you can make sure you cover all the key topics before the examination.

- You can use this plan for weekend or daily revision.
- Do not fill in more than you feel you will achieve.
- Set yourself a fixed amount of time each day or each weekend for completing what you have set out to do.
- As you complete each task that you have set yourself, tick it off. This will make you feel that you have made progress.
- If you fall behind in your plan, don't give up! Start again!

The Study Plan is on page 281.

Layout of Topics

In the Later Modern History Field of Study, there are 12 Topics, six from Irish history and six from the history of Europe and the Wider World. Every year, one of these topics is pre-nominated by the Examination Commission to be examined through documents. All students must study the pre-nominated Topic and any three other Topics chosen from the 12.

In this book we include the following Topics:

> Later Modern Ireland Topic 3: The pursuit of sovereignty and the impact of partition, 1912-1949
>
> Later Modern Ireland Topic 5: Politics and Society in Northern Ireland, 1949-1993
>
> Later Modern Europe and the Wider World Topic 3: Dictatorship and Democracy in Europe, 1920-1945
>
> Later Modern Europe and the Wider World Topic 6: The United States and the World, 1945-1989

All topics follow the same format and are examined through three perspectives:

- Politics and Administration.
- Society and Economy.
- Culture, Science and Religion.

Each perspective contains a Case Study. There are also 'key personalities' – that is people who play an important role in events. Exam questions are often drawn from case studies or refer to key personalities.

Preparing for the Examination

All students, both Ordinary and Higher Level, must do a Research Study. It can be drawn from any period of history up to 1990. Students submit the result of their work, the Research Study Report (RSR) in April before they sit the examination. The RSR is worth 20 per cent of their final result.

The remaining 80 per cent comes from the examination in June. It is important to familiarise yourself with the paper. Know what to expect from each section on the paper and make sure to have a bank of essays completed on your chosen Topics. You should also work on your timing for the examination. Divide the amount of time the examination lasts by the number of questions you have to answer and practise writing all essays within that time.

Structure of the Higher Level (HL) Paper

Your paper will have three sections.

Section 1 is a Documentary Question drawn from the Pre-nominated Topic you have studied. It will be drawn from one of the Case Studies. You will be given two sources, either written or visual and the questions on them will be divided as follows:

Sections	Explanation	Marks	
(a)	Comprehension	You will be expected to answer questions that show you understand the source.	20%
(b)	Comparison	Here you will be asked to compare or note differences between the two sources.	20%
(c)	Criticism	This section may ask you to detect bias, propaganda, opinions or to make judgments about the reliability of the sources.	20%
(d)	Contextualisation	Here you will be asked to show that you know the historical background to the documents by writing a short essay.	40%

As most marks go for part (d) it is very important that you understand the background to each of the Case Studies you have prepared. You should write about one and a half pages.

Do not spend too long on the Document question because you still have three essays to write on:
- Section 2 – your chosen Topics from Ireland
- Section 3 – your chosen Topics from Europe and the Wider World

In each of these you will be given four essay titles and must choose one to write about. You have about 35 minutes for each essay.

Structure of the Ordinary Level (OL) Paper

The OL paper has two parts, Section 1 is compulsory and is a documents-based question. You will be given two documents, written or visual, drawn from one of the Case Studies in the Pre-nominated Topic that you have studied.

You will be asked four questions on them.
(a)   asks you about the content of the documents (40 marks)
(b)   asks you to compare the two documents (20 marks)
(c)   asks you to judge if the documents are reliable or biased (20 marks)
(d)   asks you to write about the background to the documents (20 marks)

Do not spend too long on this section as you have three more to do.

Next you must look for the questions on the three other Topics you have studied. It is very important to know the names of your chosen Topics as doing the wrong one can lead to failure.

The questions on each Topic are divided into (a), (b) and (c).
- For (a) you are given a visual source or a short document and asked questions about it. This is worth 30 marks.
- For (b) you have to write a short paragraph which is also worth 30 marks.
- For (c) you answer a question. This is worth 40 marks.
- (b) and (c) are usually based on Case studies or Key Personalities.

Note the timing recommended for each part and practice answering questions within that timeframe.

Later Modern Ireland   Topic 3
The Pursuit of Sovereignty and the Impact of Partition 1912–1949

1.1 Ireland in the United Kingdom

- In 1800, the **Act of Union** made Ireland part of the **United Kingdom of Great Britain and Ireland (UK)**
- Laws and taxes for Ireland were decided in the Westminster parliament in London:
  - Irish voters elected **103 MPs** to the House of Commons
  - The English, Scots and Welsh elected 550 MPs
  - Ireland had more than its fair share of MPs, but British MPs always outnumbered Irish MPs. That meant that Irish interests always had to take second place to British interests
- The leader of the biggest party in the Commons became **Prime Minister** of the UK. He appointed his followers as Ministers
- The two Ministers for Ireland were the **Lord Lieutenant** and the **Chief Secretary**. They were responsible for the Royal Irish Constabulary (RIC/police), the civil service, the courts, education, transport, etc.

Unionists and nationalists

- Since the 1870s, Irish people had been divided about whether it was good or bad for Ireland to be part of the UK
- **Unionists** thought **Ireland gained** from being in the **United Kingdom**, which was then the greatest power in the world. They wanted to **keep the union** between Britain and Ireland
- **Nationalists** thought it would be better for **Ireland** to have its **own parliament** that could make **laws suited to Irish conditions**.

1.2 Who were the unionists?

- About 25% of Irish people were unionists. Although in a small minority over the whole of Ireland, they formed a majority in the four northeastern counties (**Antrim, Down, Armagh** and **Derry**)
- There were several reasons why a person might be a unionist:
  - **Religious**: Most Irish Protestants were unionist. In the whole UK, Protestants were a majority but in Ireland, they were only 25% of the population. **If Ireland had its own parliament, Protestants would be heavily outnumbered** and they feared they would suffer discrimination or persecution. They felt safer in the UK where they were part of the majority

○ **Ethnic**: Many unionists were descendants of British people who settled in Ireland in 16th and 17th centuries. They **felt British as well as Irish** and wanted to remain part of the British state where they felt at home

○ **Economic/social**:

   – Most owners of big businesses (e.g. Guinness, Jacobs' or Harland and Wolfe) were unionists. They sold what they produced to Britain and feared an Irish parliament would interfere with trade between the two countries

   – In the **north-east of Ulster**, the economy prospered after 1860, while other parts of Ireland declined. There were many jobs in the linen and shipbuilding industries. Protestants, who were in a majority in the north-east, did especially well. They feared that would change if Ireland left the United Kingdom.

The Unionist Party: Carson and Craig

● In the 1910 general election most unionists voted for the **Unionist Party**, led by **Edward Carson** and **James Craig**. It won 18 seats in Westminster. Two MPs were elected for Trinity College in Dublin and the rest for north-east Ulster

● Their aim was to keep Ireland in the United Kingdom.

1.3 Who were the nationalists?

● About 75% of Irish people were **nationalists**. They wanted Ireland to have a parliament which would decide on Irish laws and taxes

● A person might be a nationalist because of:

   ○ **Religion**: Most nationalists were Catholics, who made up 75% of the population. They felt the predominantly Protestant UK discriminated against them. They wanted to run their own affairs

   ○ **Ethnic identity**: Most nationalists **felt Irish**, **not British**. They wanted Ireland to be run by Irish people, not by British people

   ○ **Economics**: Outside of east Ulster, the Irish economy had declined since the Act of Union in 1800. Through the 19th century Ireland experienced famine, poverty, and emigration. Nationalists felt they could do a better job of managing the Irish economy than the British had.

Divided nationalists

● Nationalists were divided into two opposing camps – moderate and extreme. They differed in **their aims** and in **the means** they would use to achieve those aims.

Moderate/constitutional nationalists (Home Rulers)

- Most nationalists were **moderate** or **constitutional**
- They aimed to persuade the British to give Ireland a **parliament with power over local issues** like health and transport. But the Westminster parliament would still control international affairs like trade or war. This limited form of independence was called **Home Rule**
- Constitutional nationalists disliked violence. They hoped to **win Home Rule by peaceful and lawful means** (i.e. by winning elections and votes in parliament)
- In the 1910 general election, constitutional nationalists voted for the **Irish Party** (usually called the **Home Rule Party**). It was led by **John Redmond** and **John Dillon**. The Home Rulers won 85 of the 103 Irish seats in Westminster.

Extreme nationalists (republicans/separatists)

- A small minority of nationalists wanted to **cut all ties** between Ireland and Britain and have a **completely separate** and **independent** Irish state, perhaps a republic. They were called 'separatists' or 'republicans'
- Separatists believed that Britain would never listen to the moderate requests for Home Rule. Only violence, they thought, would force the British to give Ireland independence
- Some of them belonged to a secret society, the **Irish Republican Brotherhood (IRB)**, whose members took an oath to fight for an Irish republic. The IRB was led by an elected **Supreme Council**
- After 1900, extreme nationalism gained increased support. An important reason for this was development of cultural nationalism.

Cultural nationalism

- All through the 19ᵗʰ century, the Irish population had become **anglicised** (like the English). By the 1890s, most Irish people spoke English, read English books and newspapers and played English games. This undermined their claim to be different from the other people of the UK
- **Cultural nationalists** tried to reverse anglicisation by developing aspects of Irish life where the Irish were different from the English. They set up:
  - The **Gaelic Athletic Association (GAA)** to develop distinctively Irish sports and games played according to Irish rules. The IRB used GAA clubs as a cover for recruiting and drilling. The RIC always spied on them
  - The **Gaelic League** to reverse the decline of the Irish language. Many of the people who joined it like **Patrick Pearse** and **Eamon de Valera** were drawn towards republicanism because they believed only an Irish government could protect and revive Irish. In 1915, republicans

changed the constitution of the League to make it support complete separation from Britain

- The **Anglo-Irish Literary movement** tried to develop a distinctively Irish literature in English. Poets, like **W B Yeats**, and playwrights, like **Lady Gregory** and **J M Synge**, included Irish myths, place names and folklore in their work. Many of the leading people in it were Protestants, which made other nationalists suspicious of them. It had far less impact on Irish nationalists than the Gaelic League and the GAA.

The revival of the IRB

- Between the 1880s and 1900, the IRB declined. It was revived after 1900 due to:
  - ○ A new interest in republicanism after 1898, the centenary of the 1798 rebellion and Wolfe Tone, the first Irish republican
  - ○ The impact of the cultural revival
  - ○ The activities of a number of enthusiastic young men who joined after 1900. They included **Bulmer Hobson**, a Belfast Quaker and **Seán MacDiarmada** from Leitrim, who used his job as organiser for the Gaelic League to recruit young men into the IRB
  - ○ In 1907, **Thomas Clarke**, who had been in the IRB since the 1880s, returned to Ireland from the US. He joined the younger men in taking control of the IRB Supreme Council
- Fearing spies and leaks, they kept the new IRB small. To compensate for that they infiltrated other organisations like the GAA and the Gaelic League with the aim of making them support republicanism
- The Home Rule crisis of 1912–1914 (see below) gave them their chance to acquire an army by setting up the Irish Volunteers.

A new nationalist party: Sinn Féin

- Cultural nationalism also influenced **Arthur Griffith** (see page 18). He started a small newspaper called *United Irishman* in 1898. In it, he published articles on politics and economics, as well as supporting the GAA and the Gaelic League
- In 1905 Griffith set up a new political movement called **Sinn Féin**. Its aims were:
  - ○ To elect MPs who **would not go** to Westminster. Instead they would set up an Irish parliament and government to replace the British government **peacefully**
  - ○ To satisfy unionists who wanted a link with Britain, Griffith said Sinn Féin would look for a **dual monarchy** like in **Austria-Hungary** (i.e. the King would be Head of State in **both** Ireland **and** Britain, although the two countries would be otherwise separate)
  - ○ Develop Irish industry behind tariff barriers

- Griffith changed the name of his paper to *Sinn Féin* and used it to spread his ideas.

1905–1916: The 'first' Sinn Féin Party

- At first, Sinn Féin attracted cultural nationalists and Home Rulers who were fed up because the British government would not give Home Rule
- But most of them went back to the Home Rule Party after a political crisis in Britain in 1910 suddenly made Home Rule possible
- Griffith went on preaching his ideas. He won few followers, but gradually the name **Sinn Féin** became associated with extreme nationalists
- When IRB men staged the 1916 rising, many people called it a "Sinn Féin rising", even though Sinn Féin had nothing to do with it. This led to a second and very different Sinn Féin Party appearing in 1917.

Questions

For Examination questions on Later Modern Ireland, Topic 3 see page 275.

Your revision notes

Home Rule delayed 1900-1910

- In 1891, the Home Rule Party split over the divorce of Parnell's lover, Katherine O'Shea. After ten years of in-fighting it re-united in 1900 under the leadership of **John Redmond** and **John Dillon**
- They had an alliance with the **British Liberal Party**, but up to 1905 the pro-unionist **Conservatives** were in power so there was no chance of Home Rule
- Nationalist hopes rose when the Liberals won a huge victory in 1906. But the Liberal leaders told Redmond they would not bring in a Home Rule Bill because the Conservative-dominated **House of Lords** would veto it. Instead, the Liberals concentrated on social reforms like old age pensions. Redmond could do nothing about this because the Liberals did not need his votes
- Events between 1909 and 1911 opened the way for Home Rule:
  - In 1909, the Lords defeated a budget for the first time in 200 years. This caused a constitutional crisis in Britain
  - In 1911, the **Parliament Act replaced the Lords' veto** with a delaying power of **two years**
  - In two general elections in 1910 the Liberals lost seats. After that they had to depend on the votes of Redmond's MPs to stay in power. To secure these votes, the Liberal Prime Minister **Herbert Asquith** promised Home Rule
- 1912: Asquith introduced the **third Home Rule Bill**. It offered Ireland a **very limited** measure of self-government. It passed the Commons but was defeated in the Lords. However under the Parliament Act, it was due to pass finally in 1914.

Unionists oppose Home Rule

- The prospect of Home Rule horrified unionists. Led by **Edward Carson** and **James Craig**, they planned to stop it.
  - They organised public meetings and demonstrations all over Ulster and Britain to rally opposition to Home Rule. The biggest was the mass signing of the **Solemn League and Covenant** on 28 September, 1912. 400,000 men promised to use '*any means*' to stop Home Rule
  - In 1911, groups of unionists began to arm and drill. Fearing that they would discredit the Unionist cause by uncontrolled violence, Carson organised them into the **Ulster Volunteer Force** in 1913. By 1914,

they numbered about 100,000. With many wealthy supporters, they collected £1 million to buy arms in Germany. A large shipment was smuggled in at **Larne** in April 1914

- ○ Carson and Craig also set up a "Provisional government" to take control in Ulster when Home Rule passed
- Although the last actions were illegal, the Conservative leader, **Bonar Law**, and many in the British ruling class, enthusiastically supported the unionists
- Many officers in the British army were also unionists. In March 1914, some of them resigned rather than obey an order to disarm the UVF (the '**Curragh mutiny**'). After that it was impossible for Asquith to use the British army against the UVF.

1913–1914: Discussing partition

- At first Asquith and Redmond believed the unionists were bluffing. They pointed out that only 18 Irish MPs were Unionists compared with 85 Home Rulers
- But as unionist opposition became clearer and as the UVF gained strength, leading British Liberals like **David Lloyd George** and **Winston Churchill** insisted that they negotiate with Carson
- Secret talks went on through 1913 and 1914 about 'special treatment' for the north-east of Ireland where unionists were in a majority
- First Redmond offered them a Belfast parliament under Dublin control. Carson rejected this. He wrote that there was: '*A desire to settle on the terms of leaving "Ulster" out*'
- This pointed to **partition**. Ireland would be divided (**partitioned**) into two parts:
  - ○ Most of the island would have Home Rule
  - ○ But part of Ulster would remain in the UK, under British rule
- The question then emerged of how much of Ulster would remain in the United Kingdom?
  - ○ Traditional Ulster has **nine** counties. They were divided almost equally (49% Catholic and 51% Protestant). Carson did not want all nine counties because a small change in population would mean the unionists losing control
  - ○ Four counties – **Antrim**, **Derry**, **Down** and **Armagh** – had large Protestant majorities. Early on, Redmond accepted that he would have to give these up
  - ○ Three counties – **Donegal**, **Cavan** and **Monaghan** – had large Catholic majorities. Early on in the negotiations, Carson made it clear that he did not want these counties
  - ○ But two counties – **Fermanagh** and **Tyrone** – were more evenly divided, with small Catholic majorities. Each side wanted them.

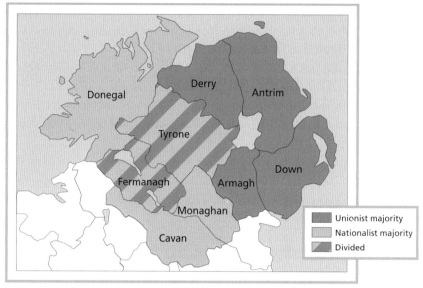

The whole province of Ulster in 1914

Nationalists set up the Irish National Volunteers

- Nationalists were angry when they heard that partition was being discussed.
- The IRB saw an opportunity to create an army like the UVF
- Bulmer Hobson suggested that **Eoin MacNeill** (one of the founders of the Gaelic League), write an article, "***The North Began***", for the League's paper, *An Claidheamh Soluis*
- MacNeill said that if the unionists could form an army to stop Home Rule, then nationalists must do the same to defend it
- In November 1913, the **Irish National Volunteers** were set up at a meeting in Dublin. MacNeill was elected Commander-in-Chief, but many other officers were members of the IRB
- By **June** 1914, the Irish Volunteers had enrolled 200,000 men
- Redmond was alarmed at the growth of a nationalist movement he did not control. He demanded the right to nominate 25 members of the governing council. Rather than split the Volunteers, MacNeill agreed
- In **July**, the IRB landed guns from Germany at **Howth**.

Threat of civil war

- There were now two large private armies in Ireland and civil war seemed likely
- In **July 1914**, King George V called the **Buckingham Palace Conference** to look for a solution. It broke down over which side would get **Tyrone** and **Fermanagh**.

Suspending Home Rule

- A week later, Germany invaded Belgium and Britain declared war on Germany. Both Carson and Redmond supported Britain's action. At that time everyone thought the war would be '**over by Christmas**'
- Carson immediately told the UVF to join the British army. He also reluctantly agreed to let Home Rule pass in September, provided it was suspended until the war ended and the issue of Ulster was sorted out.

Redmond, the war and the Volunteers

- When the war started, Redmond said the Irish Volunteers would defend Ireland. But once Home Rule passed he needed to be in a strong position when talks with Carson resumed 'after Christmas'
- In a speech at **Woodenbridge**, he called on Irish Volunteers to join the British army too. This was because:
  - ❍ He believed it was right to defend Belgium
  - ❍ He wanted to show the British that Irish nationalists would support them against a foreign enemy
- Redmond's call split the Volunteers:
  - ❍ A huge majority (about 190,000) backed Redmond
  - ❍ About 8,000 rejected his call. They were led by MacNeill and secretly controlled by the IRB. Griffith backed them and they were popularly, though inaccurately, known as the '**Sinn Féin Volunteers**'.

Questions

For Examination questions on Later Modern Ireland, Topic 3 see page 275.

Your revision notes

CHAPTER 3
Ireland and the first World War

Irish soldiers in the war

- When the war began there were already 50,000 Irish men serving in the British forces. Between 1914 and 1918, 150,000 more joined up
- About **30,000 UVF men** joined the army. The British War Office formed them into the **36th 'Ulster' Division**. Led by UVF officers, it was allowed to use Ulster unionist emblems. They suffered heavy casualties at the **battle of the Somme** in 1916
- About **32,000 National Volunteers** also joined up. The War Office refused Redmond's request to form them into an 'Irish brigade'. Most nationalists served in the 10th and 16th Divisions. They suffered heavy casualties at **Gallipoli** and other battles
- In 1914 and 1915, many men volunteered to fight but as reports of conditions in the trenches reached home, recruitment dried up. In Britain **conscription** was imposed at the start of 1916, but Redmond persuaded the British not to extend it to Ireland
- Around 30,000 Irishmen were killed in the war.

The war and the economy

- The war brought prosperity to farmers because prices for agricultural produce increased
- Demand for ships and linen for tents, uniforms, etc, created a boom in the north, but there was not much war industry elsewhere
- The wives and children of soldiers benefited from the 'separation allowances' they received as part of the soldiers' pay
- But higher prices also made life difficult for the poorest people. This caused considerable unrest in rural areas in 1917 and contributed to the rise of Sinn Féin.

How the war affected Redmond's position

Redmond was at the height of his success in 1914, but his influence declined after that.

- He had won Home Rule, but it was not in force and his Party was left with nothing to do
- His most active followers were fighting France
- In 1915, the British parties formed a **coalition** to fight the war. Asquith offered ministerial jobs to both Redmond and Carson. Carson accepted but Redmond refused. This was popular in Ireland, but it left Redmond on the outside when decisions were made.

The 'Sinn Féin Volunteers'

- The Volunteers who rejected Redmond's leadership refused to support the war. Their Commander-in-Chief was Eoin MacNeill
- Late in 1914, they re-organised on military lines, with a **Headquarters Staff**. Almost all the officers in it, apart from MacNeill, were also in the IRB
- The Volunteers drilled openly and opposed recruiting to the British army. On Redmond's advice, the British government left them alone.

The IRB plans a rising

- The IRB had a saying, *"England's difficulty is Ireland's opportunity"*, so they saw the first World War as a golden opportunity to have a rebellion against British rule
- When war began, the IRB Supreme Council set up a secret **Military Committee** to plan it. At first there were two men, **Tom Clarke** and **Seán MacDiarmada** on it; later **Pearse**, **Plunkett**, **MacDonagh**, **Ceannt**, and (from January 1916) the Labour leader **James Connolly** joined it. They did not tell other IRB leaders what they were going to do
- They sent **Roger Casement** to Germany to get soldiers and arms. Germans doubted if they had much support and would only promise to send guns
- The Military Committee drew up plans for a rising:
  - The arrival of German arms would be the signal to start fighting
  - In Dublin the Volunteers would seize important buildings
- In 1915, they planned to rise in the autumn, but this fell through. In January 1916, they chose **Easter Sunday**. Historians are unsure why they chose this date. Was it symbolic or practical?
- The IRB agreed with the Germans that arms should land near Tralee between Good Friday (21 April) and Easter Sunday, 23 April. Later, they sent a message to change the arrival date to 23 April, but it never reached the arms ship, the *Aud*.

McNeill's attitude

- The plotters planned to use the Volunteers, but MacNeill knew nothing about their plans. When he heard rumours, he made clear his views:
  - A rebellion would cause suffering and was bound to fail
  - It was only justified if the British tried to disarm the Volunteers or impose conscription on Ireland
- In the days before Easter, the plotters set out to persuade MacNeill to order the Volunteers to fight.

The week before Easter

- **Wednesday 19 April**: The *'Castle Document'* appeared. It said the government planned to arrest nationalist leaders. It was probably a forgery, but convinced MacNeill. He gave orders to resist. A rebellion was to begin on Sunday
- **Thursday 20 April**: MacNeill found he had been conned and cancelled his orders. Pearse and others decided to tell him about the German arms on the *Aud*
- **Friday 21 April**: Pearse told MacNeill. Recognising this would lead to arrests anyway, he again ordered a rebellion on Sunday. That morning the British navy arrested the *Aud* off the Kerry coast, so no arms were coming. Casement landed at the same time, hoping to stop a rising and was arrested
- **Saturday 22 April**: Word of these developments reached MacNeill. Without arms, he knew a rising was hopeless. He cancelled everything and put his orders in Sunday newspapers
- **Sunday 23 April**: (a) The Lord Lieutenant and Under Secretary met. They knew about the arms, Casement and the cancellation, and decided not to arrest any leaders until Tuesday. (b) The plotters met and decided to fight anyway on Monday.

24 – 29 April, 1916: Easter Week

- **Easter Monday**: After the confusion, only 1,500 people turned out, mostly in Dublin. The Volunteer Headquarters were in the GPO, where Pearse read the **Proclamation of the Republic**. The Volunteers took key positions around the city, but not Dublin Castle. Unaware of the IRB's role, everyone called it a "Sinn Féin" rising
- **Tuesday to Thursday**: The British imposed **martial law**, poured in troops and concentrated on capturing the GPO. They bombarded O'Connell Street. The rebels were forced to evacuate the GPO
- **Friday**: Pearse surrendered and by Saturday, all fighting had ceased.

April/May 1916: The British response to the rising

- Under martial law, the British army controlled Ireland. They rounded up 3,000 people and began to execute the leaders
- At first Irish people were hostile to the rebels, but after the executions opinion swung to their side. People admired their courage
- Home Rule leaders, **Redmond and Dillon**, were alarmed by the army's behaviour. They persuaded **Asquith** to stop executions. Those spared (e.g. Markievicz, Cosgrave, de Valera) were given life sentences
- The British response was very moderate considering that Britain was at war with Germany and the rebels were in contact with the enemy.

Home Rule and partition again

- Redmond told Asquith that the only way to stop the growing popularity of the rebels was to put Home Rule into force
- Asquith sent **David Lloyd George** to hold new discussions with Redmond and Carson
- He persuaded Redmond to let the unionists have six counties because it was for a limited period. He then told Carson that partition would be permanent. When this deception emerged, the talks collapsed
- This discredited Redmond, who, for the first time, had given up Tyrone and Fermanagh to the unionists
- But his Party was still strong because nationalists who supported the rising had no party to challenge the Home Rulers.

Patrick Pearse (1879 – 1916)

- Son of an English stonemason, he studied law but never practised. At 16 he joined **the Gaelic League** and in 1903 became **editor** of the League newspaper, *An Claidheamh Soluis*
- Pearse raised the standard of the paper, publishing news items as well as stories and poems in Irish. He hoped it would convince more people to learn Irish
- When that failed he turned to education, opening his own school, **St Enda's**, in 1908. Teaching was mainly through Irish. Students had freedom to express themselves and were encouraged to admire ancient Gaelic heroes, like Cuchulainn
- At first it was a success. Friends and family taught in it and many Gaelic Leaguers sent their sons as pupils
- Success went to Pearse's head. He moved the school to a bigger house on the outskirts of Dublin. This increased costs while reducing the number of students
- By 1912, Pearse was almost bankrupt and had to beg and borrow money to keep his school alive
- Up to then Pearse concentrated on the revival of Irish and generally ignored politics. In 1912, he spoke in favour of Home Rule alongside Redmond
- But as his school failed and as unionist opposition to Home Rule grew, Pearse linked the revival of Irish to independence, calling for *'an Ireland not free merely but Gaelic as well; not Gaelic merely but free as well'*
- He helped to found the Irish Volunteers in November 1913 and shortly after took the IRB oath
- In 1914, when Redmond called on the Volunteers to join the British army, he sided with the minority. Soon after, when the Volunteers re-organised he became **Director of Military Organisation**. This position allowed him to appoint IRB men to key positions
- Although old republicans like Thomas Clarke and Seán MacDiarmada at first distrusted him, he won them over with his passionate enthusiasm. He was elected to the IRB Supreme Council and told of the plans for a rising
- He developed a theory of **'blood sacrifice'**, i.e. the spirit of Irish independence could only be revived if men were prepared to die for it. In a speech at the funeral of the old Fenian O'Donovan Rossa in 1915, Pearse expressed this idea when he said *"Life springs from death, and from the graves of patriot men and women spring living nations"*

- The Military Committee, which plotted the rising, appointed him **President of the Provisional Government** and he read the Proclamation of the Republic at the GPO on Easter Monday
- By Friday when it was clear that any further fighting was useless, he signed the surrender
- After a court martial, he was executed by firing squad on 3 May, 1916.

Questions

For Examination questions on Later Modern Ireland, Topic 3 see page 275.

Your revision notes

Lloyd George frees the prisoners

- By the end of 1916, Britain was doing badly in the war. In December, Asquith was forced out and **David Lloyd George** became Prime Minister
- He had one main aim: to win the war by getting America to declare war on Germany
- The large Irish-American community was hostile to Britain because of its treatment of Ireland
- To appease them, Lloyd George freed the Easter Week prisoners.

New leaders for nationalists

- They got a warm welcome home. Some of them at once began to organise extreme nationalists to oppose the Home Rule Party:
  - **Arthur Griffith** started to revive the **Sinn Féin Party**
  - **Michael Collins** re-organised the **IRB** and built a spy network
  - **Cathal Brugha**, who disapproved of secret societies, began to revive **Irish Volunteers** as an open army.

The by-elections of 1917

- **In February** 1917 in a by-election in Roscommon, local people named **Count Plunkett**, whose son had been executed, as a 'Sinn Féin' candidate. (By 'Sinn Féin' they meant a supporter of the rising, not a member of Griffith's Party). Griffith, Collins and Brugha went to canvass for him. To everyone's amazement, he won
- Later 'Sinn Féiners' won two more by-elections. The candidate in the third (Clare) was **Eamon de Valera** who had just been freed by Lloyd George
- These by-elections were important because they made Griffith's Sinn Féin better known and showed militant republicans, like Collins and Brugha, the value of elections for winning popular support.

Founding a 'second' Sinn Féin

- After de Valera was elected he began talks to unite the various pro-1916 factions. They were divided about aims (republic or dual monarchy?), tactics (violence or politics?) and leadership (Griffith, Plunkett or de Valera?)
- The talks led to a new ('second') **Sinn Féin** Party in October 1917.

- They agreed to work for a **republic** which they hoped to achieve by:
  - ○ Getting MPs elected
  - ○ They would **abstain from Westminster**
  - ○ Set up a **Dáil** in Dublin
  - ○ **Elect an Irish government** to rule the country
  - ○ **Appeal for self determination to the Peace Conference** when the war ended
- De Valera was elected President; Griffith and Plunkett were Vice-Presidents
- Next day the **Volunteers** also elected de Valera as their leader, thus uniting the political and military wings of the movement
- **Michael Collins**, **Richard Mulcahy** and **Cathal Brugha** were also prominent in both organisations
- Sinn Féin grew slowly through the winter of 1917–1918.

> **Remember...**
>
> In 1917 when the US entered the war, **Woodrow Wilson** said it was to get *'self-determination for small nations'*. He didn't mean Ireland but most Irish people thought he did.
>
> EDCO REVISE WISE POINTS TO NOTE

1917–1918: The Irish Convention

- When America entered the war early in 1917, Lloyd George set up the **Irish Convention** to let the Irish find a solution to the division between unionists and nationalists
- It met between **July 1917** and **April 1918**
- Home Rulers, unionists, churches and trade unionists attended, but Sinn Féin boycotted it
- Redmond, a dying man, tried to make a deal with Carson but he was only interested in the six counties Redmond had agreed to in 1916
- The Convention ended in failure. This further discredited the Home Rule Party and strengthened Sinn Féin
- **March 1918**: Redmond died. **John Dillon** became Home Rule leader.

April–May 1918: The Conscription Crisis

- Early in 1918 the Germans launched a desperate attack on the Western Front. Britain needed more soldiers to fight them, so Lloyd George introduced **conscription** for Ireland
- Most nationalists opposed conscription:
  - ○ Dillon walked out of Westminster in protest
  - ○ The Trade Unions organised strikes against it
  - ○ The Catholic bishops denounced it
  - ○ Sinn Féin and the Volunteers threatened to fight it

- The British discovered a '**German plot**' and arrested many Sinn Féin leaders. No one believed the plot existed so it earned sympathy for Sinn Féin. With de Valera and Griffith in jail, **Collins** emerged as a leader
- By August, Germany had collapsed and the soldiers were not needed, but Sinn Féin got the credit for preventing conscription.

The 1918 election

- When the first World War ended on 11 November, Lloyd George called a general election for December 1918. It was an unusual election:
  - The first since 1910 because there were no elections during the war
  - The first time that all men over 21, and women ratepayers over 30 could vote. Women could also stand as candidates
- In the campaign:
  - The Unionist Party, still led by Carson continued campaigning against Home Rule
  - The **Labour Party** did not put up candidates so as not to confuse the issue for nationalists
  - Nationalist voters had a clear choice. Did they want:
    - (a) **Dillon's Home Rule Party** to go back to Westminster and go on negotiating for a limited self-government?

      or
    - (b) **de Valera's Sinn Féin Party** to stay in Ireland, set up an Irish republic and appeal for recognition to the Peace Conference?
- Sinn Féin did not mention violence in its election literature, but Collins, Brugha and some Volunteers were planning violence, whatever the result
- Many Sinn Féin leaders were still in jail and its campaign literature was censored. This probably helped to make them popular
- The election results were dramatic:

Parties	Before the election	After the election
Unionist	18	26
Home Rule	78	6
Sinn Féin	7 (won in by-elections since 1916)	73

- The Home Rule Party was almost wiped out. Even its leader, John Dillon, lost his seat.

Arthur Griffith and Sinn Féin (1871-1922)

EDCO REVISE WISE KEY PERSONALITY

- Dublin-born journalist, Griffith set up a small newspaper, *The United Irishman*, in 1898. In it he published articles by most of the important thinkers of the time, led 'buy Irish' campaigns and supported the Gaelic League and the GAA
- Griffith thought Home Rule would not give Ireland enough control over its affairs, but he also knew most nationalists disliked republican violence. In his 1904 book, *The Resurrection of Hungary*, he proposed a middle way between the two:
  - ○ Nationalists would elect MPs who would not go to Westminster but set up an Irish parliament and government in Dublin
  - ○ Griffith argued that the British government in Ireland would then wither away and no violence would be needed
  - ○ To reassure the British and please unionists, nationalists would agree to a "**Dual Monarchy**" with Britain (like the arrangement between Austria and Hungary)
  - ○ An Irish government should develop Irish industry behind **protective tariffs**
- Griffith set up **Sinn Féin** to achieve these aims in 1905. It attracted people involved in the cultural revival or frustrated by the delay in getting Home Rule
- Sinn Féin did well in local elections but when political developments in Britain made Home Rule likely after 1910, it declined
- Griffith continued to publish his newspaper, *Sinn Féin*, supporting nationalist causes like the Irish Volunteers. Gradually 'Sinn Féin' became a kind of brand name attached to extreme nationalists, such as MacNeill's 'Sinn Féin' Volunteers
- When violence broke out at Easter 1916, everyone called it "the **Sinn Féin Rebellion**", even though Griffith and Sinn Féin had nothing to do with it
- Griffith was arrested after the rising, but freed in December 1916. His Party grew as support for the 1916 rebels increased, though he was too moderate for republicans like Collins or Brugha
- In October 1917, de Valera united the various anti-Home Rule groups. To maintain unity, Griffith stepped aside and let de Valera become leader of the '**second**' Sinn Féin
- It
  - ○ demanded a republic rather than Dual Monarchy
  - ○ promised to abstain from Westminster
  - ○ set up a Dáil in Dublin
  - ○ to appeal for recognition to the peace conference
- Sinn Féin grew rapidly. When it opposed conscription, the British arrested the leaders including Griffith for the 'German Plot'
- He was in jail during the 1918 election when he was elected MP (TD) for East Cavan and missed the first meeting of Dáil Éireann
- When freed in March 1919, de Valera appointed him as **Vice-President** and **Minister for Home Affairs** in the **Dáil Cabinet**
- He presided over the Dáil government while de Valera was in the US and was responsible for setting up the **Sinn Féin courts**
- He disliked IRA violence but restrained his protests when faced with Black and Tan violence. Arrested in November 1920 he was in jail until the **Truce** in July, 1921

- Griffith led the **Irish delegation to London** to negotiate with Lloyd George after de Valera refused to go:
  - ○ He argued for de Valera's **"External Association"** but soon realised the British would insist on Dominion Status
  - ○ On partition, he accepted that the **Boundary Commission** would move large areas from the north to the south
  - ○ He was delighted when Lloyd George gave Ireland **full economic independence** during the final session
- He was the first delegate to agree to sign the Treaty without reference to de Valera
- In the **Dáil debates** Griffith argued that the Treaty gave much more independence – a flag, an army, full control of the economy – than Home Rule and that they got the best terms possible
- When de Valera resigned in January 1922, Griffith became **head of the Dáil government**. With Collins he began setting up the Irish Free State, but disapproved of things Collins did to try to keep the IRA from splitting
- Like everyone, he was heart-broken when the split over the Treaty degenerated into civil war in June. He died suddenly in August, 1922, aged 52.

Questions

For Examination questions on Later Modern Ireland, Topic 3 see page 275.

Your revision notes

The first meeting of the First Dáil: 21 January, 1919

- To prepare the Irish appeal to the **Peace Conference** which was to meet in Paris at the end of January, Sinn Féin leaders invited all 105 Irish MPs to a meeting of a new Irish parliament, **Dáil Éireann**
- Only 27 Sinn Féiners turned up and Unionist and Home Rule MPs were not interested. De Valera, Griffith and other TDs were still in jail
- The first meeting of Dáil Éireann took place at the Mansion House in Dublin on 21 January. It lasted two hours. The Dáil:
  - Declared a **Republic**
  - Approved a **Constitution**
  - Agreed on a '**Democratic Programme**' of social reform to please the Labour Party
  - Appointed delegates, led by **Seán T O'Kelly**, to put Ireland's case for self-determination to the Peace Conference

> **Remember...**
>
> MP: **Member of Parliament** (i.e. the House of Commons).
> TD: **Teachta Dála**: representative to the Dáil.

- All this was carried out in Irish.

De Valera elected President

- In February, Collins got de Valera out of jail and in March, Lloyd George freed the other Sinn Féin leaders
- In 1 April, the Dáil met for a second time and elected de Valera as **President** (i.e. Prime Minister). He appointed a **Cabinet**. It included:
  - **Arthur Griffith**, Vice-President and Minister for Home Affairs (i.e. Justice)
  - **Michael Collins**, Minister for Finance
  - **William T Cosgrave**, Minister for Local Government
  - **Constance Markievicz**, Minister for Labour
  - **Cathal Brugha**, Minister for Defence.

De Valera in America 1919 – 1920

- In Paris, US President Woodrow Wilson refused to meet the Sinn Féin delegates because he considered them pro-German
- In **June**, de Valera went to America, hoping to get Irish-American voters to make the US government change its position
- He failed to achieve this, but he raised $4 million for the Dáil government

- He returned to Ireland in **December 1920**. By then the whole situation had completely changed.

Achievements of the Dáil government

- While de Valera was away, **Griffith** led the Dáil government which planned to set up an Irish government and take over the country from the British. They faced huge difficulties:
  - ❍ All Sinn Féin Ministers were young and inexperienced
  - ❍ They had no civil servants or even offices
  - ❍ They were often on the run from the Black and Tans
- In spite of these difficulties, they achieved a great deal:
  - ❍ **Collins in Finance** raised loan of £358,000 which helped pay for guns and propaganda. He carefully oversaw the spending of this money and established the **Department of Finance** as the most important department in the government
  - ❍ **Cosgrave in Local Government** took over county councils after the local elections in 1920. He tried to end corruption
  - ❍ **Griffith** (and after he was imprisoned, **Austin Stack**), **in Home Affairs** encouraged the setting up of **Sinn Féin arbitration courts** which had largely replaced the British court system by 1921. In places, the Volunteers (now known as the **IRA**) acted as a police force, supporting and enforcing the decisions of the Sinn Féin courts
  - ❍ **Foreign Affairs (Seán T O'Kelly)** and **Publicity (Erskine Childers)** brought Irish issues to the attention of the world and embarrassed Britain by publicising the behaviour of the Black and Tans.

Constance Markievicz (1868–1927)

- **Constance Gore-Booth** was born into an anglo-Irish landlord family. She grew up at the family mansion in Sligo and was presented to Queen Victoria. She studied art in London and Paris
- In 1900, she married a Polish Count, **Casimir Markievicz** and they moved to Dublin in 1903. About ten years later the marriage collapsed and her husband left Ireland for good
- Contact with the cultural revival drew her into nationalist politics. She joined **Sinn Féin** and *Inghinidhe na hÉireann*, a woman's nationalist organisation set up by Maude Gonne McBride
- With **Bulmer Hobson** in 1909, she set up *Na Fianna*, a scout-type organisation to recruit and train boys to fight for Irish independence
- Friendship with **James Connolly** led her to support **socialism**. She helped to organise the feeding of workers during the **1913 lockout** in Dublin. She also joined Connolly's **Irish Citizen Army** and outraged many in Dublin by appearing in a uniform with trousers and guns
- In the 1916 rising, she fought in Stephen's Green with the Citizen Army unit led by **Michael Mallin**

- Afterwards she was court-martialled and sentenced to death. But the British did not want to execute a woman and her sentence was at once changed to life imprisonment. Like the other life prisoners she was freed in June 1917
- She joined the new **Sinn Féin Party** led by de Valera and along with other prominent members was imprisoned in 1918 as part of the 'German Plot'
- In the 1918 election, she was one of two women candidates nominated by Sinn Féin. Her victory made her **the first woman elected to Westminster** and to **Dáil Éireann**. In line with Sinn Féin policy she never took her seat in the British parliament
- When the **Dáil government** was set up in 1919 de Valera made her **Minister for Labour**, but over the next three years she was imprisoned twice which made it difficult for her to achieve much in this role
- When the Dáil Cabinet was re-organised in 1921, she was left out of the inner circle of Ministers who made the main decisions
- During the **Dáil debates on the Treaty**, she vehemently opposed Dominion Status. She supported the anti-Treaty side in the civil war and went to America to gather funds
- She lost her seat in the 'Treaty election' of 1922 but was re-elected in 1923 as a Sinn Féin TD
- She supported de Valera when he left Sinn Féin in 1926 and was a founder member of **Fianna Fáil**. She was elected a **Fianna Fáil TD** in 1927, but died soon after.

Questions

For Examination questions on Later Modern Ireland, Topic 3 see page 275.

Your revision notes

Relationship between Dáil Éireann and the Volunteers

- After the Dáil declared a republic, the Volunteers began to call themselves the **Irish Republican Army (IRA)**
- In theory, the Dáil government and its **Minister for Defence, Cathal Brugha** were in charge of the IRA, but in practice the Volunteers paid little attention to them
- The Volunteers, set up in 1913, were older than the Dáil. They had their own **Headquarters** under their own **Chief of Staff, Richard Mulcahy** who was elected to that position in 1917
- They took their orders from him, or from their own local commandants who were elected by the Volunteers, not from the Dáil
- This is seen when Volunteers in Tipperary shot and killed two policemen in an arms raid at **Soloheadbeg**, on 21 January 1919, the first day the Dáil met and well before it declared war on Britain
- This confusion about who was in charge led to friction between the two branches of the independence movement, the political wing (Sinn Féin and the Dáil) and the army (IRA)
- For example, **Collins** as **Director of Intelligence** in the IRA (and head of the secret IRB to which many IRA officers belonged) paid little attention to **Brugha**, his nominal boss as **Minister of Defence**
- These issues caused trouble after the Treaty was signed, but between 1919 and 1921, while they faced a common enemy, they stayed united.

The growth of violence

- The War of Independence developed slowly and semi-accidentally
- In 1919–1920, the IRA **raided police barracks** looking for arms (like at Soloheadbeg). In the first year, 19 RIC men were shot
- In Dublin, Collins organised a spy network and ruthlessly used his 'Squad' of gunmen to murder police spies and destroy the government's sources of information
- **Lloyd George** would not admit that it was a war. He insisted the IRA was a "*murder gang*" against which they had to use the police (RIC), rather than the British army
- But in 1919, few Irishmen wanted to join the RIC. So the British recruited unemployed ex-soldiers in Britain, the '**Black and Tans**'
- They arrived early in 1920. They did not know Ireland. When the IRA attacked them, they hit back indiscriminately, looting and burning

- This angered people like Griffith who, up to then, had disliked the brutality of the IRA. Now they felt obliged to support their own side
- Sinn Féin publicised the brutality of the Tans. This led to criticism of British policy in Britain, Europe and the U.S and forced an embarrassed British government to begin talks with Sinn Féin. It was this and not any "victory" of the IRA which led to the **Truce** (**July 1921**) and the start of peace talks.

Important episodes in the War of Independence

- The worst stage in the War of Independence was from **October 1920 to July 1921**. Most of the violence was in Dublin or in Munster
- **October 1920**: the death of Terence MacSwiney, Mayor of Cork, after being on hunger strike for 73 days
- **November 1920**: The execution of 18 year-old **Kevin Barry** for his part in ambush in which a 17 year old British soldier died
- 21 November 1920 – '**Bloody Sunday**': The British brought in new spies, the '**Cairo gang**'. Collins sent his Squad to kill them on Sunday morning. Eleven died. That afternoon, the Tans fired into crowd in Croke Park, killing 13; that night, three IRA men were killed in Dublin Castle "trying to escape"
- **December 1920**: After the IRA under **Tom Barry** ambushed and killed a troop of Auxiliaries at **Kilmichael** near Cork, the Black and Tans rioted and burned the centre of the city
- In 1921, the **British army** became more involved. It imposed martial law in places, but politicians in London were afraid of the effect on British and world public opinion if it was given a free hand
- The IRA developed '**flying squads**' of trained and paid men who moved from area to area, helping local Volunteers to organise ambushes
- **Brugha** and **de Valera** (after he returned from the US), disliked the IRA's guerrilla tactics. They argued for a more open warfare
- That led in **May 1921** to the IRA attack on the Customs House in Dublin. They burned it, but lost seven men and 70 were captured along with their arms
- By summer 1921, the IRA was weakening. Many activists were rounded up by the army and put in internment camps.

November – December 1920: The search for peace begins

- People in Britain, the US and Europe were upset by reports of British brutality and the failure to give Ireland 'self-determination'. They urged Lloyd George to talk to Sinn Féin
- Early attempts to talk ended in November 1920 after Bloody Sunday
- The return of de Valera in December 1920 gave Lloyd George a "clean" leader to talk to. He told the army not to arrest him.

December 1920 – July 1921: Partition and Truce

- In 1920, Lloyd George brought in the **Government of Ireland Act**. It **partitioned** Ireland into two states, a unionist-dominated, six county "**Northern Ireland**" and a nationalist-dominated 26 county "**Southern Ireland**". Each had its own parliament
- This satisfied the Unionists and left Lloyd George free to do a deal with Sinn Féin for the rest of Ireland
- **May 1921:** Under the Government of Ireland Act, elections were held for the two Irish parliaments in May 1921
- Sinn Féin treated the election for the 'Southern Irish parliament' as an election to the **Second Dáil**. 124 Sinn Féin TDs were returned unopposed
- In Belfast, 40 Unionists, six Home Rulers and six Sinn Féiners (who attended the Dáil) were elected to the first Northern Ireland parliament
- The Government of Ireland Act said that if the "Southern Parliament" did not meet, Britain would have to impose direct rule on the 26 counties. Lloyd George knew this would be unpopular in Britain unless he made a public attempt to get peace
- He encouraged **King George V to appeal for peace** when he opened the Belfast parliament. Then Lloyd George publicly offered talks to de Valera
- De Valera accepted because he felt nationalists might stop supporting the IRA if he did not
- 11 July 1921: A Truce (ceasefire) was agreed to allow talks begin.

Éamon De Valera, revolutionary leader (1882 to 1923)

- Born in the US, he grew up in Limerick, taught maths in Dublin and joined Gaelic League. In 1913, he joined the Volunteers and in 1916, reluctantly joined the IRB
- During the Easter Rising, he commanded at **Boland's Mills**. His death sentence was changed to life imprisonment when the executions stopped
- In prison he emerged as a leader, healing divisions among republican prisoners. Freed in June 1917, he was elected a "Sinn Féin" MP for East Clare
- In October 1917, he united the anti-Home Rule groups which emerged after the 1916 rising into the "**second**" **Sinn Féin Party** and was elected its President
- Soon after he was also elected **leader of the Volunteers**, thus uniting political and military movements
- Imprisoned during the 1918 **Conscription Crisis 'German Plot'**, he was in jail for the 1918 election and the first meeting of Dáil Éireann in January 1919
- Collins got him out and in April, the First Dáil elected him **President** (i.e. Prime Minister). He appointed a **Cabinet**, then left for the US where he stayed until December 1920
- He returned to find a guerrilla war and Sinn Féin Cabinet split between **Collins** and **Cathal Brugha**. He sided with Brugha
- As violence grew in the north, de Valera met the Northern Prime Minister, **Sir James Craig**, but the talks achieved nothing

- By June 1921, **Lloyd George** was ready to talk to Sinn Féin. He and de Valera agreed to a **Truce** (11 July) so negotiations could begin
- De Valera went to London. He demanded an independent republic and an end to partition. Lloyd George offered limited "Dominion Status" to 26 counties. But neither side wanted war and they agreed to reopen negotiations in October
- De Valera refused to be part of the delegation the Dáil Cabinet chose. He said the delegates must have someone to refer back to. He told them to demand an end to partition and offer Britain **"external association"** in return. He forbade them to sign anything without his approval
- He accepted a **Boundary Commission** as solving partition but continued to insist on 'external association' even when the British rejected it. He was furious when the delegates signed a Treaty without consulting him on 6 December 1921 and called on the Irish people to reject it
- In Dáil debates, de Valera opposed the Treaty because **(a)** it made the **king head of state** and **(b)** the **oath** would give Britain power in Ireland. His suggested alternative Treaty ("**Document no 2**") pleased no one
- When Dáil accepted the Treaty, de Valera resigned and walked out, leaving Griffith and Collins to set up the Free State. He made inflammatory speeches, and backed the IRA occupation of the Four Courts
- But he also negotiated a **Pact** with Collins to fight the June 1922 election jointly. Collins called off the Pact on the eve of the election
- The anti-Treaty side lost (35 to 58). Soon after the Free State army attacked the IRA in the Four Courts and civil war began
- Although head of a "republican government" de Valera did not control the IRA who ignored his pleas for a ceasefire until an extreme IRA leader, Liam Lynch, was killed in May 1923
- In elections in August, de Valera's anti-Treaty **Sinn Féin** Party won 44 seats, but he was arrested during the campaign and was in jail until 1924.

Questions

For Examination questions on Later Modern Ireland, Topic 3 see page 275.

Your revision notes

●●●**Case study**

8.1 Negotiating a Treaty

July 1921: De Valera in London

- 20 July 1921: de Valera went to London to meet **Lloyd George**. Each side set out its starting position:
  - ○ Lloyd George offered a limited "**Dominion Status**" (i.e. less independence than Canada had) for 26 counties
  - ○ De Valera demanded **an independent Republic** for the whole island of Ireland
- The talks broke down.

> **Remember...**
>
> **Dominion status:** the same amount of independence as the **dominions** of the British Empire (Canada, Australia, etc.). In 1921 it was unclear how much independence that was.

August–September: finding a formula for talks

- The two leaders then exchanged letters to work out a formula for talks
- Finally, they agreed an Irish delegation would go to London to discuss "*how the association of Ireland with the community of nations known as the British Empire may be reconciled with Ireland's national aspirations*".

The Irish delegation

- The seven-man **Dáil Cabinet** chose the **delegates** to represent Ireland at the negotiations
- De Valera refused to go. He said he must stay at home so they had someone to refer back to
- **Griffith** then led the delegation. Others were **Collins**, **Robert Barton** (Minister for Agriculture) and two lawyers, **Gavan Duffy**, and **Eamon Duggan**, added to give legal advice. **Erskine Childers** was a non-voting secretary. Griffith unfairly distrusted him, which caused tension
- The Irish delegation had some **serious weaknesses**
  - ○ They were more moderate than extreme republican ministers like **Austin Stack** and **Cathal Brugha** who stayed behind
  - ○ They lacked negotiating experience and had few back-up services
  - ○ They were under great pressure because they were away from home with the fate of their country in their hands.

The British delegation

- Was led by Prime Minister **Lloyd George** with Liberal **Winston Churchill**, and Conservatives **Austin Chamberlain** and **Lord Birkenhead**
- They had huge advantages:
  - They were very experienced negotiators
  - They were on their home ground
  - They had a large back-up civil service
- But Lloyd George was in coalition with the **pro-unionist Conservative Party**. This limited his freedom to make concessions to the Irish.

11 October - 6 December: Negotiating a treaty

- Negotiations began on **11 October** and lasted until **6 December**
- The leaders of the two delegations discussed the main issues. Other points like defence and trading rights were discussed by sub-committees
- The **main issues** were (i) **partition of Ireland** and (ii) **Ireland's relationship to Britain and its Empire**:
  - The British feared an independent Ireland might **undermine their security** by joining their enemies. To prevent that they wanted to keep Ireland in the Empire as a **Dominion**. They were willing to compromise on partition to achieve that
  - The Irish wanted to end partition (i.e. re-unite Ireland) and would compromise on independence to achieve that. De Valera proposed the idea of Ireland's '**External Association**' with the empire as a compromise
- There were **seven stages in the negotiations**:
  1. Some Conservative MPs disliked talking to Sinn Féin. To head off protests at their annual conference, Lloyd George got Griffith to agree to '**free partnership**' in the Empire in return for ending partition. He promised to resign if Craig (the Northern Ireland Prime Minister) rejected the idea.
  2. When Craig refused even to talk, Lloyd George did not resign. Instead he offered a **Boundary Commission** to re-draw the border between the six and 26 counties. He argued this would reduce Northern Ireland to a small, unviable area which would soon fail. Griffith accepted this argument and said so in a letter (**13 November**).
  3. By late-November they were still far apart on the other issue. Lloyd George rejected External Association repeatedly. Instead he offered Dominion Status which he defined as being '**like Canada**'. He included this and the Boundary Commission in a **draft of a Treaty** that he gave to the Irish to take back to Dublin on 2 December.
  4. **3 December**: After a heated discussion, the **Dáil Cabinet** rejected the draft Treaty. They told the delegates to go back and demand "External Association" again and to sign nothing without checking with de Valera

first. But they did not discuss what to do if war was the only alternative. The delegates rushed back to London.

5. **4 December**: They met the British that afternoon. Lloyd George again rejected External Association and the talks broke down.

6. **5 December**: In the morning, Lloyd George met Griffith and Collins and persuaded them the Boundary Commission would end partition. That night was the final session. At it Lloyd George **rewrote the oath to the king** and **agreed to let the Irish Free State impose tariffs on imports**, which was something Griffith always wanted.

7. The Irish said they must consult de Valera about the changes. Lloyd George insisted he must have an instant answer because he had to tell Craig. He then produced Griffith's 13 November letter and asked if he would break his promise. Griffith gave in and agreed to sign. Lloyd George then threatened war if the others refused. They returned home and argued for hours. At last they gave in, returned to Downing St. and signed **at 2am on 6 December, 1921.**

The Articles of the Anglo-Irish Treaty (1921)

The Treaty had 18 articles. The main ones were:
- Ireland was to be called the **Irish Free State**
- It was to be a **Dominion of the British Commonwealth** (which was defined as **having the same independence as Canada**)
- All TDs were to take an **oath of allegiance to the Constitution** of the Irish Free State and **of loyalty to the King** as head of the Commonwealth to which the Irish Free State belonged
- The Treaty was to apply to the whole of Ireland **unless** the Northern Ireland parliament objected (which everyone knew it would). When that happened a **Boundary Commission** of three men would redraw the border between north and south
- The Free State was to let the **British navy have the use of three ports** on its coast
- It was to pay a **share of the debt for the first World War**.

8.2 Debating the Treaty

De Valera responds to the treaty

- **6-8 December**: De Valera was furious that the delegates had signed without his permission. He publicly condemned the Treaty. Collins got the IRB to back it
- **8 December**: The Dáil Cabinet decided by 4 **votes to 3** to send it to be debated and voted on in Dáil Éireann.

Dáil Éireann debates the Anglo-Irish Treaty

- From **14 December**, 1921–7 **January**, 1922, with a short break for Christmas, TDs in the Dáil debated the Treaty. All TDs spoke. They were almost evenly divided, for and against.

The pro-Treaty arguments

- Few of the TDs who supported the Treaty actually liked it. They accepted it because it was the best deal they could get
- Griffith said it gave much more independence than Home Rule; Ireland would have its own flag and army and could impose tariffs
- Kevin O'Higgins said that Canada and other Dominions would defend Irish independence from British interference
- Collins said that it gave 'the freedom to achieve freedom' because the dominions were getting more freedom and Ireland would get the same
- Richard Mulcahy said that the IRA had not won the war while it had the advantage of secrecy and surprise. Could it do better if the war began again?
- The Irish public wanted peace and would not support a renewed war.

The anti-Treaty arguments

- Anti-Treaty TDs divided into **moderate** and **extreme republicans**
- **Moderates** like de Valera wanted the Dáil to reject the Treaty and renew negotiations. He produced an alternative Treaty called "**Document no. 2**" with External Association instead of Dominion Status. It annoyed both pro- and anti-Treaty sides and he dropped it
- The **moderates** urged TDs to vote against the Treaty because:
  - Dominion status gave too little independence
  - Having the British King as Head of State would let the British interfere in Ireland (de Valera)
  - Unlike Canada or Australia, Ireland is near to Britain, so the British could easily interfere (Childers)
- **Extremist republicans** wanted the Dáil to resume the war with Britain. They argued:
  - That the republic had been declared in 1916 and confirmed in 1919. It could not be undone (Mary MacSwiney)
  - If TDs took an oath to the king they would break the oath they had already taken to the republic (Brugha)
  - Only a republic would do. If the Dáil accepted the Treaty, they would ignore its decision and go on fighting.

The vote

- Over the Christmas break a few TDs found their constituents wanted peace and decided, reluctantly, to vote for the Treaty
- On **7 January**, 1922, the Dáil voted to accept the Treaty by 64 votes to 57. De Valera resigned as President and Griffith was elected to head the Dáil government in his place.

Michael Collins (1890–1922)

- Born in Cork, Collins worked in London from 1906. He studied accountancy, joined the Gaelic League and the IRB. Returned to Ireland in 1915 to avoid conscription. Fought in GPO in Easter Week and was interned
- When freed, he rebuilt the IRB and was elected President in 1917. He travelled the country, building up a network of contacts and spies
- Having helped set up the 'second Sinn Féin', he was on its **Executive Council** in 1917. He was also **Director of Intelligence** in the Irish Volunteers
- Elected a Sinn Féin TD in 1918, de Valera appointed him **Minister for Finance** in Dáil government
- As **Minister for Finance**, he raised £350,000 in the National Loan, using it for propaganda, expenses and guns
- As IRA **Director of Intelligence**, he collected information on British plans and passed it to local IRA units. In Dublin his 'Squad' intimidated and murdered Castle detectives. He ruthlessly killed British spies on **Bloody Sunday**
- The British offered a reward of £10,000 for him which made him famous. This caused tensions with **Brugha** and **de Valera** who were both jealous of him
- Collins went reluctantly to London to negotiate with Lloyd George
- He realised the British would give no more than **Dominion Status**, but found the Dominions were evolving to full independence. Lloyd George also convinced him the **Boundary Commission** would end partition
- After Lloyd George threatened war, he backed Griffith's decision to sign the **Treaty on 6 December** without referring it back to de Valera
- In the Dáil debates he defended it on the grounds that **(a)** it was the best they could get from the British, **(b)** it was only the **first step** to the republic and **(c)** that the **Boundary Commission** would end partition
- After the Treaty passed de Valera resigned and Collins became leader of the **'Provisional Government'**, to which the British were to hand over power
- Collins began **(a)** taking over from the British, **(b)** wrote a Constitution for the **Free State** and **(c)** set up police, army and civil service
- At the same time he secretly supplied guns to the IRA in the North who were still fighting the Unionist government there
- To avert a civil war, he refused to retaliate when extreme republicans under **Rory O'Connor** seized the Four Courts
- He also tried to isolate extremists by making the **Collins-de Valera Pact** to fight the June election jointly
- As part of the pact, Collins left king and oath out of the Constitution, but the British insisted on restoring them. As a result Collins called off the pact on the eve of the election
- The pro-Treaty group won a decisive victory (58 seats to 35)
- After that Collins let Free State army attack the IRA in the Four Courts. This started the **civil war**. The Cabinet appointed Collins Commander-in-Chief
- Within a week he had defeated the IRA in Dublin, then sent the army to attack them in Munster by land and sea. By August he defeated them there too
- Griffith died suddenly on 11 August. Collins took over as head of government. A few days later, he went to Cork where he was ambushed and killed at **Béal na mBláth** on 22 August, 1922.

Sliding towards civil war

- The Treaty allowed a 12-month transition period to 6 December 1922, during which the British would hand over to a Provisional **Government**. Collins became head of the Provisional Government
- **January-March** Griffith and Collins (a) took over Dublin Castle (b) set up an Irish police (Garda), army and civil service; (c) wrote a Constitution; (d) called elections for June 1922
- The British army withdrew from barracks around the country. At first they left arms for the local IRA commanders who were often anti-Treaty. When this became clear, they gave them to the Free State army which Collins was hurriedly building up
- **March**: The IRA called a conference to discuss the Treaty. When he realised that most IRA men were anti-Treaty, Minister for Defence **Richard Mulcahy** banned it as undemocratic (an army should obey decisions made by the elected parliament). The meeting went ahead and rejected the Treaty
- **April**: extreme republicans, led by **Rory O'Connor**, occupied the **Four Courts**. Not wanting to fight men who were his friends, Collins left them alone
- **May**: To isolate the extremists Collins made a **pact** with de Valera to fight the June elections jointly. He drew up a Free State Constitution which did not mention the king or the oath
- **June**: Just before the election, the British rejected the Constitution as a breach of the Treaty. They forced Collins to put back the king and the oath. He called off the Pact, which would not have worked anyway because other parties stood for election
- The election result was decisive:

Pro-Treaty	Anti-Treaty	Others: most pro-Treaty
58	35	35

The start of the civil war

- Three events sparked off the civil war;
    - The election gave Collins a mandate to act against the IRA in the Four Courts
    - On 22 June, General Wilson, an ardent unionist was assassinated in London. The British blamed the Four Courts garrison and pressed Collins to remove them
    - The IRA in the Four Courts kidnapped one of Collins's men
- On 27 **June**, 1922, Collins ordered the Free State army to attack the Four Courts.

The main events of the civil war

The civil war had three distinct phases:

- **June 1922**: The Free State army attacked buildings in Dublin held by the IRA. Within a week, they were driven from the city. Cathal Brugha was killed
- **July–August**: Munster was the republican stronghold. The IRA held most of it south of a line from Limerick to Waterford. In July, Collins launched a two-pronged attack from land and sea. By August, they were driven from all their strongholds
- **August 1922 – May 1923**: A savage guerrilla war then developed, which lasted until May 1923. During it, there were many atrocities on both sides:
  - ❍ **12 August**, 1922 Griffith died of stroke
  - ❍ **22 August**, 1922 Collins was killed in an ambush
- After their deaths, **W T Cosgrave** became President (i.e. Prime Minister) of the Free State government
- The IRA assassinated Pro-Treaty TDs. In Cork and border areas it killed Protestants or forced them from their homes
- Cosgrave's government took power to execute anyone found with guns. **Erskine Childers** and **Rory O'Connor** were among 77 people executed
- De Valera joined in the civil war as an ordinary soldier. In October 1922 he set up a "republican government", but failed to control the IRA
- The IRA commander, Liam Lynch, refused to recognise that they were beaten or to call a ceasefire. He was killed in April 1923
- His successor, **Frank Aiken**, listened to de Valera's plea for peace. He agreed to a cease-fire in **May 1923**. Guns were not surrendered but hidden away for another day which never came
- There were about 1,000 republicans in jail and in August 1923, de Valera was arrested during an election speech. But they were all released, unconditionally by August 1924 and allowed to resume peaceful political activity.

Impact of the civil war

- About 4,000 people died, including many able leaders
- The centre of Dublin was destroyed. Other towns were damaged, houses burnt, roads, bridges and railways were destroyed. Money, badly needed to deal with social problems, had to be spent repairing the damage
- It created great bitterness among political leaders that took a generation to heal
- Our modern political parties have come from the split in the second Sinn Féin which led to the civil war.

The Pro-Treaty side took the name **Cumann na nGaedheal**, and in 1933 became **Fine Gael**.	The Anti-Treaty side kept the name **Sinn Féin** until 1926, when de Valera left it and set up **Fianna Fáil**.

In 1920, the **Government of Ireland Act partitioned (divided)** Ireland into two parts – Northern Ireland with six counties, and Southern Ireland with 26 counties. This is how it came about:

Unionists opposition to Home Rule leads to talk of partition

- 1912: Ulster Unionists opposed Home Rule for Ireland. They wanted Ireland to be divided, with **six Ulster** counties remaining in the UK when the remaining **26 counties** got Home Rule
- Redmond was willing to let them have **four counties**, but did not want to give up **Tyrone** and **Fermanagh** where the majority were nationalists
- The first World War began before any agreement was reached. The Home Rule Bill was passed in September 1914, but suspended until the war ended and the details of partition worked out. No one expected that the war would last so long.

Talks on partition during the first World War

- In 1915, with the war going badly for Britain, the Liberals and Conservatives (allies of the Unionists) formed a Coalition government. Carson became a Minister. Redmond refused to become one. This reduced his influence on the British and increased Carson's
- 1916: After the 1916 Rising in Dublin, Lloyd George re-opened negotiations with the two leaders. He got Redmond to agree to let the unionists have all six counties in return for a promise that partition would be "temporary", while at the same time promising Carson that it would be permanent. When Redmond realised he was conned, he repudiated the deal, but it was too late. He had given up Tyrone and Fermanagh
- 1917: To please Irish-Americans, Lloyd George set up the **Irish Convention** to let the Irish sort out the problem themselves. Carson insisted that Redmond had agreed to six counties and would not negotiate on any other terms.

Lloyd George and partition

- **December 1918 – the general election:** In nationalist areas, **Sinn Féin** replaced the Home Rule Party. They wanted a totally independent republic. That was even more unacceptable to unionists
- Carson's Unionist Party won 26 seats. Because Sinn Féin refused to go to Westminster, the Unionists were the biggest Irish party there.

- **The first World War ended** when the Peace Treaties were signed in Paris in 1919. Lloyd George then turned his attention to Ireland, which was due to get Home Rule. But with few Home Rulers and no Sinn Féiners in Westminster, he talked mainly to Unionists
- His solution was "**Home Rule all round**" – i.e. a Home Rule parliament in Belfast for the Ulster unionists and another in Dublin for the nationalists
- After some hesitation, the unionists saw the advantage of this. With their own parliament they would no longer be at the mercy of British politics in Westminster
- But Lloyd George wanted the Belfast parliament to control all **nine** counties of Ulster (see map on page 8). He believed that with Catholics and Protestants fairly evenly balanced (51% Protestants to 49% Catholics) there was less chance of one discriminating against the other
- The unionists rejected nine counties. They only wanted six, because that guaranteed them a permanent majority of about 65%. Lloyd George had to give way because they had the support of the Conservatives, whose votes Lloyd George needed to maintain his Coalition Government.

The Government of Ireland Act, 1920

- The Government of Ireland Act was passed in **December 1920**. It **partitioned Ireland** into two states. 'Northern Ireland' had six counties, 'Southern Ireland' (which never functioned) had 26
- Carson retired and **Sir James Craig became first Prime Minister of Northern Ireland**, which officially came into existence in May 1921
- 1921: Soon after Lloyd George began negotiating with Sinn Féin (see page 20). De Valera wanted to **end partition and reunite the country**. Craig was alarmed but determined to hold onto all six counties. The Conservatives backed him and the Ulster Unionists
- Lloyd George's solution was to include a '**Boundary Commission**' in the Treaty with Sinn Féin
- It would consist of **three men**, (i) one from the North (ii) one from the Free State and (iii) a British-appointed neutral chairman
- They would redraw border between north and south according to:
  - ❍ The **wishes of the people**
  - ❍ Economic and geographic considerations
- Lloyd George convinced Collins and Griffith that the Commission would give mainly nationalist areas, like Tyrone and Fermanagh, to the south. Most nationalists accepted this idea.

1924–1925: The Boundary Commission

- The Boundary Commission did not begin work until 1924 because:
  - ❍ of the civil war in the Free State
  - ❍ the refusal of Craig to name anyone to it

- Finally, the British appointed **J Fisher** (a friend of Craig's) as the Unionist representative and a South African, **J Feetham**, as the neutral chairman. Cosgrave appointed his Education Minister, **Eoin MacNeill** to represent the nationalists
- On 7 November, 1925, London papers reported that they planned to alter the border only a little and to give some Free State land to Northern Ireland
- Horrified, Cosgrave and O'Higgins flew to London. They agreed with British to suppress the report, leaving the six county/twenty-six county border, set in the 1920 Government of Ireland Act, unchanged.

Partition consolidated

- Partition was a compromise between the wishes of nationalists and unionists. No one wanted it and it left no side fully satisfied
- After 1920 the two parts of Ireland moved further apart
- The Irish Free State moved away from the United Kingdom to full independence, while Northern Ireland remained loyal to the British connection
- Each state developed different economic, education and health systems
- Catholic sectarianism became dominant in the South and Protestant sectarianism in the North
- The experience of the second World War, when the south remained neutral, while Northern Ireland was fully involved, sealed the difference.

Questions

For Examination questions on Later Modern Ireland, Topic 3 see page 275.

Your revision notes

Under the terms of the Anglo-Irish Treaty, **the Irish Free State** was officially set up on 6 December, 1922, exactly one year after the Treaty was signed.

- The **Cumann na nGaedheal Party** (the pro-Treaty section of the "second" Sinn Féin) formed the government.
  - It was led by **William T Cosgrave** as President (PM)
  - The Vice President was **Kevin O'Higgins**, who was also Minister for Home Affairs (Justice)
  - **Richard Mulcahy** was Minister for Defence
  - **Patrick Hogan** was Minister for Agriculture
  - **Ernest Blythe** was Minister for Finance
- Their aims were to set up the new state and establish a democratic form of government.

Ending the Civil War

- The greatest threat to democracy was the civil war. It began when republicans refused to accept the people's support for the Treaty
- Cumann na nGaedheal responded to the IRA's campaign of terror and assassination by executing over 70 republicans and imprisoning hundreds of others without trial
- Though brutal, this policy was successful and in 1923 the IRA called a ceasefire
- The return to peace and stability was helped by:
  - Having unarmed **Gardaí** who were able to win the trust of resentful republican supporters
  - Freeing republican prisoners within a year of the ceasefire.

Setting up the Irish Free State

- At the same time the Cumann na nGaedheal government set up the machinery of government
- They wrote a **democratic Constitution**:
  - There was a **Dáil** and a **Senate**
  - Men and women had equal citizenship
  - Freedom of speech and religion were guaranteed
- Under the terms of the Treaty **King George V** was **Head of State**. He was represented by the **Governor General**, who, Cosgrave insisted, must be an Irishman. They appointed **Tim Healy** as the first Governor General

- TDs had to take an oath of allegiance to the Constitution and of loyalty to the King
- They set up government departments and civil service and re-organised the courts.

The Army Mutiny

Another threat to democracy came in 1924 with the **Army Mutiny**:
- In the War of Independence, the Dáil had not controlled the IRA and in the civil war the **Free State army** was often undisciplined. It also grew big and expensive
- When the war ended, Mulcahy began to demobilise it
- Some officers who had fought with Collins resented this. They complained that preference was given to ex-British soldiers
- O'Higgins feared they planned a military coup. He sacked the leaders and forced Mulcahy to resign
- Although he over-reacted, his actions made it clear that from then on the Irish army must be under government control.

The Boundary Commission

- A bigger crisis for the Cosgrave government was the **Boundary Commission** (see page 35)
- When it became clear that it would not give large areas of Northern Ireland to the South, Cosgrave and O'Higgins got it suppressed. This angered many of their own followers and some TDs left the Party
- These events weakened Cumann na nGaedheal, but they could not be defeated in the Dáil because the only opposition there came from the small **Labour Party**.

The origin of Fianna Fáil 1923-1926

- In 1922, when the second Sinn Féin Party split over the Treaty, the anti-Treaty faction kept the name **Sinn Féin**
- Led by de Valera, it won 44 seats in the 1923 election. These TDs **abstained from Dáil Éireann** because of the oath to the king
- In 1924, Cosgrave freed the republicans and Sinn Féin set up its own "republican Dáil" (like in 1919). This failed because an Irish government was now in place
- But because Sinn Féin was not in the Dáil, it was unable to embarrass Cosgrave over the Army Mutiny and the Boundary Commission
- By 1926, de Valera realised the **abstention policy was futile**. He proposed that Sinn Féin get the oath removed and then enter the Dáil
- When the IRA rejected this, he left Sinn Féin and set up a new party, **Fianna Fáil**

- Most Sinn Féin TDs and branches joined the new party. By 1930, de Valera and **Seán Lemass** had built it into a well organised, nationwide party.

1927: A year of change

- By 1927, Cumann na nGaedheal was getting unpopular because:
  - ○ The Boundary Commission failed to end partition
  - ○ The economy was doing badly
  - ○ It had cut the small old age pension by 10%
  - ○ It planned to reduce the number of pubs
- Some of its own TDs broke away and voted with the Labour Party against Cosgrave's government.

In June, Cosgrave called an election.
- Cumann na nGaedheal won 47 seats (down from 63 in 1923)
- Discontented voters turned to Labour which won 22 seats (up from 14)
- Fianna Fáil only won 44 seats (the same as Sinn Féin in 1923)
- If all the parties were in the Dáil, Cosgrave would be beaten, but because Fianna Fáil still abstained from the Dáil, he was safe.

In July, IRA men murdered Kevin O'Higgins.
- Determined to strengthen democracy, Cosgrave brought in the **Electoral Amendment Bill**. It said a TD must enter the Dáil within six months or lose his seat
- Faced with this ultimatum, de Valera took the oath and entered the Dáil
- He then put down a motion of no confidence in Cumann na nGaedheal, but Cosgrave survived by one vote.

In September, Cosgrave called another election.
- Now that Fianna Fáil was in the Dáil, dissatisfied voters backed it. It won 57 seats (up from 44)
- But people who feared another civil war, went back to supporting Cumann na nGaedheal which went up to 62. Cosgrave continued to lead the government until 1932
- These events are important because they established normal democratic politics (a government and a strong opposition) in the Irish Free State.

1927–1932: The rise of Fianna Fáil

- Although now in the Dáil, Fianna Fáil TDs still rejected the Free State Constitution. They attacked Free State institutions (Governor General/ Senate/Commonwealth membership) and kept close ties with the IRA
- Seán Lemass said Fianna Fáil was a "slightly constitutional" party

- But that frightened off voters, who feared another war with Britain, so Fianna Fáil also developed a new economic policy. They proposed:
  - To keep £5 million land annuities in Ireland to invest in industry
  - To protect Irish industries and jobs with tariffs on imports
  - To encourage farmers to grow food products to replace imports (**self-sufficiency**)
- These proposals became popular with voters when the **Great Depression** began in 1930.

> **Remember…**
> Land annuities: money the British Government lent to Irish farmers so they could buy their farms. They paid it back in annual instalments (annuities).

Cumann na nGaedheal and the 'red scare'

- In the Great Depression unemployment rose and several left-wing movements appeared:
  - **Saor Éire**, a breakaway from the IRA, organised small farmers in the west against land annuities
  - A small **Communist Party**
- The existence of a Communist Party in Ireland led to a 'red scare'. Bishops and Cumann na nGaedheal leaders denounced the 'communist menace'
- Cosgrave introduced **Article 2A** into the Constitution to set up a military tribunal to try "subversives"
- The first trial was of the editor of the Fianna Fáil newspaper, *The Irish Press*
- To many, this looked like an attack on democracy and it actually helped Fianna Fáil.

The 1932 election consolidates democracy

- Cosgrave called an election in January 1932
- He pointed to Cumann na nGaedheal's record since 1922, but had no solution to the Depression
- Fianna Fáil put forward its economic policy and promised to dismantle the Treaty
- Fianna Fáil won 72 seats, enough to take power with the backing of the Labour Party
- Many wondered if Cosgrave would accept the election result, but he told army, police, civil service and the British to accept the wishes of the voters.
- The **hand over of power was trouble-free**, a big step on the way to making the country a democracy – quite an achievement in Europe in the 1930s.

William T Cosgrave (1880–1965)

- Born in Dublin, Cosgrave helped found **Sinn Féin** and was elected a Sinn Féin member of Dublin Corporation. He joined the Volunteers and fought in 1916. His death sentence was reduced and he was freed in 1917
- Elected Sinn Féin MP for Kilkenny, de Valera appointed him **Minister for Local Government** in the first Dáil Cabinet in 1919
- After delegates signed the **Treaty**, he supported their demand that it be sent to the Dáil. In the debate, he accepted Collins's argument that it was the best deal they could win. He remained as Minister in the Griffith/Collins government
- After Collins was killed in August 1922, a frightened Cabinet chose **Cosgrave** as leader because he was the oldest, had the longest political experience and no military connections
- Quiet but firm, Cosgrave backed the execution of leading republicans in retaliation for the murder of a pro-Treaty TD. This hard-line policy helped to end the civil war in May 1923. He then encouraged democratic politics by holding free elections in 1923 and freeing most republicans by 1924
- In 1923, Cosgrave formed **Cumann na nGaedheal**. It was poorly organised and never won an over-all majority in any election
- From **1923** to **1927**, with only the small Labour Party to oppose them in the Dáil, Cosgrove's government **(a)** wrote a democratic Constitution, **(b)** set up an army, police and civil service, **(c)** established civilian control over the army, **(d)** re-organised the courts and **(e)** made **Irish compulsory** in schools
- When the **Boundary Commission** failed, Cosgrave negotiated the **Anglo-Irish Agreement** which left the border unchanged
- In **economic policy**, they resisted demands for protection, kept free trade and low taxes
- In **foreign policy** they joined the League of Nations and sent diplomats to Washington, Paris, etc
- In **Anglo-Irish policy** they expanded the sovereignty of the Dominions through **the Balfour Declaration** (1926) and the **Statute of Westminster** (1931)
- In **June 1927 election**, Cumann na nGaedheal lost seats. After the murder of O'Higgins, Cosgrave's **Electoral Amendment Bill** forced Fianna Fáil into the Dáil. This was good for Irish democracy, though bad for his party
- They recovered most of the lost seats in September 1927 election and stayed in power until 1932
- Alarmed by the growth of left-wing movements in 1931, Cosgrave put **Article 2A** into the Constitution, taking power to try them in military courts
- Cumann na nGaedheal had no answers to the economic problems in 1930, and Fianna Fáil won the 1932 election
- To their surprise, Cosgrave handed over power peacefully and told the army and civil service to accept the democratic decision of the people
- In opposition, he did not trust Fianna Fáil to uphold democracy. When IRA men broke up Cumann na nGaedheal meetings, he joined with Eoin O'Duffy's Blueshirts to form a new party, Fine Gael, with O'Duffy as leader
- But O'Duffy had fascist sympathies. After a year, he was sacked and Cosgrave took over again
- From 1934–1943, Cosgrave led Fine Gael. He criticised Fianna Fáil policies, but never won popular support. Fine Gael declined steadily and Cosgrave retired in 1944. He died in 1965.

General policies

- Fianna Fáil won the 1932 election on a promise to:
  - ○ Dismantle the Treaty
  - ○ End land annuity payments to Britain and invest the money in Ireland
  - ○ Seek economic self-sufficiency by getting farmers to switch from pasture (raising animals) to tillage (growing crops) to replace imported food
  - ○ Create jobs by protecting Irish industries with tariffs on imports (see economic policies on page 50).

1932 – 1935: The 'economic war' with Britain

- Once elected, Fianna Fáil began to keep its promises:
- De Valera's Bill to **abolish the oath** was delayed by the Cumann na nGaedheal-controlled Senate, but finally passed in 1933
- The British protested, but were unable to do anything because of the **Statute of Westminster** (see page 44)
- The 1932 budget **imposed tariffs** on 43 imports (mostly from Britain) and **withheld £5 million in land annuities**
- The British retaliated by imposing **a tax on Irish cattle** equal to the £5 million. Their aim was to make Fianna Fáil unpopular
- This policy gave Fianna Fáil an excuse to impose more tariffs (1,000 by 1933). This hit farmers and consumers, but de Valera was able to present it as standing up to Britain and so avoided blame
- These policies combined into the 'economic war' with Britain. It damaged the economy severely until it was eased by **the Coal-Cattle pact** in 1935 (see Fianna Fáil economic policy on page 50).

Republican violence

- In 1932, the IRA had 30,000 members and backed Fianna Fáil in the 1932 election. After it, triumphant IRA men attacked Cumann na nGaedheal meetings
- Cumann na nGaedheal leaders asked a group of former Free State army men, the **Army Comrades Association (ACA)** to act as bodyguards
- In January 1933, de Valera called a sudden election. During the campaign, there were riots between the IRA and the ACA.

The 'Blueshirts' episode

- When Fianna Fáil won an over-all majority, de Valera demanded the resignation of Garda Commissioner, **Eoin O'Duffy**
- He then became head of the ACA, renamed them the **National Guard**, dressed them in **blueshirts** and adopted a programme based on Mussolini's Corporate State. In August, he announced a rally in front of Leinster House
- Fearing a coup (like Mussolini's "march on Rome"), de Valera banned it. He also used Article 2A to outlaw the National Guard and set up a special police unit (the "**Broy Harriers**"), to deal with it
- Cosgrave and others, knowing how Mussolini and Hitler took power, and distrusting De Valera, feared a dictatorship
- In September 1933, **Cumann na nGaedheal**, the **National Guard** and a newly formed **Centre Party**, joined together to stop him. They called themselves **Fine Gael** and elected O'Duffy leader
- Fine Gael gained support from bigger farmers, badly hit by economic war. They **refused to pay rates (local taxes)**
- In late-1933, riots between Broy Harriers (collecting the rates) and the Blueshirts (defending the farmers) were common
- This embarrassed Cosgrave who always backed law and order. It became worse when O'Duffy threatened to invade Northern Ireland
- **September 1934**: At their first annual Ard Fheis, Fine Gael replaced O'Duffy with Cosgrave. The Blueshirts declined in number, and in 1936, O'Duffy led the remnant to Spain to fight for Franco.

De Valera and the IRA

- In 1932, the IRA backed Fianna Fáil, hoping it would destroy the hated Treaty and reunite Ireland
- Many were satisfied when de Valera abolished the oath. Others were won over by getting pensions for the War of Independence, or by joining the Broy Harriers or the army
- But this was not enough for deeply committed republicans. By 1934 they were disillusioned with de Valera
- Between 1934 and 1936, the IRA murdered a number of people. De Valera pleaded with the leaders to give up their guns. When they refused, he outlawed the IRA in June 1936
- In January 1939, the IRA set off bombs in Britain and, although de Valera did not yet know it, they were also in contact with Germany
- Fearing this would give Britain an excuse to invade, de Valera got the Dáil to pass the **Offences against the State Act** which let him intern IRA men without trial
- During the war, over 500 were interned and about a dozen died on hunger strike or were hanged for murder.

Éamon De Valera, the statesman (1924 – 1959)

- By 1925, de Valera realised abstention was futile, but when the IRA would not agree he left **Sinn Féin** in 1926 and set up **Fianna Fáil**. Most Sinn Féin TDs and branches went with him
- Fianna Fáil won 44 seats in the June 1927 election. In July, after O'Higgins's, murder, Cosgrave's **Electoral Amendment Bill**, forced de Valera and Fianna Fáil TDs to take the oath and enter the Dáil. In the September election they won 57 seats. From then until 1932, they were the main opposition Party in the Dáil
- Fianna Fáil won the 1932 election. De Valera at once abolished the oath and withheld £5 million in land annuities, leading to an **economic war** with Britain
- De Valera left economic issues to his economic Ministers. His main interest was in **foreign** and **Anglo-Irish policy**. He appointed himself **Minister for External Affairs** to deal with them
- He supported the **League of Nations**, went frequently to Geneva for meetings, and backed its policies like sanctions against Italy over Abyssinia
- He dismantled the Treaty bit by bit, removing the Oath and Senate and downgraded the Governor General. The British could do nothing because the 1931 Statute of Westminster allowed Dominions to change British laws
- In 1937, de Valera wrote a new **Constitution**. He hoped an Irish-written Constitution would win the support of all Irish people
- As a European war loomed in 1938, de Valera and British Prime Minister **Chamberlain** made the **Anglo-Irish Agreements** which restored the Treaty ports and made neutrality possible
- When war began, de Valera declared neutrality, but to avoid a British invasion he followed a **pro-Allied policy**. He personally dealt with the representatives of the warring countries in Dublin
- After France fell in 1940, he turned down Churchill's offer of Irish unity in return for joining in the war
- After America joined in December 1941, pressure on Ireland increased. On the eve of D-Day, the "American Note" demanded de Valera close German and Italian embassies. When he refused, all travel to Britain was stopped for six weeks
- When Hitler died, de Valera visited the German embassy to formally offer condolences, which gave the impression of support for Germany
- From 1932 to 1948, Valera dealt firmly with anyone who threatened his government. He **(a)** banned the Blueshirts **(b)** weakened the IRA by enrolling IRA men in the army and police and giving them pensions. When hard-line republicans returned to violence he **(c)** outlawed them
- In 1939, when the IRA threatened neutrality with bombs in Britain, he passed the **Offences against the State Act**. During the war, 500 people were interned and he allowed several to die on hunger strike or be executed for murder
- An **astute politician**, de Valera won six general elections. He often called a snap election catching the opposition unprepared
- By 1948, post-war economic problems made Fianna Fáil unpopular. De Valera called a sudden election. Other parties formed a Coalition and he lost power.

13.1   The start of Irish foreign policy

- From 1919 Irish governments had to decide how to deal with neighbouring countries. This led them to develop a **foreign policy**
- Irish foreign policy began when the First Dáil appealed to the Paris Peace Conference to recognise the Irish right to self-determination
- Later, the Dáil sent representatives to Rome and Berlin to counter British propaganda and set out the case for Irish independence.

The Importance of Anglo-Irish Policy

- In the Irish Free State, the main part of foreign policy had to be **Anglo-Irish policy** (i.e. relations with Britain) because:
  - ❑   Britain is Ireland's closest neighbour
  - ❑   Most of Irish trade was with Britain
  - ❑   Many Irish people lived in Britain
  - ❑   The Anglo-Irish Treaty made the Free State a **Dominion of the British Commonwealth**.

Did the Treaty give Ireland Full Sovereignty?

- The Treaty made the Irish Free State a **Dominion of the British Commonwealth**. But was a dominion really a sovereign (i.e. fully independent) nation or was it still under the control of Britain? This was the issue that divided the two sides during the Treaty debates
- After 1922, both Cumann na nGaedheal and Fianna Fáil used foreign and Anglo-Irish policy to assert Irish sovereignty.

13.2   Cumann na nGaedheal Foreign/Anglo-Irish Policy

Asserting Irish sovereignty

- Although Cumann na nGaedheal leaders argued that the Treaty made the Free State a **fully sovereign state**, they feared that the British might go on interfering in Irish affairs. To counter British power and demonstrate Irish independence:
  - ❑   They joined the League of Nations
  - ❑   They registered the Treaty at the League as an "inter-national agreement". The British objected, saying it was just an internal British matter, but the Irish had their way

○ Other Dominions were content to let the British ambassador represent them in Paris, Washington, etc. But Cosgrave sent Irish diplomats to these countries.

Expanding Dominion Status

- British and Dominion leaders met regularly at **Imperial Conferences**
- In 1923, O'Higgins attended his first **Imperial Conference**. He found the British treated the Dominions as equals. But he returned home determined to get a legal basis for this informal equality
- Canada and South Africa wanted the same. O'Higgins worked with them at the 1926 Imperial Conference to get the **Balfour Declaration**, which stated: "*all Dominions are equal to each other and to Britain*"
- In 1931, the British turned this declaration into law with the **Statute of Westminster**. It gave the Dominions full legal right to change any law passed for them by the Westminster parliament
- When de Valera changed the Treaty, he was acting within British law and there was nothing the British could legally do about it.

13.3 Fianna Fáil's Foreign and Anglo-Irish Policy

In the 1932 election, Fianna Fáil promised to dismantle the Treaty and assert full Irish sovereignty. From 1932 to 1945, de Valera kept control of foreign and Anglo-Irish affairs in his own hands.

De Valera and the League of Nations

- De Valera was more active in the League than Cosgrave and often spoke at meetings in Geneva. He hoped its policy of 'collective security' would protect Ireland if Britain retaliated when he dismantled the Treaty
- Later he also hoped the League could prevent another European war. He supported its sanctions on Mussolini over Ethiopia and backed Chamberlain at the time of the Munich Crisis (see page 188).
- By 1939, he realised that nothing could stop Hitler.

De Valera's Anglo-Irish policy

- Dismantling the Treaty was de Valera's priority. This led to a kind of 'cold war' with Britain from 1932 to 1938
- In 1932, he removed the oath to the king and withheld £5 million in land annuities
- The British feared Ireland would leave the Commonwealth. The Statute of Westminster prevented them from doing anything about the oath, so they focussed on the annuities, which were a valid debt. They put taxes on Irish cattle exports to Britain equal to £5 million. They hoped to make de Valera unpopular, but instead helped him win the 1933 election

- Contact with Britain almost ceased up to 1938, apart from **the Coal-Cattle Pact** (1935) which eased the tariffs on these two items.

A new Constitution: Bunreacht na hÉireann

- De Valera took the Treaty apart, step by step. He removed the oath, downgraded the role of Governor General, abolished the Senate and ended appeals to the Privy Council
- In 1936, he used the abdication of King Edward VIII as an excuse to remove the king as Head of State (the **External Relations Act**)
- De Valera wanted to replace the 1922 (Treaty-dominated) Constitution with one he wrote himself. He consulted many people including heads of various religions
- In 1937, he introduced his new Constitution, *Bunreacht na hÉireann.* Important provisions in it were:
  - ❍ The Head of State was a **President** elected every seven years. This made the country a republic in fact – although it was 1949 before Ireland was actually named a republic
  - ❍ Rights to freedom, justice, ownership of property, etc, were guaranteed
  - ❍ The Catholic Church had a "special position" because it was the Church of the vast majority. This was less than the Pope and many Catholic clergy wanted. Other Churches and the Jewish community were also guaranteed rights
  - ❍ Divorce was outlawed
  - ❍ The influence of Mussolini's Corporate State ideas (popular with Catholics in the 1930s) are seen in the title of the head of government (*Taoiseach*) and in a Senate elected by "vocational panels"
- In the first **referendum** in Irish history, people voted to accept it
- The British Cabinet were unsure if this meant Ireland was still in the Commonwealth, but decided to go on treating the country as if nothing had changed.

Mending fences

- By 1938, both countries wanted to improve relations
- De Valera had, with his new Constitution, asserted Irish sovereignty. Now that war loomed in Europe, he needed to make peace with Britain
- In Britain, a new Prime Minister, **Neville Chamberlain**, was willing to appease de Valera in the hope that Ireland would support Britain against Hitler.

1938: The Anglo-Irish Agreements

- De Valera and other Ministers went to London and after negotiations, signed the Anglo-Irish Agreements:
  - ○ Ireland paid £10 million to settle the land annuities
  - ○ Trade barriers on agricultural produce were to be reduced
  - ○ As a gesture of appeasement (and because they were too costly to maintain) Chamberlain gave the three "Treaty ports" to Ireland. De Valera guaranteed that no other country would be allowed to use them. Without this neutrality in the second World War would have been impossible
- De Valera had hoped to achieve something on partition, but Chamberlain said that was a matter for the Northern Ireland government.

Questions

For Examination questions on Later Modern Ireland, Topic 3 see page 275.

Your revision notes

14.1 1922 – 1932: Cumann na nGaedheal's Economic Policies

Deciding on an economic policy

- The Cumann na nGaedheal government had to decide on an economic policy, but **Cosgrave**, **Blythe** and the other leaders had no economic experience
- They asked advice from civil servants who had worked in the British system and bankers/businessmen who traded mostly with Britain. They urged the government to continue the economic policy the British had followed since the 1890s
- As a result, Cumann na nGaedheal:
  - Retained **free trade** and **refused to introduce protection** (taxes on imports)
  - Concentrated on **improving agriculture**
  - Kept **taxes low** and cut spending (e.g. reduced the old age pension by 10%).

Agricultural policy

- Agriculture was badly hit by (i) the post-first World War fall in food prices and (ii) damage to creameries, etc, in the civil war. It also had serious structural weaknesses: 60% of farms were under 30 acres, too small for economic development; 25% of farmers were over 60, too old to adopt new techniques
- **Patrick Hogan**, the Minister for Agriculture, tackled these problems in the way the British had by:
  - Completing land purchase with the 1923 **Land Act**
  - Letting the **Land Commission** buy up under-used big farms and distribute the land to raise farm size
  - Setting up the **Agricultural Credit Corporation** to give farmers cheap loans
  - Getting the Department of Agriculture to **instruct farmers** on new techniques and **set quality standards** on eggs, butter, etc, to recover the British market lost after the first World War
- Cumann na nGaedheal policy favoured big farmers at the expense of small holders. It was successful in recovering lost British markets by 1930.

Industrial policy

- Advised by civil servants like **J J McElligott**, the Minister for Finance, **Earnest Blythe**, did not intervene in industry (which provided 60% of GNP in the 1920s)
- The only exception was the state-financed **Shannon Scheme** in 1923 and the establishment of the state-owned **ESB** to provide cheap power through a national grid in 1927
- Some Cumann na nGaedheal TDs wanted to **protect industry** from British competition with tariffs, but Blythe resisted
- He set up an enquiry which proposed tariffs on a handful of items. In 1926 a **Tariff Commission** was to look at individual demands for protection. By 1930 it had agreed to impose tariffs on three items
- After the Depression developed, they agreed to several more in 1931.

The Depression and the defeat of Cumann na nGaedheal

- The Depression hit in 1930. Industries closed and foreign goods were dumped here. The demand for protection grew
- Like most governments, Cumann na nGaedheal cut spending (wages for teachers/guards, etc.) making them unpopular
- In the 1932 election, they pointed to the success of economic policies
- But Fianna Fáil promised to create jobs by (i) investing the land annuities in Ireland (ii) protecting Irish industries (iii) self-sufficiency (making everything possible in Ireland to replace imports). This was popular and they won.

14.2 1932–1948: Fianna Fáil's Economic Policies

1932–1935: The Economic War

- Fianna Fáil's two aims of protection and dismantling the Treaty led to an 'economic war' with Britain in 1932
- Their first budget put tariffs on over 40 items, mostly coming from Britain. It also withheld £5 million in land annuities
- The British retaliated with a tax on Irish cattle, to collect the equivalent of the £5 million
- Fianna Fáil then imposed tariffs on 1,000 items
- This damaged trade between the two countries. Irish exports to Britain fell from £47 million in 1929 to £18 million by 1934.

Agricultural policy: 1932–1939

- The economic war hit farmers badly. It was almost impossible to find a buyer for cattle
- Fianna Fáil encouraged farmers to switch to growing wheat and sugar beet to replace imports. Fianna Fáil called this 'self-sufficiency', which was a popular idea in the 1930s
- It made little difference. Up to 1936, **arable farming** (i.e. crop-growing) only increased by 10%
- Fianna Fáil policy did little for small farmers of the west. In 1937, some farmers formed a new party, Clann na Talmhain.

Returning to normal

- By 1935, both Britain and Ireland needed to end economic war
- The **1935 Coal-Cattle Pact** eased tariffs on these items
- The **1938 Anglo-Irish Agreement** was intended to restore trade in agriculture to what it had been in the 1920s, but the second World War started before it could work.

Industrial policies: 1932–1939

- Fianna Fáil was more concerned about industry than agriculture

Seán Lemass dominated industrial policy as **Minister for Industry and Commerce** from 1932–1948:

- ❍ He controlled imports by tariffs and licences
- ❍ He fostered **new industries** with grants, cheap loans from the **Industrial Credit Corporation** and by giving them monopolies
- ❍ Most new industries were small, making things like cloth, cutlery or carpets for the Irish market only – not for export
- ❍ To satisfy Fianna Fáil's nationalist ideals, the **Control of Manufacturers Act**, insisted new industries be Irish-owned, but Lemass applied the Act flexibly
- ❍ He set up **semi-state companies** to develop areas where there was not enough private capital, e.g. Aer Lingus, Bord na Móna.

Results of Lemass's industrial policy

1. It increased the number of industrial jobs by 50% and developed industrial experience – useful in the depressed 1930s
2. But tariffs damaged the old exporting industries like Guinness which relocated their factories to Britain
3. The new industries were small, inefficient and did not earn their way by exporting. This was a problem by 1939, but the war masked it. It finally produced an economic crisis in the 1950s.

J J McElligott (1893-1974)

- Kerry-born James J McElligott graduated from UCD and joined the British civil service. In 1913, he enrolled in the Volunteers, and fought in the GPO in 1916. After being sacked he worked in London as a financial journalist
- In 1923, he became **Assistant Secretary** in the **Department of Finance** and worked with **Joseph Brennan**, the Department Secretary
- In 1927, he replaced Brennan as **Secretary of the Department of Finance**, the top job in the civil service, a post he held through several changes of government until 1953
- Under Cumann na nGaedheal, McElligott worked closely with Finance Minister, **Ernest Blythe**. To help big businesses and farmers, they kept government spending and taxes low, while maintaining free trade. But this policy left little to spend on health care, education and housing
- Blythe appointed McElligott Chairman of the **Tariff Commission** to look at requests for tariffs, one by one. By 1930, they dealt with 12 requests, but granted only three – on rosary beads, margarine and flour
- McElligott opposed government involvement in industry. He opposed spending on the **Shannon Scheme** or setting up the **ESB** as a state-run company
- The Depression in 1930 led to a new policy. McElligott was removed from the Commission and tariffs imposed, even before Fianna Fáil came to power
- McElligott was uncomfortable with **Fianna Fáil's policy** of protection, high government spending and government interference in the economy
- He clashed with **Seán Lemass**, but got on better with Minister for Finance, **Seán MacEntee**, who came to share his views
- McElligott approved of de Valera's decision to talk to Britain in 1938. He was on the Irish delegation and was closely involved in negotiating the end of the dispute over land annuities
- When Fianna Fáil set up a **Banking Commission** in the mid-1930s, McElligott strongly influenced its report which recommended **keeping the Irish pound linked to sterling** and setting up a **Central Bank**. This was done in 1943
- McElligott was involved in the government's preparation for war. Wartime conditions forced him to accept more government involvement in the economy, e.g. he supported a government-owned **Irish Shipping**
- In 1943, when planning for post-war conditions began, McElligott successfully resisted Lemass's suggestion that the economic ideas of **John Maynard Keynes** be adopted
- He also opposed Irish involvement in post-war international financial organisations like the International Monetary Fund (IMF) and all new economic thinking up to his resignation in 1953.

The policy of neutrality

- When Hitler invaded Poland on **1 September, 1939**, de Valera told the Dáil that Ireland would be neutral. He did this because:
  - ○ It divided people less than the other options
  - ○ It showed the reality of Irish independence
  - ○ It protected the people from suffering
  - ○ He said partition made co-operation with Britain impossible
- On 2 September, the Dáil declared a **state of emergency**. It gave government extensive powers to run the country while the 'emergency' lasted
- This allowed them to **censor** newspapers, letters, radio, etc. Censorship kept Irish people from learning what was going on
- Thousands of men volunteered to join the army, but it had been neglected for years and had very few modern weapons.

Feeding the people

- In 1939, 95% of imports were carried in by foreign ships, leaving the country vulnerable to British pressure
- The government set up a **Department of Supplies** under **Seán Lemass**, to deal with the problem
- Wheat was the main imported food. Lemass ordered farmers to grow more wheat and bakers to use whole-grain flour. Fertiliser for farming was scarce after Britain cut off supplies in 1942. Farm productivity fell, but bread rationing was avoided
- **Strict rationing** was imposed on imported tea. Fruit like bananas and oranges disappeared from the shops
- Imported **coal and oil were very scarce** and tightly rationed. Horse transport and turf for cooking and heating were partial substitutes. But many new industries had to close or go on part-time working
- Lemass set up **Irish Shipping** in 1941 to carry imports but only a few elderly ships were available to purchase
- The poor did badly as wages were controlled more than prices. Diseases of poverty like TB increased.

The IRA threatens neutrality

- In 1939, the IRA made contact with the Nazis and bombed Britain. This was a serious threat to Irish neutrality
- Before the war began, the Dáil passed the **Offences against the State Act** taking powers to intern them without trial

- During the war over 500 IRA men were interned, several died on hunger strike or were hanged for murder
- The German Intelligence Department (**Abwehr**) sent IRA Chief of Staff, **Seán Russell** to Ireland in a U-boat, but he died on the way
- German spies landed to make contact with the IRA, but were easily rounded up. Only **Hermann Goertz** lasted more than a few weeks, but he had no radio to contact Germany.

Managing neutrality

- De Valera, as **Minister for External Affairs**, kept the management of neutrality in his own hands
- He dealt directly with the British representative, **Sir John Maffey**, the German representative, **Edward Hempel** and the American representative **David Gray**
- Only Gray was hostile to Irish neutrality. The others explained Irish difficulties to their own governments. Hempel disapproved of the Abwehr's links with IRA, which threatened Irish neutrality.

Churchill's offer of unity

- The **most dangerous time** for Irish neutrality was **from May to July 1940**, after the fall of France
- British Prime Minister Churchill sent **Malcolm McDonald** to offer de Valera Irish unity in return for joining in the war
- He turned the offer down, possibly because he did not believe they could deliver the Unionists or because he thought Germany was winning and did not want to join the losing side
- For a while, de Valera feared a British invasion, but it did not come
- Churchill sent another offer in 1941 when the US entered the war, but it did not develop further
- In 1944, on eve of D-Day, Gray delivered the "**American Note**" demanding that de Valera close the German and Italian offices. When he refused, all travel to Britain was stopped for six weeks.

A pro-Allied policy

- When Hitler died in 1945, de Valera visited the German embassy to sympathise with Hempel. This gave the impression of support for Germany, but in practice Irish neutrality was **pro-Allied**:
  - ❑ Irish people fought with the Allies, worked in British munitions factories and sold food to Britain
  - ❑ The Irish army drew up plans with the British army for joint action against a German invasion
  - ❑ De Valera sent the British information gathered in Irish embassies in Europe and by eavesdropping on Germans in Ireland

○ British soldiers and airmen landing in Ireland were freed, but Germans were interned

- These policies enabled Irish neutrality to succeed because the Allies got what they wanted without an invasion

- Neutrality also succeeded because (**i**) Ireland was too far for the Germans to get here easily. (**ii**) As democracies fighting tyranny, Britain and the US could not easily invade a small democratic country.

Questions

For Examination questions on Later Modern Ireland, Topic 3 see page 275.

Your revision notes

1945–1948: Post-war problems

- After the war, the economy was in difficulty:
  - ○ Inflation rose when wartime wage restraint ended and strikes followed as workers tried to catch up
  - ○ The wet summer of 1946 caused a bad harvest and bread was rationed for the first time
  - ○ The bitterly cold winter of 1946–1947 caused shortages and made life miserable for many people.

Forming the first Coalition

- This made Fianna Fáil unpopular, but opposition parties (**Fine Gael**, **Labour** and **Clann na Talmhain**) seemed too divided to threaten it
- In 1946, **Sean MacBride**, a former leader of the IRA, formed a new Party, **Clann na Poblachta**. It attracted young people, fed up with the old 'civil war' parties
- The Clann grew quickly, winning several by-elections in 1947
- To catch the Clann before it grew stronger, de Valera called a snap election early in 1948. Although Fianna Fáil lost eight seats it could have formed a government
- But Opposition Parties had one thing in common: they wanted to get rid of de Valera, so they formed a Coalition (or "Inter-party") government. **John A Costello** was Taoiseach and MacBride Minister for External Affairs.

Declaring a Republic

- By 1948, only the **External Relations Act** linked Ireland to the Commonwealth. MacBride had campaigned to repeal it, but the government had not decided what to do when Costello visited Canada
- There, apparently without consulting the Cabinet, he told a reporter, they planned to leave the Commonwealth and declare a republic
- The British, who were not consulted, passed the **Ireland Act** in 1949. This accepted the Irish decision, left Irish citizens free to travel to and live in the UK but for the first time guaranteed that Northern Ireland could not be forced to join the South without the consent of its parliament.

17.1 Language, Religion and Art

Developing a new cultural identity

When the Irish Free State became independent, its leaders wanted to create a distinctively Irish cultural identity.

- Many of the leaders, both pro- and anti-Treaty who had been influenced by the Gaelic League, wanted to **revive Irish as a spoken language**
- Since the Free State was over 90% Roman Catholic, many leaders and most of the Catholic bishops and clergy wanted a country that reflected **Catholic moral values**
- These ideals often came into conflict with the views of a minority who wanted a country that would reflect **the best liberal values** of Europe, such as democracy, freedom of religion and the right to explore new ideas and new ways of expressing them without interference.

Reviving Irish

- As soon as the British left, nationalists changed place names to their Irish form – e.g. Kingstown became Dún Laoghaire and Maryborough became Portlaoise
- The Minister for Education, Eoin MacNéill, made Irish compulsory in primary schools
- To train Irish speaking teachers, free second level '**Preparatory Colleges**' were set up where all teaching was through Irish
- Gaeltacht students got scholarships to attend the Preparatory Colleges and their students got priority in admission to teacher training colleges
- In secondary schools, students had to pass Irish to get Intermediate and Leaving Certificate examinations and students who answered through Irish got extra marks
- Teachers and school children got grants to attend Irish colleges in the Gaeltacht
- People looking for jobs in the Garda Síochána or civil service had to pass an examination in Irish
- In 1937, de Valera made Irish the '*first official language*' in his Constitution, *Bunreacht na hÉireann*

Assessing the revival programme

- By the 1940s, over 70% of primary teachers could teach through Irish, 14% of primary schools used only Irish and 64% of secondary students did several subjects through Irish
- A modern literature in Irish had begun to develop, with fine poets like Seán Ó Ríordáin and novelists like Brian O'Nolan
- But overall the attempt to revive Irish failed because:
  - ❏ Outside the Gaeltacht few people used Irish as their everyday language because government departments, shops, the courts etc. still used English
  - ❏ New, attractive new forms of entertainment like films and radio used English not Irish
  - ❏ The policy of making Irish compulsory in schools angered many parents and students and turned them against Irish.

The power of the Catholic Church

- In the Irish Free State over 90% of the population were Roman Catholics
- Catholic priests and bishops had enormous influence. They controlled the schools where Catholics were educated and when they spoke on an issue, most Catholic voters listened to them.

The Catholic Church and political leaders

- Cosgrave, de Valera and most nationalist leaders were devout Catholics
- On **political issues**, they felt entitled to make up their own minds. De Valera and the republicans showed this when they ignored the bishops who condemned them during the civil war
- But on moral issues like divorce or contraception, they felt obliged to obey the teaching of the Pope and the Catholic bishops
- They listened when the bishops urged them to pass laws which would stop modern developments of which they disapproved.

A 'moral panic'

- Bishops and political leaders shared the 'moral panic' that was widespread across the western world after the first World War. Like older people everywhere, they believed that the moral standards of the young were declining due to:
  - ❏ New forms of entertainment like cheap magazines, films, radio and popular music like jazz
  - ❏ Motor cars and motor cycles which made it easier for the young to escape the watchful eyes of their parents
  - ❏ Young women who now enjoyed political and economic freedom which they showed by wearing short skirts and make up

- Bishops and priests in sermons and pastoral letters condemned these 'moral evils'
- Both the Cumann na nGaedheal and Fianna Fáil governments passed laws to limit their effects.

Censorship

- In 1923, censorship of films was introduced
- Even before independence, devout Catholics and Gaelic League supporters demanded the exclusion of British newspapers and magazines and at times the IRA seized and burned them
- In 1929, Cumann na nGaedheal set up the Censorship Board. It could ban books or magazines it considered 'indecent or obscene' or which advocated contraception
- The Board was free to decide what 'indecent or obscene' meant and it banned many books by the finest world authors for the flimsiest of reasons
- It was especially hard on books by Irish authors who presented a view of Ireland of which the Board did not approve. This made it very difficult for them to make a living.

Divorce

- Up to 1922, wealthy people could get a divorce by having a special act of parliament passed
- When asked if the Dáil would do the same, Cosgrave consulted the bishops and on their advice refused to continue this practice
- De Valera went further and outlawed divorce in *Bunreacht na hÉireann*.

Limits on entertainment

- In 1924, the hours public houses could open was cut, and in 1927, a new licensing system reduced their number in half
- In 1935, Fianna Fáil regulated dance halls. Many closed or were replaced by parish halls controlled by the clergy
- These changes reflected the growing influence of the Catholic Church in the Irish Free State. The most obvious sign of this was the Eucharistic Congress which was held in Dublin in 1932.

17.2 The 1932 Eucharistic Congress

Background

- Eucharistic Congresses were held every three years in different cities
- In 1929, Cosgrave's government established diplomatic relations with the Vatican. Following that the Pope agreed to allow the 1932 Eucharistic Congress to take place in Dublin. It was to celebrate the arrival of St Patrick in 432
- An election was due late in 1932, but to avoid a clash with the Congress, Cosgrave held it early. To his surprise he lost, so that it was de Valera and Fianna Fáil that enjoyed the limelight during the Congress.

Preparations

- Planning for it had begun in 1930 under the direction of Garda Commissioner, **Eoin O'Duffy**
- Around the country Catholics collected money to decorate their areas and held discussions and prayer meetings about the Eucharist
- In Dublin, every street was decorated with flowers, flags and altars
- Thousands of pilgrims poured in from around the world. The biggest contingent came from the United States. They were housed in tent cities around or in ships anchored in Dublin bay.

20–27 June, 1932: Congress week

- The week began when the Papal Legate (Pope's representative), **Cardinal Lauri**, landed in Dun Laoghaire. De Valera greeted him and crowds cheered him as he drove into Dublin
- Each day there were lectures on the Eucharist, special masses and receptions for the dignitaries
- The climax was mass in Phoenix Park attended by hundreds of thousands
- For the first time **radio** was used to let the Pope give his blessing personally and to allow people around the country to share in the ceremonies and listen as world-famous tenor, John McCormack, sang *Panis Angelicus*.

The impact of the Congress

- The success of the Congress made Irish people proud of their new state and its ability to organise a large international event
- It also showed the strength of belief among Irish Catholics
- It allowed de Valera and Fianna Fáil to draw close to the Catholic bishops and forget their disagreement over the civil war
- It increased the power and influence of the Catholic bishops.

A Catholic State?

- Under Fianna Fáil, the South became more obviously Catholic in its attitudes and laws
- In 1931, de Valera told the Fianna Fáil Ard Fheis that he was "a Catholic first"
- In *Bunreacht na hÉireann* in 1937, he gave the Catholic Church a '*special position*' because it was the church of the vast majority of Irish people. This was less than the Pope wanted, but far more than in the 1922 Constitution which merely guaranteed freedom of religion
- Fianna Fáil made contraception illegal and outlawed divorce in the Constitution
- Censorship of books and films was more thoroughly applied
- These changes made the south less attractive for Irish Protestants
- The proportion of Protestants in the population fell by 12% between 1926 and 1936, and by 14% from 1936 to 1946
- This was due to inter-marriage (Catholic priests insisted that children in a mixed marriage be brought up as Catholics) and to emigration caused by the weakness of the economy.

17.3 Developments in literature and art

- Censorship and the desire of the political and religious leaders to present an image of a pure, religious and Gaelic Ireland made life difficult for writers and artists who did not conform
- Work by older writers like J M Synge or W B Yeats, were acceptable.

W B Yeats

- Yeats was generally acknowledged as Ireland's greatest poet, especially after he won the Nobel Prize in 1923
- He wrote some of his best poetry in the 1920s
- Cosgrave made Yeats a Senator in 1923. In the Senate he opposed the moves towards censorship and the ending of divorce
- He was one of the group which designed the new Irish coins.

The Abbey and Séan O'Casey

- Yeats and Lady Gregory continued to run the Abbey. In 1924, they persuaded the government to give them an annual grant
- They put on three plays by Seán O'Casey, which dealt with the period from 1916 to 1921, and they defended him when some nationalists were offended by *The Plough and the Stars*
- But O'Casey's next play, *The Silver Tassie*, was experimental and they refused to put it on. O'Casey left Ireland and never returned
- The Abbey went into decline. Writers had to turn to the **Gate Theatre**, founded in 1930, to have more adventurous plays presented.

Younger writers

- Younger writers like Frank O'Connor, Seán Ó Faoláin, Patrick Kavanagh or Kate O'Brien who did not conform to the official attitude, found their novels banned by the Censorship Board
- In the 1940s, Seán Ó Faoláin set up a small magazine, **The Bell**. As well as publishing poetry, short stories and articles on current affairs, it campaigned against the stupidities of the censorship.

Developments in art

- The visual arts were neglected in the Free State, though images which reflected the Celtic designs of the Book of Kells, or paintings like those of **Paul Henry** which showed an idealised rural Ireland, were acceptable.

Jack B Yeats

- The greatest painter of the period was **Jack B Yeats**, the poet's brother. In his early years, he painted pictures of the people of the Gaeltacht – which can be seen as a visual equivalent of Synge's writings
- He supported the republicans during the civil war and painted pictures sympathetic to them which were popular
- But from the 1920s, he painted in an increasingly complex, expressionist style which did not appeal to most viewers and his pictures did not sell. Only in the 1960s was his genius appreciated.

The impact of European ideas

- Younger artists were influenced by new ideas in art, such as cubism, which were emerging in Europe in the early 20th century.
- One of them was **Evie Hone.**

Eva Hone (1894 – 1955)

- Born in Dublin, **Hone** came from a family that contained several distinguished Irish artists. At age 12, she contracted polio which left her lame and with one weak hand
- She studied art in London and Paris with her friend and fellow-artist, **Mainie Jellett**. In Paris, they came into contact with cubism and studied under Albert Gleizes. Under his influence, Hone arranged her paintings into harmonic abstractions of colour and shape
- In 1924, she and Jellett organised Dublin's first exhibition of abstract art, which shocked conservative Irish opinion. Hone also exhibited paintings at art shows in England, the US and Paris
- Hone was deeply religious, and in 1925 she briefly entered an Anglican convent. Later, in 1937, she became a Catholic. This may have influenced her desire to work in stained glass
- In 1933, she joined *An Túr Gloine*, a co-operative for making stained glass and mosaics which Sarah Purser set up around 1900. Her images in glass were simple, bold and often abstract, showing that cubist ideas continued to affect her work
- She quickly gained recognition and was commissioned by the Department of Industry and Commerce to make a window, *My Four Green Fields*, for the **Irish pavilion** at the 1939 World Fair in New York. It won first prize for stained glass and today is in the Government Buildings in Merrion Street, Dublin
- When *An Túr Gloine* closed in 1943, she set up her own studio in her home. She produced over 100 pieces of stained glass, many of them windows for churches. The most important is a huge window for the chapel of Eton school near London
- Although Hone is best remembered for her stained glass work, she also continued to paint. She and Mainie Jellett were founder members of the Irish Exhibition of Living Art in 1943, which aimed to make modern Irish art **known** the general public. They also exhibited pictures at the avant-garde White Stag Group of artists in Dublin in the 1940s
- Evie Hone died suddenly in 1955.

Questions

For Examination questions on Later Modern Ireland, Topic 3 see page 275.

18.1 Early years

The Constitution of Northern Ireland

- Northern Ireland, set up by the 1920 **Government of Ireland Act**, was part of the **United Kingdom of Great Britain and Northern Ireland**. The king was represented by the **Governor**
- It had a parliament consisting of a **Senate** and a **House of Commons**, with 52 MPs, elected by Proportional Representation (PR)
- It had a government with a **Prime Minister** and **six Ministers**. They controlled internal affairs like health and education
- But most taxation and all foreign policy and trade remained under the control of the Westminster parliament
- Northern Ireland elected 13 MPs to Westminster
- In the 1921 election, 40 Unionist MPs were elected. Their leader, **Sir James Craig** became the first Prime Minister of Northern Ireland. His Home Affairs Minister was **Richard Dawson Bates**.

1921 – 23: A violent beginning

- About two thirds of the people in Northern Ireland were unionists and one third were nationalists
- Nationalists refused to recognise the new state and the IRA attacked it. Riots and sectarian killings were common in border areas and Belfast in 1920–1922. About 400 people were killed – over 60% of them Catholics
- To defeat the IRA Craig and Dawson Bates introduced the **Special Powers Act** which allowed them to intern IRA men. Over 500 were imprisoned without trial
- They formed the Royal Ulster Constabulary (**RUC**) as an armed police force and allowed the re-establishment of the UVF to counter the IRA in border areas
- Dawson Bates created '**Special Constables**' to assist the RUC. Exclusively Protestant and often ex-members of the UVF, the '**Specials**' were used against the Catholic community until disbanded in the 1970s
- By 1923, peace was restored but the violence left a legacy of bitterness.

Nationalist divisions

Nationalists were divided in their attitude to Northern Ireland:

- Moderates, led by **Joseph Devlin**, belonged to the **Nationalist Party**
- They hoped the Boundary Commission would re-unite many of them with the south. When it failed, they entered the Northern Ireland parliament in 1928
- But unionists excluded them from all power and influence and they left again after Devlin's death
- Republicans in the IRA and Sinn Féin refused to have anything to do with Northern institutions
- Nationalists kept to themselves, with their own newspapers, schools, hospitals, etc.

Unionists' attitudes to Catholics

- Craig promised fair treatment to Catholics, but most unionists resented their attitude to the new state. They saw it as proof that they were disloyal and not to be trusted
- Unionists were also uncomfortably aware that there was a huge majority of Catholics on the island of Ireland and that southern political leaders talked a great deal about ending partition
- These feelings made it easy for political leaders like Dawson Bates, who disliked Catholics, to **discriminate** against them.

Ensuring Unionist control

- To protect the Catholic minority, Lloyd George introduced the **Proportional Representation (PR)** system of voting for local councils and the Northern Ireland parliament
- The 1920, local elections produced many nationalist-controlled local councils. Dawson Bates suspended them, then changed the method of voting to the less fair '**first past the post**' system
- Later he re-drew election boundaries to ensure that unionists always won (**gerrymandering**)
- When divisions appeared among unionists during the 1925 election to the Belfast Parliament, Craig blamed PR and abolished it in 1929
- 'First past the post' voting encouraged 'tribal politics'. All elections became straight fights between unionists and nationalists. Other parties like Labour were squeezed out
- The **Orange Order**, which excluded Catholics, also encouraged unity. Unionists of all classes met in their local Orange hall and no man could hope to lead the Unionist Party if he did not belong to it
- Craig (known as **Lord Craigavon** from 1927) won every election with a comfortable majority and remained Prime Minister until he died in 1940.

The failure of education reform

- **Lord Londonderry** was the first Education Minister. An enquiry he set up found serious weaknesses in education
- This led to 1923 **Education Act**. Schools that **transferred** from church to state control would get generous building grants. But 'transferred schools':
  - ○ Had to accept children from all religions
  - ○ Could not teach religion in school hours
- Catholic bishops objected and would not transfer their schools, even though it meant a loss of grants
- Protestant clergy also objected, but since Catholics were not involved, they transferred their schools. Later they got the rules about religious education changed, so that Protestantism could be taught in 'transferred' state schools
- After that, state schools were really Protestant schools. They had better resources than Catholic schools and Catholics resented this.

Richard Dawson Bates (1873–1949)

- Born in Belfast in 1873, he studied law and became a solicitor. An active member of the Orange Order, he was appointed secretary of the **Ulster Unionist Council** in 1906
- In this post he had played an important part in Unionist opposition to Home Rule from 1910, and in the 1912 signing of the **Solemn League and Covenant**
- When Northern Ireland was set up, Craig appointed him **Minister for Home Affairs**. His most important task was to defeat the IRA
- He achieved this with the **Civil Authorities (Special Powers) Act** which allowed him to intern anyone, by having an armed police, the RUC and by forming units of **special constables** to assist them. Many of the 'B Specials' were former members of Carson's UVF and this exclusively Protestant force became a permanent feature of northern life
- Bates also ensured unionist dominance by **ending Proportional Representation** (PR) in local government elections in **1922** and redrawing the constituency boundaries to ensure that unionists won even in areas like Derry and Fermanagh where there was a clear nationalist majority
- In **1929**, he abolished PR for elections to the Northern Ireland parliament
- Bates was a religious bigot who refused to employ Catholics in the civil service and encouraged businesses to do the same
- When Craig died in 1940, his successor **J M Andrews** kept Bates on as Minister for Home Affairs
- When Belfast was bombed in 1941, his lack of preparation became clear and was blamed for the high loss of life. This made Andrew's government unpopular
- When Sir Basil Brooke became Prime Minister in 1943 Bates finally retired.

18.2 The Northern economy 1920-1939

Taxation and welfare

- The Northern government could only raise 20% of taxes spent in Northern Ireland. The rest was set by Westminster
- In the 1920s, enough money came from London to keep social services in Northern Ireland at the same level as in Britain
- The 1930s Depression hit Britain severely, so little money flowed into Northern Ireland. As a result, pensions and dole payments were lower than in Britain or the south.

Industry and employment

- After the first World War the north's big industries, **linen** and **shipbuilding** declined due to falling demand
- This decline increased greatly in 1930s Depression. Many industries closed and Harland and Wolfe needed government aid to survive
- Unemployment was over 30% from 1930 to 1940. Very low dole payments led to hunger and malnutrition
- In 1932, Catholic and Protestants workers protested jointly against their conditions
- The unionist government improved welfare, but Craig and other unionist leaders encouraged Protestant businessmen to employ only Protestants
- This divided the workers and there were sectarian riots in Belfast in 1935.

Agriculture

- Agriculture was an important part of the Northern economy, employing over 25% of workers and earning more than shipbuilding
- The **1925 Land Act** completed land purchase
- To hold British markets, the government encouraged new farming methods and imposed quality control
- In the 1930s, northern farmers had protected access to British markets while southern farmers were excluded by the economic war. This gave them a modest prosperity
- **Sir Basil Brooke** as Minister for Agriculture, encouraged specialisation in poultry farming and pig-rearing.

18.3 Northern Ireland in the second World War

Craigavon and the start of the second World War

- When Britain declared war on Germany on 3 September, 1939, Lord Craigavon announced that Northern Ireland would loyally support the war effort
- He wanted to impose conscription, but had to drop the idea after nationalist protests were backed by Churchill
- He was very shocked in May 1940, when Churchill offered de Valera re-unification in return for the South's involvement in the war (see page 54).

Nationalists and the war

- Many nationalists saw it as 'England's war' and it was not their business. Until Belfast was bombed, some even hoped for a German victory
- The IRA got support, especially in Belfast. The government interned over 700 of them and any who escaped to the south were interned there.

Belfast bombed

- Northern leaders believed Belfast was too far from Germany to be bombed, so did little to protect it until late in 1940
- There were few anti-aircraft guns, barrage balloons or bomb shelters. Only 3,000 people were evacuated from the city
- German bombers came three times in April and May 1941
- The worst raid was on the night of 15/16 April. 90 bombers dropped thousands of tonnes of high explosives, which missed the shipyards and fell on tightly packed workers' houses
- Bombs also knocked out telephone cables and water mains, making it difficult for rescue workers and firemen
- After an appeal for help, de Valera sent fire brigades from the south, but they could do little
- At least 900 people died. Many were never identified but buried in mass graves
- Another raid on 5 May killed fewer people, but badly damaged the Harland and Wolfe shipyard
- Thousands of refugees fled south or to nearby towns and villages
- For months, about 100,000 left the city each night and slept in barns or fields.

The economy and the war

- The North's economy (unlike the south's) benefited from the war
- Food, fuel and clothing were rationed, though not as tightly as in Britain.

The impact of war on industry

- The war revived North's main industries, linen and shipbuilding:
  - ○ Northern farmers grew flax and linen mills made it into uniforms, tents, parachutes, etc
  - ○ Demand for ships grew as U-boats sank so many. Over 700 ships were built
  - ○ Engineering firms produced guns and tanks
  - ○ Shorts aircraft factory, set up in 1938, made 1500 bombers
- Large numbers of British and American troops were stationed in Northern Ireland. Building barracks and providing services for them created work
- Wages rose and unemployment fell to 5%.
- Workers from the south went to work in Northern Ireland. Fearing an increase in nationalist numbers, the unionist government insisted on work-permits limiting the time they could spend in the North.

The impact on agriculture

- Government controlled what farmers grew through compulsory tillage orders
- Farm production trebled, with most of it going to Britain
- But Northern farmers got the same guaranteed prices for their produce as British farmers, which saved them the cost of transport.

Northern politics during the war

- Unionist leaders made no attempt to involve nationalists directly in the war effort
- Official recruiting was mainly through unionist organisations
- **J M Andrews** became Prime Minister in 1940 when Craigavon died but kept all the old Ministers, including Dawson Bates
- In 1943, discontent inside the Unionist Party led to him being replaced by the younger, more energetic **Sir Basil Brooke** (later Lord **Brookeborough**)
- He included a Labour MP in his government, but made no attempt to win over nationalists.

Northern Ireland's contribution to the war effort

- Northern Ireland made a significant contribution to the Allied victory over Germany
- Food from Northern Ireland helped Britain to avoid starvation

- About 38,000 people joined the British forces in Northern Ireland. About half came from the south
- From Northern Ireland:
  - The **RAF** patrolled the Atlantic searching for U-Boats
  - The **Royal Navy** sent convoys to protect ships carrying food and munitions from America to Britain
- British and, from 1942, American troops trained in Northern Ireland for the North African campaign and for the D-Day landings.

The impact of the second World War

- The war widened the gap between Northern Ireland and the south
- The North prospered, while the south grew poorer
- After the war Britain set up the **Welfare State**. It gave northern people of both communities social welfare benefits that the south could not afford for its people
- British leaders saw the unionist government as their allies in contrast to neutral de Valera
- The gap increased when the south left the Commonwealth in 1949 and declared a republic
- As a result, in **1949** the British passed the **Ireland Act**, which guaranteed that Northern Ireland could not be reunited with the south without the consent of its parliament.

Questions

For Examination questions on Later Modern Ireland, Topic 3 see page 278.

Your revision notes

Later Modern Ireland   Topic 5
Politics and Society in Northern Ireland 1949-1993

CHAPTER 1
The Origin of Northern Ireland

Ireland in the United Kingdom

- Up to 1920 the whole island of Ireland was united with Britain, forming the **United Kingdom of Great Britain and Ireland (the UK)**.
- Laws and taxes for Ireland were decided in the Westminster parliament in London.
- Irish voters elected **105 MPs** to represent their interests there.

Nationalists

- Some Irish people disliked being part of the United Kingdom. They were called **nationalists**. They wanted Irish people to control Irish affairs.
- Most nationalists were **Catholics**. They made up 75% of the population. They did not feel the British had treated them fairly.
- Nationalists also believed that the Irish economy had suffered from being part of the UK. They thought Irish people would manage it better.

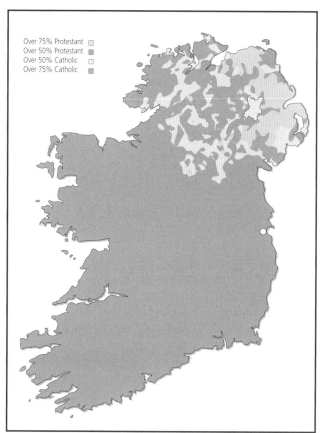

Over 75% Protestant
Over 50% Protestant
Over 50% Catholic
Over 75% Catholic

This map is based on the census taken in 1911. In an official document like a census it was not possible to ask people what their political views were but they could be asked about their religion. And since almost all Protestants were unionists and almost all Catholics were nationalists, the religious census also reflected the political divide across the island

Unionists

- Irish people who thought that union with Britain was good for Ireland were called **unionists**.
- Most unionists were **Protestants**. They were only 25% of the population in Ireland but were a majority in the north east of Ulster (see map).
- That part of Ireland was prosperous in the 19th century. It sold linen and ships to Britain and its empire. Ulster unionists feared they would lose the British market if Ireland left the UK.
- Many Protestants also **felt that they were British as well as Irish** because their ancestors had come from Britain to Ireland during the 17th century plantations. They were loyal to the British monarch and because of that were sometimes called **loyalists**. They felt at home in the UK and wanted to remain in part of it.
- Protestants also feared that they would suffer discrimination in jobs and education if Ireland was ruled by the Catholic majority.

The partition of Ireland

- When nationalists demanded an Irish parliament, unionists said they would resist it by force if necessary.
- In 1918 a majority of nationalists voted for the **Sinn Féin Party** which wanted to cut all ties with Britain and make Ireland a **republic**. Their army, the IRA, began to fight the British forces in Ireland.
- This made the unionists more determined than ever to resist Irish independence. In 1920 they got the British government to pass the **Government of Ireland Act**. It partitioned (divided) Ireland into two parts:
  1. 'Southern Ireland' had 26 counties. In it, 93 per cent of the population were Catholic.
  2. **Northern Ireland** had 6 counties. In it, 66 per cent of the population Protestant and 33 per cent Catholic.
- Nationalists refused to agree to this. Their war continued until 1921 when they made the **Anglo-Irish Treaty** with Britain. This turned 'Southern Ireland' into the **Irish Free State**. In 1949 it became a republic, completely independent of Britain.

For a fuller account of the event from 1912–22 see section on p. 34

The Constitution of Northern Ireland

- Northern Ireland remained part of the United Kingdom, though it had its own locally elected parliament and government.
- The Northern parliament controlled industry, transport, agriculture, education and health and had a limited power to raise taxes.
- There were 52 MPs in the Northern Ireland House of Commons. They elected a **Prime Minister** and a **Cabinet** which contained ministers responsible for Finance, Home Affairs, Education, etc.

- The first Prime Minister was **Sir James Craig** (later **Lord Craigavon**) who remained in office until he died in 1940.

> ### Remember…
>
> After the Unionist government built a splendid home for the Northern Ireland parliament at Stormont Castle, it was usually called the *Stormont parliament.*

Northern Ireland and the Westminster parliament

- Because Northern Ireland was still part of the United Kingdom, the Westminster parliament was still supreme over it. Because of this, Northern Ireland voters elected 12 MPs to represent their interests in Westminster.
- Westminster decided on most of the taxes Northern Irish people paid. The British then handed the money raised to the Northern government to spend.
- Although the Westminster parliament was supposed to control Northern Ireland, in reality it refused to discuss anything happening in the North. The British said this was because Northern Ireland had its own parliament to look after its affairs.

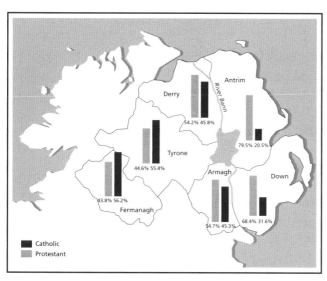

The Bann river, that flows through Lough Neagh, divides Northern Ireland into two halves. East of the Bann, Protestants are in a clear majority. West of the Bann there are Catholic majorities in many areas

Nationalists and Northern Ireland

- Nationalists throughout Ireland refused to accept partition. They believed that the whole of Ireland should be united under one government.
- Within Northern Ireland nationalists (almost all Catholics) were a third of the population. They wanted to be part of the Free State but the British made them part of Northern Ireland without any consultation.

- In areas **West of the Bann**, like Fermanagh, Tyrone, south Down, south Armagh and Derry city, nationalists formed a local majority (see map). In 1920 they elected local councils which supported the Dublin government rather than the unionist government in Belfast.

- To stop this, the Unionist government changed the method of voting for local councils from **PR** to 'first past the post'.

- They also re-organised the constituency boundaries to ensure that unionists would control most of these councils in the future. This is called '**gerrymandering**'.

> **Remember...**
>
> Proportional Representation (PR): In an election seats are given **in proportion** to the votes cast. This system is used in the republic.

> **Remember...**
>
> 'First past the post' voting: The person with the most votes wins, even if, overall, others got more votes. This system is used in Britain.

- These changes meant that up to the 1970, the Unionist party controlled most local councils in Northern Ireland, even in areas where Catholics were in a majority.

The RUC, the 'B' Specials and the 'Special Powers Act'

- When Northern Ireland was set up, the Unionist government formed its own police force, the **Royal Ulster Constabulary (RUC)**.

- The IRA attacked it even after there was peace in the South.

- To combat the IRA, especially near the border, the Unionist government appointed '**Special Constables**' to assist the RUC. They were heavily armed part-time policemen, all of them Protestant.

- They patrolled the areas where they lived. By 1923 their local knowledge had helped to defeat the IRA.

- The '**Specials**' were supposed to be temporary but the Unionist government kept the part-time B unit in existence up to 1970. '**B Specials**' patrolled country areas and their often undisciplined behaviour earned the hatred of Catholics.

- To combat the IRA the Belfast parliament also passed the **Special Powers Act** in 1922. It gave the Northern government the right to **intern** (imprison) suspected IRA men without trial.

- Like the 'B Specials' the Special Powers Act began as an emergency response to IRA activity but was made permanent in 1933. It was used almost exclusively against nationalists.

How nationalists fared in Northern Ireland

These developments did nothing to win Catholic support for Northern Ireland.

- Its police force the RUC was mainly Protestant and the few Catholics in it did not get promotion.
- The 'B Specials' and the Special Powers Act were used mainly against the Catholic community.
- The political system, especially at local level, was rigged against them by gerrymandering and the use of 'first past the post' voting, so that they could not win power even when they were in a majority.

The Nationalist Party, Sinn Féin and the IRA

- After 1925 most nationalists reluctantly accepted that Northern Ireland existed. They voted for the moderate **Nationalist Party**.
- It won seats in the Stormont parliament but was unable to achieve much for its voters.
- A small minority of northern nationalists were **republicans**. Their party was **Sinn Féin**, but it usually refused to take part in elections.
- A few republicans joined the IRA and occasionally attacked the RUC. These attacks achieved nothing but gave Unionists an excuse to keep the 'B Specials' and the Special Powers Act.
- From 1922 until the 1960s, many northern Catholics bitterly resented Unionist government policies but apart from occasional IRA violence, did little about them.

Sectarian politics

- From 1921 to 1972 the Unionist Party formed the government of Northern Ireland. It was exclusively Protestant.
- At first Protestants of all classes, who feared Catholic rule, voted for it. But in the late 1920s, when peace returned and the economy declined, some working-class Protestants began to vote for the **Northern Ireland Labour Party** (NILP).
- Craig feared this would weaken unionist power. To stop it he changed the method of electing MPs to Stormont from PR to 'first past the post'.
- The result was that every election in Northern Ireland became a straight fight between Protestant unionists and Catholic nationalists. That kept **sectarian differences** at the centre of northern politics and made it almost impossible for non-sectarian parties like Labour to emerge.

Remember...

Sectarian: Relating to a particular religion (sect).
Sectarianism: Judging people or issues according to their connection to a religious group.

Unionists feel under siege

After 1923 Unionists were firmly in control of Northern Ireland but they never felt secure.

- They knew that in Ireland as a whole they were a small minority. They grew nervous when Southern politicians like de Valera demanded that Northern Ireland be forced to unite with the South.
- They feared that northern Catholics supported this idea and resented the way they refused to get involved in Northern Ireland affairs.
- Catholics had bigger families than Protestants and 40% of school children were Catholic. Unionists feared that eventually that might lead to a Catholic majority within Northern Ireland.

Discrimination

This insecurity made unionists discriminate against Catholics:

- They refused to give them important jobs in the civil service because they did not think a Catholic would be loyal to Northern Ireland.
- Catholics were not encouraged to join the RUC and if they did they did not get promoted to the higher ranks.
- Although there were many qualified Catholic lawyers, very few were made into judges.
- They reorganised local government so that even in areas where Catholics were in a majority, the Unionist Party controlled local councils. These councils controlled many jobs but they seldom gave them to Catholics.
- Discrimination left many Catholics with a strong sense of injustice which eventually contributed to the outbreak of violence.

Questions

For Examination questions on Later Modern Ireland, Topic 5 see page 274.

Your revision notes

Culture in a divided society

Partition created a divided society in Northern Ireland.

- There were two communities, the Catholics/nationalists and the Protestants/unionists.
- Each community kept to itself and had little to do with the other.

Nationalist cultural activities

- Catholics/nationalists believed they were Irish and rejected the northern state. They kept their cultural ties with the rest of the island and developed them through their schools, newspapers and clubs.
- Catholic schools taught students the Irish language and Irish history that were not part of the official school curriculum. They usually played hurling or Gaelic football, rather than rugby or soccer.
- The **Gaelic Athletic Association** (GAA) was the most public expression of nationalist identity. Most Catholic parishes had a GAA club, which was often the centre of social activity.
- Some Catholic men also belonged to the **Ancient Order of Hibernians** (**AOH**). It was like a Catholic version of the Orange Order though it was much less powerful. It had links with the Nationalist Party.
- The AOH organised parades on St Patrick's Day and on 15 August. The RUC only allowed them to march in Catholic areas and would not let them to go through town centres.

Unionist cultural identity

- Protestants/unionists felt they were British and looked to London for cultural inspiration and leadership.
- The official school curriculum required students to study English literature and English history, with very little reference to Ireland.

The Loyal Orders and the tradition of parades

- The most distinctive part of the unionist culture was the tradition of loyalist parades.
- These were organised by the **loyal orders** – the **Orange Order**, the **Apprentice Boys of Derry**, and a number of smaller organisations.
- These parades commemorated significant events in the history of Protestants in Ireland. Their aim was to give Protestants a sense of shared identity and unite them in their determination to resist any threat from the Catholic/nationalist majority within Ireland.

The Orange Order

- The Orange Order was by far the biggest of the loyal orders.
- It had close ties to the Unionist Party. It was represented on the party's governing body, the **Ulster Unionist Council** and no unionist politician could succeed unless he was an Orangeman.
- The Orange Order has a lodge (branch) in almost every town and village. Usually it met in the Orange hall, where the Protestant community also held dances, band practices and other meetings.
- Lodges organise parades. The most important parade is on 12th **of July**. It celebrates the victory of the Protestant King William of Orange over his Catholic father-in-law, King James II at the **battle of the Boyne** (1690).
- Thousands of Orangemen and women march behind bands playing traditional airs. After the march families picnic while listening to speeches from unionist leaders.
- When Orange marches passed through mainly Protestant districts they were usually peaceful. But when they went through Catholic areas there was tension and sometimes violence.
- Catholics resented having to put up with Orange marches when the RUC stopped them marching in Protestant areas. They also disliked the anti-Catholic nature of some Orange songs and speeches.

●●●Case study

The Apprentice Boys of Derry

- Another of the loyal orders is the **Apprentice Boys of Derry**. It is much smaller than the Orange Order but just as important to unionist cultural identity.
- Its main purpose is to commemorate the **Siege of Derry**. That took place in 1688–9 during the war between William and James.

The Siege of Derry

- In 1690, after the Protestant William ousted the Catholic James from the British throne, Irish Catholics stayed loyal to James.
- Protestants in Ulster feared for their lives and fled for safety to the walled city of Derry.
- On 7 December King James's army arrived before the walls and demanded to be let in. While the city's leaders considered what to do, **13 apprentice boys**, shouting '*no surrender*', locked the gates against the Catholic forces.
- A long siege followed. No food got through. People were starving but when the governor of the city, **Colonel Lundy**, suggested giving in, they expelled

him. From then on, the name 'Lundy' meant a traitor to the Protestant cause.

- During the siege about 4,000 people died of hunger and disease. At last a ship, the *Mountjoy*, laden with food, broke through and Derry was saved.

Why the story of the siege mattered to Ulster Protestants

- Later Protestants saw the siege of Derry as a symbol of their heroic defence of their freedom against Catholic rule.
- And because Catholics outnumbered Protestants in modern Ireland Ulster unionists felt they were still under siege, just as their ancestors had been in 1688–9.
- In speeches, Unionist leaders used the language of the siege to show what they felt. Like those heroic ancestors, they too were brave and defiant (*no surrender*) and they too had to be constantly on the alert against traitors (*Lundys*) who might sell them out.

The Apprentice Boys of Derry

- An organisation called the **Apprentice Boys of Derry** was set to commemorate the siege. It is based in Derry where its headquarters is the **Memorial Hall**.
- The Apprentice Boys hold two main events each year:
  - A smaller parade in December commemorates the original apprentices closing Derry's gates. At it, an image of 'Lundy' is symbolically burnt.
  - The larger parade on 12 August commemorates the arrival of the *Mountjoy*. It is an important date in the North's marching season. In the 1960s up to 40,000 people from Ulster and abroad went to Derry every year to take part.
- On the day of the parade, the city was decorated with crimson flags and bunting. The marchers gathered on the Mall wall. This looked down on the Catholic ghetto of the Bogside and symbolically showed the supremacy of Protestants over Catholics.
- Led by their bands, the Apprentice Boys then marched around the walls of Derry. The march ended with a service in St Columb's Church of Ireland Cathedral.
- Like the Orange Order, the Apprentice Boys had close ties to the Unionist Party.
- Many prominent Unionist politicians, including Lord Brookeborough, Terence O'Neill, and Brian Faulkner were members of the Apprentice Boys. Ian Paisley remained a member even after he left the Orange Order in 1965.

The Apprentice Boys and the 'Troubles'

- Apprentice Boy marches in Derry were one of the sparks that set off the troubles.
- A reason for this was that Derry was 60 per cent Catholic but the Council that ran the city was Unionist controlled as a result of gerrymandering (see page 76).
- Nationalists resented the marches because they stressed Catholic defeat and the marchers often behaved in a disrespectful way.
- In October 1968 when civil rights demonstrators planned to march inside the city walls, the Apprentice Boys called a special parade. The Home Affairs minister, William Craig used this as a reason to ban both marches and violence followed.
- But Craig refused to ban their August 1969 march even though violence was likely. This was because of its symbolic importance within the Protestant community.
- The parade sparked off the 'battle of the Bogside' and led to the introduction of British troops (see page 102).
- For most of the 1970s and 1980s Apprentice Boys parades were banned completely or confined to Protestant areas.
- But as community relations in Derry improved at the end of the 1980s, the nationalist-dominated council let parades start again. In 1989, at the third centenary of the siege, it organised a pageant to celebrate it.

● ● ●

Ulster writers

- There were other aspects to Ulster culture, although they received little support from the Stormont government.
- Northern Ireland produced several fine writers.
  - ○ **John Hewitt** wrote poetry and published ballads sung by the weavers who made Ulster's prosperity in the 18th and 19th centuries. He urged Ulster artists to develop a 'regional identity' to which both communities in the North could relate.
  - ○ **Sam Thompson** was an important playwright. Working in the Belfast shipyards, he lost his job for attacking sectarianism but used his experience in his most successful play, *Over the Bridge*.
- After the Welfare State made higher education more common, a new generation of poets, both Catholic and Protestant, emerged in the 1960s. Seamus Heaney was typical of them.

Seamus Heaney (1939–)

- Born in 1939, Heaney's home was a farm called Mossbawn and his memory of it later shaped his poetry.
- At 12 he won a scholarship to St. Columb's College, a Catholic boarding school in Derry city. This move, which he describes as from *'the earth of farm labour to the heaven of education'* has been a recurrent theme in his work.
- While in school, his four year old brother Christopher was killed in an accident, an event that inspired two poems, *Mid-Term Break* and *The Blackbird of Glanmore*.
- Heaney lectured in Queen's University in Belfast until 1972 when he moved to Co Wicklow where he worked as a poet and lecturer. As his reputation grew, Harvard University gave him a part-time post which allowed him to spend more time writing. In 1966 he won the Nobel Prize for Literature.
- In 1966 Heaney published his first collection of poems, *Death of a Naturalist*. People associated him with several other young writers like Michael Longley and Derek Mahon, saying they formed part of a new "Northern School" of Irish writing.
- After the troubles began in 1969 Heaney had to consider his attitude to violence. Should a poet be free to concentrate on his work or should he reflect his place in a divided society? Heaney discussed these issues in a book called *The Government of the Tongue* (1988).
- Generally his poems do not refer directly to violence but it often appears indirectly in them.
- In the 1980s and 1990s his poems were concerned with Ireland's Gaelic past. He produced several long poems based on Gaelic stories, among them *Sweeney Astray* (1982).
- In 1980 Heaney became involved in the Derry-based **Field Day Theatre Company**. Working with other poets and with the playwright, Brian Friel, Field Day explored the crisis in Northern Ireland through plays, poems and pamphlets.

Cultivating cultural diversity

- From the 1980s the British and Irish governments gave grants to cultural activities, hoping to build bridges between the two communities.
- They encouraged conferences and summer schools where people from all communities could discuss the things that united and separated them.

Trying to heal a divided community

- In the 1960s the **ecumenical movement** encouraged Christians to look at the things they had in common rather than the things that divided them.
- This led to meetings and discussions between Catholics and Protestants.
- Many thought that separate schools for Catholic and Protestant children contributed to the conflict.
- To counter this, the British government in 1989 added **Education for Mutual Understanding** to the school curriculum. It encouraged pupils from Catholic and Protestant schools to meet and talk, work and play together.

Lord Brookeborough and the British government

- **Lord Brookeborough** was Prime Minister of Northern Ireland from 1943 to 1963.
- World War II ended shortly after he took over. It had strengthened the unionists because British leaders resented the South's neutrality and were grateful to Northern unionists for their support.
- When the South declared a republic and left the British Commonwealth in 1949, the British brought in the **Ireland Act**. It guaranteed that Northern Ireland would remain part of the United Kingdom as long as the majority of people in the North wanted it.

The Labour Government and the Welfare State

- In 1945, the British Labour Party won the general election. It introduced reforms in education, health and social welfare which were known as the **Welfare State**.
- Because Northern Ireland was part of the United Kingdom, its people shared in these reforms. But because Northern Ireland was poorer than Britain, the British tax-payer paid most of the extra cost.

Reforms in Education

- In 1947 a new system of primary, secondary and third level education was set up.
  1. All children in their last year at Primary school did an exam called the 'Eleven Plus'.
  2. The top 25 per cent of pupils got free places in **grammar schools**. If they did well, they got scholarships to go to university.
  3. The remaining 75 per cent went to free **secondary modern schools**. They got a practical education and most of them left school at fourteen or fifteen.
- Schools under the control of local councils got full grants for building and maintenance. Their pupils did not have to pay fees. Catholics would not send their children to these schools so they were mainly Protestant.
- Catholic-owned schools got 65 per cent of the cost of building and maintenance. Up to 80 per cent of their pupils received scholarships but the rest had to pay fees.

The impact of educational reforms

- The new education system gave bright but poor boys and girls a first class education that their families could never have afforded to pay for.
- Children from both communities benefited, but as there were more poor Catholics than Protestants, Catholics gained most.
- By the 1960s the education reforms had produced a generation of well educated young Catholics. They resented the discrimination they experienced under Unionist rule and led the struggle to reform it.

Reforms in Health

- The **National Health Service** (NHS) was set up in 1946. It gave free medical care to all patients.
- A **Hospitals' Authority** took over the supervision of hospitals.
- There was a problem over **the Mater Hospital**. It was run by nuns, who feared the Hospitals' Authority might interfere too much. But the Unionists would not agree to a special arrangement, so the Mater did not get any government grants.

Reforms in Social Welfare

- A system of National Insurance was introduced in 1948. All employed people paid a national insurance contribution and got generous children's allowances, old age pensions or unemployment pay.
- In the 1950s and 1960s Unionist politicians often pointed out that this made northerners much better off than people in the south.

Reforms in housing

- In 1943 a report said that 200,000 new houses were needed in Northern Ireland.
- The 1945 **Housing Act** gave local councils and a new body called the **Northern Ireland Housing Trust** power to clear slums and build new houses.
- By 1961 these two bodies had built 56,000 houses across Northern Ireland. These houses were given to poor people for a low rent.

Household franchise and discrimination in housing

- The Housing Trust gave houses on the basis of need (e.g. how bad their present home was). Most of Northern Ireland's 73 local council did the same but 12 councils followed a different policy.
- These councils included Fermanagh, Tyrone, Derry city, Dungannon and Omagh. In all of them, Catholics were in a majority but the Unionist Party controlled the council.

- This was partly due to gerrymandering (see page 76) but also to the 'household franchise'. That was a law which said that only 'householders' (i.e. people who occupied a house) could vote in local elections.
- But household franchise meant that giving a Catholic a house also meant creating more Catholic voters and so endangering Unionist control.
- As a result, these Unionist councils often left poor Catholic families in overcrowded slums while giving houses to less needy Protestants.
- Catholics bitterly resented this and the issue of housing was the spark which set off the civil rights movement in the 1960s. (see page 94)

Brookeborough's economic policies

Agriculture was the North's most important industry in the 1940s. 14 per cent of people still worked on the land. Most farm produce was sold to Britain.
- After the war the British government gave generous subsidies to farmers to get them to grow more food.
- This helped northern farmers to buy tractors and other machinery and encouraged the development of intensive pig and poultry farming.
- This made farmers more prosperous but the number of people working in farming steadily declined.

The **North's industry** faced major problems.
- The linen industry declined and many jobs were lost. Shipbuilding did well into the 1950s but in the 1960 lost out to more efficient shipyards in Poland and Japan.
- To deal with these problems, Brookeborough introduced a number of measures:
  1. The 1945 **Industries Development Act** gave loans and grants to new industries to set up in Northern Ireland.
  2. The **Northern Ireland Development Company** was set up 1956 to bring in foreign firms.
  3. To improve transport, the government took over the railways and closed uneconomic lines. It also improved the roads and built Ireland's first motorway in 1962.
- As a result industrial production in Northern Ireland rose by 50 per cent between 1950 and 1962 and the number of jobs went up by 10,000. But unemployment stayed high and Northern Ireland was the poorest part of the United Kingdom.

Brookeborough and the nationalists

- Up to the mid-1950s Brookeborough was more generous to Catholics than many unionists wanted.
  1. He supported increasing the grant to Catholic schools against the wishes of some unionists, including the young **Ian Paisley**.

2. He supported the easing of the **Special Powers Act** and encouraged the RUC to stop Orange parades in nationalist areas.

- But he did nothing that might undermine unionist supremacy. When the British replaced household franchise for local elections with 'one person, one vote', he insisted on keeping it in Northern Ireland.

Northern nationalists and the IRA border campaign

- After the war, nationalists still wanted a united Ireland.
- In the late 1940s southern leaders began an **anti-partition campaign**. They made speeches demanding a united Ireland but in reality they did little about it.
- This inspired a few young nationalists to join the IRA. Mostly from the South they knew little about Northern Ireland and even less about the unionists.
- In December 1956 the IRA announced a campaign against "British imperialism" and called on all the people of the North to help them.
- It attacked border posts and police barracks. Two policemen and several IRA men were killed.
- Brookeborough used the Special Powers Act to intern IRA suspects without trial. In the South Valera also interned IRA men.
- The campaign faded away and the IRA called it off in 1962. It was a complete failure and got almost no support from northern nationalists.

The end of the Brookeborough government

- In 1963 the economy declined. Unemployment was growing, especially in the shipyards where many Protestants worked. Some of them voted for the Northern Ireland Labour Party which won seats in Stormont.
- Unionists began to criticise Brookeborough. Was he too old to cope with the problems Northern Ireland faced?
- In March 1963 Brookeborough suddenly retired.

Questions

For Examination questions on Later Modern Ireland, Topic 5 see page 274.

REVISE WISE
QUESTIONS

The rivals for power

- Two leading members of the Unionist government hoped to replace Brookeborough as Prime Minister.
  - One was the Finance Minister, **Terence O'Neill**. He wanted to modernise Northern Ireland through planned economic development.
  - The other was the Minister for Home Affairs, **Brian Faulkner**. He had used internment in 1959 to defeat the IRA's border campaign. This made him popular with traditional unionists who disliked O'Neill's modernising ideas.

Terence O'Neill (1914–1990)

- Born into an aristocratic family in Co Antrim, O'Neill grew up in England and served in the British army during World War II. Afterwards he settled in Northern Ireland and was elected to Stormont.
- Brookeborough made him Minister for Home Affairs in 1955 and Minister for Finance in 1956.
- When Brookeborough retired, O'Neill became PM. He wanted to modernise Northern Ireland, through economic planning and development.
  1. He encouraged multinational companies to set come to Northern Ireland to replace jobs lost in the traditional industries of linen and shipbuilding.
  2. He also set up committees to suggest reforms in education, transport and town planning.
- To encourage economic co-operation with the republic he invited Taoiseach Seán Lemass to visit Belfast and went to Dublin himself.
- To improve relations with the Catholic minority, he made some small gestures like visiting a Catholic school.
- But even these gestures were too much for some unionists. Led by Ian Paisley, they mounted an 'O'Neill must go' campaign.
- At the same time, Catholics noted that he made no significant concessions. After he agreed to put the North's new university in Protestant Coleraine rather than Catholic Derry, some of them decided that only direct action could lead to reform. This led to the civil rights campaign in 1967.
- When violence broke out in Derry, O'Neill tried to strengthen his own position by calling an election for February 1969. The gamble failed.
- Violence grew and in April he resigned as Prime Minister. O'Neill moved to England and was given a seat in the House of Lords.
- His English background and stiff manner made it hard for him to persuade unionist voters that Stormont had to reform if it was to survive.

Brian Faulkner (1921 – 1977)

- Faulkner was elected as a Unionist MP to Stormont in 1949. In 1959, during the IRA border campaign, Brookeborough made him Minister for Home Affairs.
- His tough policy towards the IRA made him popular with the ordinary unionists.
- He hoped to become Prime Minister but when Brookeborough resigned, he was in America and the leaders of the Unionist Party chose O'Neill instead.
- O'Neill made him Minister of Commerce and he got foreign companies to set up in Northern Ireland.
- But his relationship with O'Neill was always tense and he resigned in January 1969 in protest at the reforms O'Neill introduced on the orders of the British government.
- When O'Neill resigned in April Faulkner lost the leadership by one vote to James Chichester-Clarke. He become Minister of Development in Chichester Clarke's government and worked hard to push through the reforms he had previously opposed.
- After violence grew, Chichester Clarke resigned in March 1971 and at last Faulkner was elected leader.
- As a gesture to nationalists, he proposed powerful committees in Stormont which nationalist MPs would chair.
- But unionists wanted him to take a hard line with the IRA and he introduced internment on 9 August 1971.
- Because of the way it was imposed, it alienated moderate nationalists and strengthened the IRA. Violence grew over the rest of the year, culminating in Bloody Sunday in Derry in January 1972.
- After that the British Prime Minister, Edward Heath took responsibility for security and Faulkner resigned in protest.
- That ended the Stormont government and began the period of 'direct rule' from London. At first Faulkner opposed direct rule but soon realised that power-sharing was the only way forward.
- After talks with the SDLP and the British and Irish governments late in 1973, he signed the **Sunningdale Agreement**.
- It set up a power-sharing Executive with Faulkner as First Minister.
- But the plan for a **Council of Ireland** angered many unionists who saw it as the first step to a united Ireland. When his own Unionist Party rejected the Agreement in December 1973, Faulkner left and set up the **Unionist Party of Northern Ireland**.
- The power-sharing Executive began work in January 1974 but was undermined when Heath called a general election and unionists opposed to the Executive won 11 out of the 12 Westminster seats.
- It fell in May when the **Ulster Workers' Council** strike paralysed Northern Ireland.
- Faulkner lost influence after that and he retired from politics in 1977. He died shortly afterwards in a hunting accident.

O'Neill becomes Prime Minister

- When Brookeborough resigned, Faulkner was in America. A small group of Unionist leaders quickly chose O'Neill to be Prime Minister without an election.
- The lack of an election and O'Neill's English accent and aloof manner meant that he never got the whole-hearted support of Unionist MPs.

The impact of ecumenism

- When O'Neill took over the **ecumenical movement** had eased traditional rivalries between Catholics and Protestants around the world.
- In Rome Pope John XXIII (23rd) supported **ecumenism** and encouraged Catholics to work with Protestants. He also held the second **Vatican Council** to reform the Catholic Church.
- In the republic **Seán Lemass** became Taoiseach in 1959. He was more interested in economic development in the South and co-operation with the North than in talking about Irish unity.
- Around Ireland some Catholics and Protestants felt the old enmities were meaningless. They began to attend each other's churches and support each others' charities.
- In the North, some people wanted to forget the old Catholic/nationalist and Protestant/unionist divide and work together to make Northern Ireland a better place.
- But more traditional Protestants were opposed to the ecumenical movement. Their most prominent spokesman was **Ian Paisley**.

> ### Remember...
>
> **Ecumenism:** The idea that the various Christian Churches should leave aside past enmities. Instead they should stress the ideas they shared and work together for the common good.

O'Neill and the nationalists

- Influenced by ecumenism, O'Neill made some small gestures of good will towards northern Catholics.
  1. He was the first northern Prime Minister to visit a Catholic school.
  2. When Pope John XXIII died in 1964, he had flags fly at half mast.
- O'Neill also invited Taoiseach Seán Lemass to visit Belfast in January 1965 and soon afterwards visited Dublin himself. This led to talks on cross-border co-operation in tourism and agriculture.
- This was popular in the South and among northern nationalists. But it angered traditional unionists and Paisley gained attention by attacking O'Neill's policies.

Planning for Economic Development

- O'Neill faced big economic and political problems. Unemployment was up, especially among Protestant workers in the shipyards. Some of them voted for the **Northern Ireland Labour Party (NILP)** rather than the Unionists.
- O'Neill hoped to win them back by developing the North's economy. He set up several committees to suggest new economic policies. Catholics noted that, in spite of his fair words, he did not appoint any Catholics to these committees.
  1. The **Matthew Committee** suggested having new 'growth centres' outside Belfast. Many people though this meant Derry, the North's second city but O'Neill decided to build a completely new city near Lurgan and called it Craigavon. This decision was unpopular with people West of the Bann.
  2. The **Wilson Committee** wanted to encourage foreign firms to set up in Northern Ireland. Brian Faulkner as Minister for Commerce was successful in attracting some multinationals.
- By 1965, unemployment had fallen but most of the new industries and jobs went to the Protestant heart-lands East of the Bann.

●●● Case study

The Coleraine University controversy

The need for more university places

- O'Neill also wanted to increase the number of students going to university. Northern Ireland's only university was Queens in Belfast. The problem was: should the extra students go there or should a completely new university be set up?
- In Britain, the Robins Committee had looked at this issue and recommended several new universities.

The Lockwood Committee 1963–5

- In 1963 O'Neill set a committee to consider what should be done in Northern Ireland. Chaired by **Sir John Lockwood**, it had eight members, three of whom were English. One Catholic was invited to serve on it but when he was unable to do so, no other Catholic was appointed.
- The **Lockwood Committee** quickly decided that Queens should not expand. The question then was where to put the new university.

Where to put the new university?

- Derry, Coleraine, Armagh and Craigavon all competed to be the site of the new university, which would create jobs and boost the local economy.
- Most people assumed that Derry would win. It already had a small third-level college, **Magee**. This looked like the ideal basis for a new university but its building was small and in poor repair and there was nowhere for students to live.
- The Lockwood Committee quickly decided against Armagh and Craigavon and focused on Derry and Coleraine. The Committee members visited both places and talked to their representatives.
- They were looking for
  - ○ a site where the new university could be built and
  - ○ a place to accommodate students.
- Derry offered Magee but was so sure of success that they did not discuss other sites or accommodation for students.
- Coleraine offered a site for the university. They also said that the nearby holiday resorts of Portstewart and Portrush had plenty of boarding houses which were empty all winter, so students could live there at no cost to the government.

Lockwood decides on Coleraine

- The Derry case did not impress the Lockwood Committee members. They thought Magee was too small. New buildings would be needed and costly student hostels would have to be built.
- They also felt that Derry's sectarian tensions and lack of industrial development made it unsuitable for a university.
- Coleraine, on the other hand, had offered a site and could house students cheaply. It was also solidly Protestant and so free of sectarian tensions.
- As a result they recommended that Magee be closed and a new university be built in Coleraine.

Derry's response to the Lockwood report

- Derry people were angry when word of this decision got out. In January 1965 a **University for Derry Committee** was set up. Its members included unionists and nationalists. One of them was a young teacher, **John Hume**.
- They organised protest meetings and met with O'Neill and his Minister of Education.
- On 18 February the Unionist mayor of Derry and the Nationalist MP led a 2000 strong motorcade to Stormont, while back in Derry pubs and shops closed in protest.

O'Neill and the Derry Unionists

- The following day, O'Neill met secretly with leading Derry Unionists. They persuaded him to keep Magee open but did not press him to give the university to Derry.
- It seems they feared that it might draw new people, some of them Catholic, into the city. That could upset the delicately balanced Unionist control of the city council.
- In the end O'Neill decided to put the new university in Coleraine, although he also decided to keep Magee open.

Why did the Lockwood Committee choose Coleraine?

- Many people in Derry believed that O'Neill's government had influenced Lockwood's choice but there is no evidence to support that theory.
- It seems more likely that the committee members made their decision on the kind of rational grounds – a site and student accommodation – that the Robbins Committee had applied in England.
- Several Lockwood members were English and others had spent their working lives there.
- But Northern Ireland was not England. Its political realities were very different and the Lockwood report ignored these.

Why did O'Neill accept their recommendation?

- O'Neill did not have to accept their recommendation. He could have put the new university in Derry.
- But like Derry Unionists, he feared that it would disturb their control of the city.
- He also knew that it would please unionist voters outside Derry if it was put in the mainly Protestant town of Coleraine.

Questions

For Examination questions on Later Modern Ireland, Topic 5 see page 274.

New nationalist attitudes to Northern Ireland

- About the time O'Neill came to power, the attitude of younger nationalists to Northern Ireland was changing.
- They still wished for a united Ireland but knew it was unlikely to come because a million unionists were opposed to it.
- Many of them were well educated, thanks to the Welfare State and they knew they would not have got that in the poorer South.

What the Catholics complained about

- But there were a number of things about Northern Ireland that left Catholics with a sense of injustice.
  1. Because of **gerrymandering**, and the **household franchise**, 12 local councils West of the Bann were controlled by the Unionist Party even though the majority of the people living in them were Catholics.
  2. Derry was a particularly clear example of this. Sixty percent of the population was Catholic but because of the way election boundaries were gerrymandered, 7,500 Protestant voters elected 12 local councillors while 10,000 Catholics only elected 8.
  3. Derry and other Unionist controlled councils **discriminated** against Catholics by giving almost all important and well paid jobs to Protestants.
  4. They were also reluctant to give council houses to Catholics, even when they lived in very bad conditions. This was because the household franchise meant that when a person got a house he/she also got a vote and too many new Catholic voters might undermine Unionist control of some of these councils.
  5. The Stormont government also discriminated against Catholics. There were no Catholics in the Unionist Party and the government did not appoint Catholics to any of the top jobs in the civil service, the police or the law.
  6. There were few Catholics in the police (RUC) and none in the paramilitary 'B Specials' who patrolled country areas and harassed Catholics.
  7. The government also kept the **Special Powers Act** and used it mainly against nationalists.

Faith in O'Neill undermined

- Younger nationalists thought that neither the passive attitude of the Nationalist party not the violence of the IRA had improved the situation.

- They put their hopes in O'Neill. If he could get the unionists to treat them fairly, they would settle down and work within Northern Ireland.
- **John Hume** was typical of this new attitude. Thanks to the educational opportunities of the Welfare State, he had become a teacher in Derry and was a leader of the University for Derry Committee.
- But O'Neill's decision about the university undermined the hope of people like him. They came to believe that only direct action would make the Unionist government give justice to the Catholic minority.
- The civil rights movement grew out of this feeling.

John Hume (1937–)

- Derry-born John Hume came from a poor family but the Welfare State enabled him to get a good education and become a teacher.
- He joined the campaign to get a university for Derry and in January 1965 became chairman of the **University for Derry Committee** which opposed the Lockwood Committee's report.
- This experience convinced Hume that only direct action would make the Unionist government give justice to the Catholic minority and he became involved in the civil rights movement.
- After the violence which followed a civil rights march on 5 October 1968 he was elected on to the **Derry Citizens' Action Committee** and tried to ensure that later protests were peaceful.
- In 1969 he was elected to the Stormont parliament. In 1970 he worked with other anti-unionist MPs to create a new party, the **Social Democratic and Labour Party (SDLP)** of which he was deputy leader.
- He was one of the first people to suggest peace would only come when a way was found for nationalists to share power with unionists.
- He was one of the SDLP delegates in the negotiations leading to the Sunningdale Agreement in December 1973. In the Executive he was Minister of Commerce, dealing with the economic problems caused by the Loyalist workers' strike.
- The failure of Sunningdale convinced Hume that any settlement in Northern Ireland must involve political leaders from the United States and Europe as well as from Northern Ireland, the republic and Britain.
- In 1979 Hume replaced Fitt as leader of the SDLP. He was also elected to the European Parliament and in 1983 to Westminster. These positions allowed him to meet foreign leaders and try to persuade them to support his ideas.
- He refused to get involved in attempts by the British government to find an internal solution to Northern Ireland's problems but he played an active part in Garret FitzGerald's New Ireland Forum in Dublin in 1983–4.
- The 1985 Anglo-Irish Agreement was the first sign that his ideas might be influencing developments. But this had only a limited impact while the Provisionals continued to bomb and kill.
- Hoping to persuade them to consider an alternative to violence, Hume secretly talked to Gerry Adams and other republicans. At the time the talks were heavily criticised but they laid the basis for the IRA ceasefire in 1994.

The Campaign for Social Justice (CSJ)

- The civil rights movement started with protests about housing in Dungannon, Co. Tyrone. In 15 years the council built 194 houses but gave most of them to Protestants even though there were several hundred poor Catholic families living in crowded slums.
- Inspired by the civil rights movement in America, local women formed the **Homeless Citizens League** and began to picket council meetings.
- They were joined by **Patricia McCluskey** who, with her husband **Conn**, a local doctor, set up the **Campaign for Social Justice (CSJ)** in 1964.
- They collected facts about injustices to Catholics which they published in a pamphlet, *The plain truth* and presented to British politicians.
- They argued that if northern Catholics were part of the United Kingdom they were entitled to the same rights as other UK citizens.

Patricia and Conn McCloskey

- Patricia McShane worked as a social worker in Glasgow before returning to Northern Ireland to marry Conn McCluskey, a medical doctor in Dungannon, Co Tyrone.
- Disturbed by the refusal of the unionist controlled town council to give council houses to Catholics, even when they were living in very bad conditions, she helped to found the **Homeless Citizens League** in 1963.
- To put pressure on local councils and the Unionist government to give justice to Catholics, the McCluskeys helped to found the **Campaign for Social Justice** (CSJ) in 1964. Unlike earlier Catholic groups, their aim was not Irish unity but civil rights. They arguing that if they lived in the United Kingdom they were entitled to the same rights as other citizens of the UK.
- To support their case they systematically collected data about gerrymandering and discrimination in employment, housing, and public appointments. In 1964 they published their findings in a pamphlet called: *Northern Ireland, The plain truth*.
- The CSJ presented this to prominent politicians in Westminster where MPs set up a Campaign for Democracy in Ulster but the British and Northern Ireland governments took no effective action at this time.
- The McCluskeys were members of the Northern Ireland Civil Rights Association (NICRA) when it was founded in 1967 but withdrew from public life after its aims were achieved and violence erupted in 1970.

Ian Paisley and the 'O'Neill must go' campaign

- But O'Neill was powerless to deal with Catholic complaints. Even his little gestures towards them angered many unionists. **Ian Paisley** began an 'O'Neill must go' campaign.
- The violent language he used encouraged a group of extreme unionists, calling themselves the **Ulster Volunteer Force**, to murder three innocent Catholics.
- Paisley denounced the murders but his 'O'Neill must go' campaign still won the backing of a large part of the Unionist Party and of the Orange Order.

Ian Paisley (1926–)

- A fundamentalist Protestant who believed the Bible to be the word of God, Ian Paisley founded the **Free Presbyterian Church** of which he was Moderator (head) in 1951.
- He first attracted public notice with attacks on the ecumenical movement for encouraging contacts between Protestants and Catholics. He saw O'Neill's meeting with Lemass in 1965 as betraying unionists and launched an "O'Neill must go" campaign.
- More unionists supported him after the civil rights movement began. His **Ulster Protestant Volunteers** held counter-demonstrations to coincide with civil rights marches. Although he always denied any link to loyalist paramilitaries, some of them supported him and claimed to be acting in his name.
- In 1968 Paisley founded the **Protestant Unionist Party**. In the 1969 he fatally undermined O'Neill by almost defeating him in the Stormont general election. O'Neill resigned soon after and Paisley then won his Stormont seat. In 1970 he was elected to the Westminster parliament as the MP for North Antrim.
- In September 1971 Paisley founded **Democratic Unionist Party** (DUP). Many members also belonged to his Free Presbyterian Church and gave unquestioning loyalty to the leader.
- The DUP opposed the reforms that Chichester-Clark and Brian Faulkner introduced in response to pressure from Britain.
- After direct rule was imposed in March 1972, the DUP worked for the restoration of Stormont. They opposed power-sharing but took their seats in the Northern Ireland Assembly elected in 1973. Although Paisley played little part in the Ulster Workers' Council strike that destroyed the Sunningdale Agreement, he got much of the credit.
- When the British rejected the demand of the Constitutional Convention (1975-6) to restore Stormont, Paisley led another workers' strike but it was defeated in 1977. In spite of that he topped the poll in the first direct election to the European Parliament in 1979.
- The DUP and the Ulster Unionist Party joined together against the **1985 Anglo-Irish Agreement**. But Paisley's links to loyalist paramilitaries put off many moderate unionists.
- Paisley opposed the 'peace process' especially any talks with the SDLP or the Dublin government. He condemned the Downing Street Declaration of 1993, attacked the 1998 Good Friday Agreement and campaigned for a 'No' vote in the referendum that followed.

Gerry Fitt and the Labour government

- In London the Campaign for Social Justice had influenced members of the Labour Party which won the 1964 election. But the Prime Minister **Harold Wilson** refused to interfere in the North.
- This changed in 1966 when **Gerry Fitt** was elected as a Republican Labour MP for West Belfast. At Westminster, he insisted on asking questions about unionist discrimination against northern Catholics.
- This encouraged Labour MPs to ask why the British taxpayer should subsidise a government responsible for so many injustices.

The Northern Ireland Civil Rights Association (NICRA)

- In 1967 frustrated Catholics decided to put pressure on the Unionist government and they set up the **Northern Ireland Civil Rights Association (NICRA)**.
- Although most members came from a nationalist background, they had a wide variety of aims
  - ○ Some were moderate nationalists like John Hume and the McCluskeys, who wanted full civil rights and the end of discrimination.
  - ○ There were also socialists, communists and militant students like **Bernadette Devlin**. They hoped for a socialist revolution.
- After the IRA's border campaign failed, some of its leaders turned to socialism. They too supported NICRA.
- NICRA demanded
  - ○ an end to the Special Powers Act and the B Specials,
  - ○ council houses to be given on a fair points system,
  - ○ 'one man, one vote' in local elections and an end to gerrymandering.
- Unionists could not accept these demands which would have reduced their power, especially West of the Bann. Instead they claimed that NICRA was a republican and/or communist conspiracy to destroy Northern Ireland.

> **Remember...**
>
> *'One man one vote'* was a demand to end the household franchise which only allowed people with a house to vote. Of course it included women too!!

Bernadette Devlin (1947–   )

- Bernadette Devlin became involved in the civil rights movement while a student at Queens University in Belfast in 1968.
- After taking part in the early demonstrations organised by the Northern Ireland Civil Rights Association, she joined a radical leftwing student group, the **People's Democracy (PD)**.
- In the 1969 Stormont election, she stood against Chichester Clarke. Her youth and energetic way of speaking attracted media attention and she was selected as the 'unity' candidate to oppose the unionists in a by-election to the Westminster Parliament in 1969.
- She won the seat, and at 21 became the youngest woman ever elected to the House of Commons. She kept the seat until 1974.
- She took part in the 'Battle of the Bogside' in Derry in August 1969 and in 1970 received a six months jail sentence for her activities. In the House of Commons, after Bloody Sunday (January 1972) she punched the British Home Secretary, Reginald Maudling when he said that the British army fired in self-defence.
- After she lost her Westminster seat she helped to found the **Irish Republican Socialist Party** (IRSP) when it broke away from the Official IRA. But she later left it when it was involved in violence.

- In 1979 she stood for election to the European Parliament to publicise the blanket protests by republican prisoners opposed to the British government's policy of treating them as criminals. She got over 38,000 votes. This showed that many nationalists would support republicans if they rejected violence and it helped to encourage Sinn Féin's move towards a political solution.
- In 1981 loyalist paramilitaries attacked her and her husband Michael McAliskey, leaving them seriously wounded.
- After she recovered she continued to campaign on left wing issues and criticised Sinn Féin's part in the peace process.

August 1968: the NICRA march in Dungannon

- In Dungannon, the local Nationalist MP, **Austin Currie**, encouraged Catholic families to squat in council houses. After the RUC evicted them the Unionist-controlled council gave one house to an unmarried Protestant girl.
- To attract attention to the case, NICRA staged a march from Coalisland to Dungannon in August 1968. Led by Currie and Fitt, the marchers sang the American civil rights anthem, '*We shall Overcome*'.
- When Ian Paisley organised a counter demonstration, the RUC stopped the NICRA marchers from getting to the centre of Dungannon.

October 1968: the clash in Derry

- In Derry a Housing Action Committee then persuaded NICRA to back its march on 5 October.
- The Apprentice Boys announced that they planned to march on the same day.
- The hard-line Minister for Home Affairs **William Craig** then forbade both marches from going to the centre of Derry. Moderates like the McCluskeys and John Hume wanted to postpone the march for a week but local radicals insisted on going ahead.
- Only 400 people turned up but they included Gerry Fitt and three British Labour MPs who came to watch.
- The RUC blocked the marchers, then used their batons to beat the peaceful demonstrators, including Fitt.
- Within hours, images of the violence appeared on TV around the world. In response reporters and camera men flocked to Northern Ireland, to see what was going on.
- Across the North, Catholics organised demonstrations in sympathy with the Derry marchers.
- In Belfast radical students led by Michael Farrell set up the **Peoples' Democracy**. Influenced by Marxist ideas, they hoped to bring about a socialist revolution.

O'Neill introduces some reforms

- The London government warned O'Neill that they would withhold subsidies to Northern Ireland unless he introduced reforms.
- Reluctantly O'Neill agreed
  - ○ to introduce a points system for council housing,
  - ○ to review the Special Powers Act and
  - ○ to set up a Development Commission to replace Derry city council.
  - ○ But he did not include 'one man, one vote'.
- **William Craig** and some members of the Unionist Party criticised O'Neill for giving in to London.

The People's Democracy march: January 1969

- On 9 December 1968, O'Neill appeared on TV, asking for support. Warning that '*Ulster is at a crossroads*' he told unionists that their way of life depended on British subsidies and begged nationalists to give his reforms time to work.
- Unionists and nationalists backed O'Neill. NICRA called off marches and he felt strong enough to sack Craig.
- But the young radicals in the People's Democracy were opposed to NICRA's moderation. On 1 January they set out to march from Belfast to Derry.
- At **Burntollet Bridge** near Derry, hundreds of extreme unionists, including some off-duty B Specials, attacked them with stones and clubs. Films of the attack showed the RUC did little to protect the marchers.
- As they reached Derry there were riots. The RUC followed some rioters into the Catholic Bogside district and used excessive force against them.
- This undermined support for moderation among nationalists and Hume announced that NICRA marches would resume.

January to March 1969: the Cameron Report and the election

- O'Neill appointed Judge Cameron to enquire into the causes of the violence. (Later he produced the **Cameron Report** which was critical of unionist rule in Northern Ireland.)
- In protest, Brian Faulkner resigned and twelve Unionist MPs called for O'Neill to go. Hoping the public would back him, O'Neill called an election.
- But of the 39 Unionist MPs elected, only 27 backed O'Neill. Ian Paisley almost defeated him in his own constituency.
- On the nationalist side several members of the civil rights campaign including John Hume won seats.

O'Neill's resignation

- After the election, O'Neill agreed to accept 'one man, one vote' in local elections but violence increased.
- There were riots in Derry and one man, beaten by the RUC, died. A few days later loyalist paramilitaries set off bombs in Belfast's water mains to undermine support for O'Neill.
- More Unionist MPs called for O'Neill to go and he resigned on 28 April 1969.
- O'Neill had few contacts among ordinary unionist voters and his stiff manner and aloof personality made it hard for him to win their support for the reforms that were essential to preserve unionist rule.

Questions

For Examination questions on Later Modern Ireland, Topic 5 see page 274.

Your revision notes

James Chichester Clarke becomes Prime Minister

- Faulkner sought the leadership but the Unionist Party elected **James Chichester Clarke**. A landlord like O'Neill, he lacked the political skill needed to restore peace to Northern Ireland.
- He promised to continue O'Neill's reforms and freed people imprisoned for rioting. In return NICRA called off its marches.

12 August 1969: The 'Battle of the Bogside'

- But he would not ban the annual Apprentice Boys parade in Derry even though it seemed likely to cause trouble.
- In the Bogside, young men stockpiled stones and petrol bombs to defend themselves against the RUC.
- Rioting began after some Apprentice Boys threw pennies from the walls onto the Bogside below.
- Chichester Clarke called in the B Specials but that only made things worse.

The violence spreads

- The violence spread to Belfast. For four days Catholic and Protestant mobs in the Lower Falls and Ardoyne areas attacked each other.
- Seven people died, five of them Catholic and 180 buildings, mostly Catholic owned, were burnt out. The Catholics claimed the RUC sided with the Protestants
- In the republic, people were horrified at the violence. On 13 August, Taoiseach **Jack Lynch** spoke on TV saying the South could '*no longer stand by and see innocent people injured*'. He sent Irish army units to the border to help refugees.
- Lynch's speech infuriated unionists who thought he meant to invade Northern Ireland. That made the violence worse.

The British army arrives

- After two days, Chichester Clarke asked Harold Wilson to send in the British army to help the exhausted RUC.
- British soldiers arrived in Derry on 14 August and in Belfast the following day. Catholics welcomed them, hoping for protection.
- The troops restored peace, often by allowing barriers to be built between Catholic and Protestant areas.

The civil rights campaign's aims achieved

- Because British soldiers were there, the British government was now directly involved in Northern Ireland.
- Harold Wilson insisted that the unionists continue to reform and by the end of 1969 most of the aims of the civil rights movement had been achieved.
  1. Local government was reformed. All citizens over 18 could vote and the fairer PR system, replaced 'first past the post' voting.
  2. A **Housing Executive** took over all public housing and was to distribute it on a fair points system.
  3. An English police officer was sent to reorganise the RUC and Catholics were to be encouraged to join it.
  4. The B Specials were replaced by the **Ulster Defence Regiment (UDR)**. It was controlled by the British army, not the unionists.

The growth of Loyalist paramilitary groups

- Violence encouraged people in both communities to join paramilitary groups in order to defend their areas.
- Various Protestant paramilitaries had existed since the mid-60s. In 1971 some of them combined into the **Ulster Defence Association (UDA)**. At its height in 1971–3 it had about 40,000 members who manned barricades and patrolled their areas.
- A small group, who used various names like the **Ulster Freedom Fighters (UFF)**, said they would kill republicans. But most of their victims were unlucky Catholics who crossed their path by chance. In 1972–3 they killed over 200 people.

Remember...

Paramilitary: an unofficial army containing men who carry arms and wear uniforms.

The Provisional IRA (PIRA or Provos)

- During the 1960s the IRA's leaders had turned to away from violence and supported the civil rights campaign.
- In 1969 when Protestant mobs attacked Catholic areas of Belfast, there was no one to defend them. The words *IRA, I Ran Away*, appeared on walls. Belfast republicans resented their helplessness.
- In December 1969 at an IRA convention in Dublin, the leaders suggested that they recognise the Dublin and Belfast governments.
- Traditional republicans rejected this and the IRA split.
  - A majority stayed with the leadership and they became known as the '**Official IRA**'.
  - The minority elected a 'provisional executive' as a temporary measure and after that became known as the '**Provisional IRA**'.
- A similar split occurred in the republican party, Sinn Féin.

What the Provisionals believed

- The Provisionals were traditional republicans. For them the enemy was Britain. They believed that it was Britain which partitioned Ireland and kept partition in existence.
- Therefore they would fight the British until they left, after which, they thought, there would be a united Ireland with Protestants and Catholics living peacefully together.
- The Provisionals ignored the wishes of a million Northern unionists who considered themselves British and wanted to remain part of the United Kingdom.
- They got money and guns from Irish Americans and from some members of Fianna Fáil who preferred their ideas to those of the socialist 'Officials'.

June 1970: A new government in Britain

- In Britain, Harold Wilson lost the general election in June 1970.
- The new Conservative government was led by **Edward Heath** and his Home Secretary **Reginald Maudling**.
- They knew little about Northern Ireland and left most decisions about it to the Unionist government and the British army commander. This led to the disastrous Falls Road curfew.

The Falls Road curfew, 3–4 July 1970

- After shots were fired at soldiers, the army imposed a 36 hour curfew on the Catholic Falls Road area of Belfast.
- 20,000 people were trapped in their houses as soldiers went from house to house, pulling up floor boards and smashing furniture. They found 100 guns.
- In an exchange of fire with the IRA the army killed four Catholics.
- Afterwards they escorted two Unionist ministers around to see the result of the curfew.
- The 'Falls curfew' changed Catholic attitudes to the British army. It no longer seemed neutral but had sided with the unionists.
- Angry young nationalists joined the IRA and the Provisionals felt strong enough to begin bombing hotels and other public buildings. They wanted to undermine the economy of Northern Ireland so that the British would leave.

Founding the Social Democratic and Labour Party (SDLP)

- Most nationalists rejected violence and supported democratic politics but when the old Nationalist Party almost disappeared in 1969 they had no party to represent them.

- In August 1970, Gerry Fitt and John Hume got anti-unionist MPs to form the **Social Democratic and Labour Party (SDLP)**. It was led by Gerry Fitt, with Hume as his deputy.

The SDLP aims at 'power sharing'

- By 1970, the aims of the civil rights movement had been achieved and a united Ireland was impossible, so what should the SDLP aim for?
- Usually political parties hope to form a government but that could not happen in Northern Ireland. Because over 60 per cent of the people were Protestant and because most people voted along sectarian lines, a mainly Catholic party could not be part of the government.
- Hume said this was because of the unfair way Northern Ireland had been set up. To overcome this inbuilt injustice, he said that some way must be found to allow the two communities to **share power** between them.

The Alliance Party

- This idea also influenced the **Alliance Party** which was set up in 1970.
- Its founders hoped to create a non-sectarian party in which both Catholics and Protestants work together for the good of all.
- But Alliance also supported Northern Ireland's Union with Britain, most of its supporters were moderate unionists, not nationalists.
- Although it never got more than 10 per cent of the vote, that was enough to allow it to play a part in the formation of power-sharing governments.

Brian Faulkner becomes Prime Minister

- Violence got worse in 1971. Early in the year Provisionals blew up a BBC radio transmitter, killing three men. In March they kidnapped and killed three teenage soldiers.
- The Unionist Party was divided about what to do.
  - ❏ **Brian Faulkner** and other moderates backed Chichester Clarke in continuing reforms.
  - ❏ **William Craig** and other hard-line unionists wanted the army to get tough with the IRA and intern its leaders. Craig had a lot of support among unionists West of the Bann. They were upset at the loss of the B Specials whom they regarded as their defenders against republicans.
- After the young soldiers were killed, Chichester Clarke asked Heath to take tougher action against the IRA. When the request was refused he resigned.
- Faulkner defeated Craig to become the next Prime Minister.

Faulkner's policies

- A shrewd politician, Faulkner hoped to win over nationalists while also dealing with the men of violence.

- He offered to let members of the SDLP chair committees of the Stormont parliament which oversaw the work of the government. This was a limited form of power-sharing.
- He banned all marches across Northern Ireland, much to the annoyance of the Orange Order.
- But he got the British government to let soldiers fire on rioters.
- The SDLP began talks on his committee idea but withdrew after the army killed two innocent men during riots in Derry.

> **Remember...**
>
> **Internment:** rounding up people suspected of violence and imprisoning them without trial for as long as was needed to restore peace. Both Irish governments used internment against the IRA during World War II and again in the 1950s.

Internment, 9 August 1971

- Faulkner thought internment would end the violence as it had ended the IRA's 1950s border campaign. After 300 bombs, mostly from the Provisionals, British leaders agreed with him.
- On 9 August soldiers and RUC Special Branch officers rounded up 340 men and took them to an old army camp at **Long Kesh** for interrogation.
- The operation was very badly managed.
  - ❏ It was completely one-sided. No loyalists were arrested, even though they too had engaged in violence.
  - ❏ Most of the men arrested were not active in the IRA and most current IRA leaders escaped.
  - ❏ Several men arrested were subjected to what the European Court later described as 'inhuman and degrading treatment'.

> **Remember...**
>
> The government later built a new prison at **Long Kesh** and renamed it **The Maze** to improve its image.

- By 1972 over 2000 had been rounded up though most were freed within days.

The impact of internment

- To protest against internment, the SDLP organised demonstrations, withdrew from local councils and supported a rent and rates strike.
- They hoped to keep the protests peaceful but internment unleashed a new wave of violence.
- There were riots between the army and the two IRAs. The worst were in Belfast. On 10th August alone 11 people died and over 400 houses were burnt.
- 7000 Catholic refugees fled for safety to the South and several hundred Protestants fled to Britain.
- The number of deaths rose sharply. From January to 9 August 1971 34 people died. For the rest of the year the death toll was 150.

- Thousands moved out of mixed housing estates to segregated areas, well away from people of the other community.
- The Provisionals grew as Catholics turned to them for protection. They became more confident because they thought they were winning and expanded their bombing campaign.
- Loyalist paramilitary groups came together to form the UDA. They responded to IRA violence, though they used assassination more often than bombs.

> **Remember...**
>
> **Rent strike:** council tenants would not pay rents.
>
> **Rates strike:** property owners would not pay local taxes (rates) to councils.
>
> *EDCO REVISE WISE POINTS TO NOTE*

Bloody Sunday in Derry, 30 January 1972

- In Derry, moderate nationalists persuaded the British army not to enter the 'no-go areas' of the Bogside and Creggan.
- They hoped this would keep the peace but most nights young men (whom the army called **Young Derry Hooligans**) went out to throw petrol bombs and stones at the soldiers. They retaliated with rubber bullets and CS gas.
- IRA snipers also fired on the soldiers from the 'no-go' areas. In January 1972 there were over 80 shooting incidents and the IRA killed two soldiers.
- General Ford, the army commander, wanted to deal with the Young Derry Hooligans. He brought in the Parachute Regiment to help.
- His chance came when the Civil Rights movement organised an illegal anti-internment march on Sunday 30 January.
- About 15,000 people turned up. Both IRAs later said they told their people to leave their guns at home.
- Halfway through the march, the Parachute Regiment fired into the crowd, killing 13 men and wounding 12 men and one woman.
- Later the soldiers claimed that someone had fired on them first but no one in the crowd heard any other shots, no guns were found on any of the victims and no soldier was injured.

Reactions to Bloody Sunday

- Like internment, Bloody Sunday made things worse. Many young people joined the Provisional IRA and it expanded its bombing campaign.
- In London, when the House of Commons met, Bernadette Devlin ran across to slap Maudling in the face.
- In the South, Jack Lynch declared a day of mourning. There were protest marches and on 2 February a mob burnt down the British embassy.
- In February the Official IRA set off a bomb in the London headquarters of the Parachute Regiment. It killed a Catholic priest, a gardener and five women who worked in the canteen.

107

- The London government asked Lord Chief Justice Widgery to investigate events in Derry. The **Widgery Report** defended the soldiers' actions and nationalists regarded it as a whitewash.

The end of Stormont: 23 March 1972

- Up to Bloody Sunday, Prime Minister Edward Heath hoped that Faulkner could sort out Northern Ireland's problems. After Bloody Sunday, he began to look for an alternative policy.
- He considered various options like a united Ireland or giving part of Northern Ireland to the South (re-partition) but rejected them all in favour of **power-sharing** between unionists and nationalists.
- On 22 March Heath called Faulkner to London and told him they planned to take control of the police. Rather than accept this, the Unionist government resigned.
- At once Heath appointed **William Whitelaw** to be the **Secretary of State for Northern Ireland**. He would run the North directly from London.
- This decision ended 50 years of **devolved government** in Northern Ireland and replaced it with **direct rule**.

> ### Remember...
> **Devolved government:** a Belfast based government dealing with Northern Ireland issues, and overseen by the British government.
> **Direct rule:** The British ruling Northern Ireland directly from London.

Questions

For Examination questions on Later Modern Ireland, Topic 5 see page 274.

Your revision notes

William Whitelaw's aims

- William Whitelaw was the first **Secretary of State for Northern Ireland** under direct rule. A leading English Conservative, he knew little about Northern Ireland but he learned quickly.
- Whitelaw hoped to win the trust of the Catholic community by restraining the British army, ending internment and getting the IRA to stop its violence.
- But to keep the trust of the Protestants he had to restore order and send the police into the 'no-go' areas from which the IRA launched most of its attacks.
- Once peace was restored he hoped to organise a power-sharing government in Northern Ireland and end direct rule.

The Ulster Unionist Party (UUP) after direct rule

- The loss of Stormont badly damaged the once mighty **Ulster Unionist Party**. For fifty years it had won every election in Northern Ireland without effort, so it had not modernised its organisation.
- Party leaders did not control its governing body, the **Ulster Unionist Council** and in elections, each constituency could pick any candidate it wished without consulting the leaders.
- As the violence got worse, the UUP lost moderate members to the Alliance Party and hard-line unionists to William Craig's Vanguard and Ian Paisley's Democratic Unionist Party.

William Craig and Ulster Vanguard

- After direct rule began, one of Faulkner's ministers, William Craig left the UUP and set up the **Vanguard Party** to campaign against it.
- At first Craig looked powerful but he was not a clever politician.
  - His close links with loyalist paramilitaries frightened off moderate unionists.
  - And working-class unionists did not like his idea that Northern Ireland should become independent of Britain because they feared losing British subsidies.
- Although Vanguard helped to destroy the Sunningdale Agreement, it disappeared soon afterwards.

Ian Paisley and the Democratic Unionist Party (DUP)

- In 1972, Ian Paisley seemed less important than Craig but he was a shrewder politician. When he saw that voters did not like his views he changed them.
- At first he formed the **Protestant Unionist Party** and became an MP at Stormont and Westminster. But many unionists disliked his strident anti-Catholicism and he gradually toned it down.
- He also began to appeal to working class Protestants who felt that the UUP had neglected them.
- This led to the foundation of the **Democratic Unionist Party (DUP)** in 1971. It was a tightly disciplined party, with one undisputed leader and a band of devoted followers, many drawn from Paisley's own Free Presbyterian Church.
- After direct rule, Paisley first suggested that Northern Ireland be integrated with Britain. But this was never popular and he soon replaced it with a demand for the restoration of Stormont.

Direct rule and the nationalist community

- Most nationalists welcomed the end of Stormont.
  - ○ Moderates like the SDLP hoped for peace and power-sharing
  - ○ Both wings of the IRA saw it as a victory for their violence. One more push, they believed, could drive out the British and bring about Irish unity. Declaring '*the war goes on*' they stepped up their bombing and shooting.

Violence intensified

- Rioting continued, mainly in Belfast and Derry. People died in crossfire between the army or loyalists and the IRA. IRA car bombs killed innocent passers by from both communities. On 14 April alone the Provisionals set off 30 bombs across the North.
- Loyalists retaliated with bombs but also tortured and killed individual Catholics who crossed their path.
- This led to a demand for peace. In Belfast 50,000 people signed a petition calling on both wings of the IRA to put aside their arms.
- On 29 May the Official IRA called a ceasefire but the Provisionals would not because they thought a truce would undermine the will to go on fighting.

Whitelaw's reforms

- Whitelaw hoped that ending internment would bring peace. He freed hundreds of internees and gave '**special category status**' to those who remained. That meant they could wear their own clothes and did not have to work.

- He replaced the old and discredited Special Powers Act with the **Northern Ireland (Emergency Provisions) Act**. It introduced the **Diplock Courts** in which one judge, sitting without a jury, tried political cases. This was necessary as terrorist groups could easily intimidate jury members.

Remember...

Diplock Courts: Named after Lord Diplock who recommended this way of dealing with terrorist cases.

Talks with the Provisionals fail

- Whitelaw also made contact with the Provisionals. On 26 June they called a ceasefire and six leading Provisionals, including **Gerry Adams**, met Whitelaw secretly in London.
- They asked Whitelaw to promise that the British would leave Northern Ireland within three years. He said that was impossible because the British could not abandon the unionists against their wishes.
- Some Provisionals wanted to continue the ceasefire but others, including Adams did not. They were afraid it would let the British army gain the upper hand.

Bloody Friday, Operation Motorman and bombs in Claudy

- On 9 July, during riots in Belfast, Provisionals opened fire and violence resumed. Ten people died over the next few days.
- On the afternoon of **Friday 21 July**, as people were out shopping, the Provisionals set off 18 bombs in Belfast as well as 3 in Derry and 16 in other areas. They killed 9 people and seriously injured hundreds of others.
- Meanwhile 5 more died during fierce gun battles between the Provisionals and the British army.
- People across Ireland were horrified at the scale of the slaughter on **Bloody Friday**.
- This allowed Whitelaw to launch **Operation Motorman** on 30 July. The army took over the 'no-go' areas in Belfast and Derry which had been largely controlled by the IRA. After this it was harder for the Provisionals to build bombs or attack the army.
- On 31 July the Provisionals retaliated by leaving 3 car bombs in the mixed and peaceful village of **Claudy**, near Derry. Nine people died, five Protestants and four Catholics, and thirty were horribly injured.
- July 1972, when 92 people died, was the worse month of the troubles.

Loyalist violence

- Loyalist violence also increased, especially as they heard that Whitelaw had talked to the Provisionals. They petrol bombed Catholic homes and killed Catholics who crossed their paths.

- In December 1972 they set off bombs in the republic, killing two people in Dublin and two more in Cavan.
- Overall, 467 people died violently in 1972 which was the worst year of the troubles.

The impact of the troubles on the South

- Before the northern troubles began, many people in the south knew little about Northern Ireland but they had plenty of prejudices.
- They did not understand that unionists felt British and wanted to be part of the United Kingdom.
- They felt Ireland should be united and blamed the British, not the unionists, for partition.
- They knew about discrimination against Catholics and backed the civil rights movement.
- At first southerners even sympathised with the IRA and believed they were continuing the struggle that won independence for the rest of the country in 1921.
- But from 1972 attitudes changed. The aims of the civil rights campaign had been achieved. Even the Stormont government was no more. And still republican violence continued.
- Many in the South were sickened when IRA car bombs killed innocent men, women and children. Was a united Ireland worth such slaughter?

Dealing with the IRA

- These changing views made it easier for southern governments to take a tougher line against the IRA.
- They strengthened the **Offences against the State Act** which had been used against the IRA since 1939. They also set up the '**Special Criminal Court**'. In it, three judges, acting without a jury, tried people accused of IRA activity.
- They closed down the Sinn Féin offices in Dublin and stopped RTÉ broadcasting interviews with IRA leaders.
- Irish army and Gardaí patrols were stepped up along the border, though it was far too long and winding to be closed completely.

The republic changes as a result of Northern developments

- As southerners got better informed about Northern Ireland, they began to understand the unionists' fear of Irish unity and their desire to preserve their British identity.
- They also became aware of the things about the South that the unionists disliked. These included the power of the Catholic Church and the ban on contraception and divorce.

- This led to a debate:
  - ○ Should these things be changed?
  - ○ And if so, was that because they were obstacles to unity or because they were bad in themselves?
- In 1972 a large majority voted in a referendum to remove the 'special status' that the Constitution gave to the Roman Catholic Church.
- Later the law against contraception was eased. A referendum to remove the ban on divorce in the Constitution failed in 1986 but a second one succeeded in 1995.
- People also began to look again at the idea of Irish unity. Some even suggested that it would be better to encourage the two communities in the North to share power and live as good neighbours with the South.

●●●●Case study

The Failure of the Sunningdale Agreement

Seeking peace

- In 1972 the British thought direct rule was only temporary. They hoped to end it as soon as the **constitutional politicians** in Northern Ireland agreed to share power.
- All through 1972 Whitelaw talked to them behind the scenes. By 1973 he was ready to act.

Remember...

Constitutional parties/ politicians: Political groups and leaders who operated peacefully and within the law.

The 'Border Poll' and the White Paper

- To reassure unionists, Whitelaw organised a referendum on the border (known as the 'border poll') in March 1973.
- Nationalists, who were still protesting about internment, did not vote. Of the people who did, 99 per cent voted to keep Northern Ireland in the United Kingdom.
- Whitelaw then produced a **White Paper** called *Northern Ireland Constitutional Proposals*. It said:
  1. Northern Ireland would remain part of the United Kingdom as long as the majority wanted that.
  2. It would have an **Assembly**, elected by PR.

Remember...

'Assembly' was used instead of 'parliament' and 'Executive' instead of government to stress the change from the old Stormont.

3. The Assembly would elect a **Northern Ireland Executive** (government) but it must contain representatives from both communities within Northern Ireland (i.e. power-sharing).

4. London would then hand over control of health, education and local government. Control over the police and courts could be handed over later if the Executive was successful.

5. To satisfy nationalists, a **Council of Ireland** would be set up to encourage co-operation with the republic.

> **Remember...**
>
> **White Paper:** When a government wants to consult about an issue it produces a 'white paper' saying what it intends to do. This allows people to comment and suggest changes.

Responses to the White Paper

- The SDLP welcomed the White Paper because it supported power-sharing.
- Republicans rejected it because it accepted partition.
- Faulkner and moderate unionists gave it a cautious welcome but in the Ulster Unionist Party (UUP), a minority led by **Harry West**, opposed power-sharing.
- Craig, Paisley and the Orange Order condemned it completely.

The Assembly election: 28 June 1973

- Elections to the new Assembly were held on 28 June. They showed up the divisions on the unionist side.
- While Paisley and Craig were united against power-sharing, Faulkner's UUP was divided. He asked candidates to sign a pledge to follow him but some constituencies picked candidates who sided with West and refused to sign the pledge.
- Faulkner tried to reassure doubters by promising not to share power with people '*whose **primary objective** is to break the Union with Great Britain*'. He later claimed this only meant Sinn Féin but some unionists thought he meant SDLP too.
- The election results disappointed Whitelaw.
  1. The 'neutral' parties, Alliance and the NILP won only 9 seats.
  2. Faulkner only won 24 seats compared with 26 for the combined anti-power-sharing unionists. Later two of the 24 changed sides.
  3. The SDLP did well but republicans boycotted the election, so it was impossible to say how much support they had among nationalists.

Party	SDLP	Alliance	NILP	UUP (Faulkner, pledged)	UUP (West, unpledged)	DUP (Paisley)	Vanguard (Craig)	Loyalists
No. of seats	19	8	1	24	8	8	7	3
% of vote	22%	10.50%	2%	29.00%	10%	10%	11.50%	4.20%

Key: red text, against power sharing; black text, in favour of power sharing.

Agreeing to talk

- When the Assembly met, DUP and Vanguard members attacked other unionists, often physically.
- But a majority favoured talks. It was agreed to have them in two phases:
  1. First the Northern Irish parties would agree among themselves to set up an Executive and accept a Council of Ireland.
  2. Then they would meet with the British and Irish governments to decide how much power the Council of Ireland would have.

Talking about an Executive

- Whitelaw chaired the first phase of talks. They began on 5 October and ended on 21 November 1973.
- Six Unionists led by Faulkner, six SDLP members led by Gerry Fitt and three members of the Alliance Party took part.
- The issues before them were:
  1. forming an Executive (government) and
  2. the powers of a Council of Ireland.
- On the Executive, the main problem was how many ministries each party should get. In the end it was agreed that there would be six ministers from the UUP, four from the SDLP and one from Alliance.
- There was disagreement about how much power a Council of Ireland should have.
  - ○ Faulkner wanted it to contain only members of the two Irish governments and to deal with uncontroversial issues like tourism.
  - ○ John Hume and the SDLP wanted it to contain members of the Dáil and the Assembly and deal with important issues like the police.
- Whitelaw backed the SDLP, hoping this would undermine support for the IRA. Reluctantly, Faulkner gave way.
- The SDLP agreed to end the rent and rate strike which had begun after internment.

Starting talks at Sunningdale: 6–9 December 1973

- The second phase of the negotiations took place in England. The British and Irish governments and the Northern parties met at **Sunningdale** between 6th and 9th December. Here the main issue was the Council of Ireland.
- Shortly before it began the Prime Minister, Edward Heath replaced Whitelaw with **Francis Pym**. This robbed the talks of Whitelaw's negotiating skill and experience. Pym knew little about Northern Ireland and played no part in the talks.
- Heath presided over the negotiations. He was impatient with the unionists and admired John Hume. He backed his line on the Council of Ireland.
- The Irish delegation was led by the Taoiseach, **Liam Cosgrave**, whose Fine Gael/Labour Coalition government was formed in February. They too supported John Hume's views.

The Sunningdale Agreement

- Faulkner was forced to agree to a Council of Ireland with strong powers but he hoped for something in return. He wanted Cosgrave to promise:
  1. to **extradite** IRA people to Northern Ireland to stand trial there and
  2. to remove **Articles 2 and 3** from the Irish Constitution. These articles offended unionists because they claimed that the Dublin government had the right to rule the whole island of Ireland.
- But Cosgrave could not do either of these things. He pointed out that:
  1. it was the courts, not the government, that could order a person to be extradited and
  2. that Articles 2 and 3 could only be changed by a referendum. Fianna Fáil was bound to oppose the change so it would not pass. Anyway, he assured, Faulkner, the two articles were only words and had no practical meaning.
- In the end all Faulkner got was:
  1. a promise that Cosgrave would acknowledge the right of Northern Ireland to exist as long as the unionist majority wanted it and
  2. a promise to do more about policing.
- The lack of concessions made it very difficult for Faulkner to sell the Agreement to a sceptical unionist community.

> **Remember...**
>
> **Extradite:** send a person accused of a crime in another country to that country to stand trial

Opposition to power-sharing

- On 6 December, as the talks began in Sunningdale, the DUP, Vanguard, Harry West's followers and the Orange Order formed the **United Ulster Unionist Council (UUUC)** to oppose power-sharing.
- After the Agreement was signed, the **Ulster Unionist Council** (the governing body of Faulkner's party) met to discuss it. By 427 votes to 374 they voted to reject a Council of Ireland.
- After this defeat, Faulkner resigned as party leader and was replaced by Harry West. With his remaining pro-Agreement followers, he set up the **Unionist Party of Northern Ireland**.

Power-sharing begins

- The power-sharing Executive took over on 1 January 1974. **Brian Faulkner** was **Chief Minister** and **Gerry Fitt** was his deputy.
- At first many unionists were prepared to give the Executive a chance to prove itself. But unfortunately events in Northern Ireland, in the republic and in Britain made this impossible.

Undermining the Executive

- In the North, the Provisionals believed they were on the way to victory and they continued to bomb and kill.
- In the republic a former Fianna Fáil minister, **Kevin Boland** went to the Supreme Court claiming the Agreement was against the Constitution because it accepted partition. Although Boland lost, the case damaged Faulkner because:
  1. In court Cosgrave's lawyers had to claim that Articles 2 and 3 were important even though he had tried to persuade unionists that they were not and
  2. Cosgrave could not make the statement on the existence of Northern Ireland which he had promised until it was over. When he finally issued it on 13 March, it was too late.
- But the worst blow to the Executive was Edward Heath's decision on 28 February to call a **general election** in the United Kingdom.
- The United Ulster Unionist Council treated the election like a referendum on the Agreement. They put up just one anti-Agreement candidate in each of the North's 12 Westminster constituencies, while all the pro-Agreement parties competed with each other.
- The result undermined Faulkner's credibility. The UUUC won 11 of the 12 seats and 51 per cent of the votes. Paisley, Craig and West were all elected, with only Gerry Fitt winning on the pro-Agreement side.

A Labour government

- In Britain, Heath lost the election and Harold Wilson returned to power. He appointed **Merlyn Rees** to be Northern Secretary.
- Rees, a hesitant and indecisive man, promised to support the Sunningdale Agreement.

The Ulster Worker's Council (UWC)

- Although weakened by these blows the Executive continued to work.
- This infuriated some loyalist workers who formed the **Ulster Worker's Council (UWC)**. Many of them worked in electric power stations where past discrimination against Catholics meant that almost all the workers were Protestants.
- On 15 May, after the Assembly passed a vote of confidence in the Executive, they called a strike.

The UWC strike: May 1974

- The strikers controlled the power stations. Within days they had cut electricity output by 60 per cent. As a result people could not cook, factories closed, sewerage plants did not work and in hospitals, life support systems began to break down.
- Loyalist paramilitaries supported the strikers. They formed 'tartan gangs' who blocked roads and 'persuaded' workers not to go to work.
- They were probably also responsible for bombs that went off in Dublin and Monaghan on 17 May, killing 32 people.
- The RUC did not interfere in the strike and Rees failed to order the British army to dismantle the barricades. This was partly because it was soon clear that many Protestants supported the strikers.
- Their support grew even stronger after Wilson, in a badly-judged broadcast on 25 May, accused Northern Irish people of 'sponging' on the British taxpayer.

The Executive falls

- Hoping to buy time, Faulkner begged the SDLP and the Dublin government to reduce the powers of the Council of Ireland. They agreed but it was too late.
- When the strikers heard of a plan to use the army to protect petrol supplies, they cut electricity supplies even more.
- Fearing a break-down in society, the Executive resigned.

Why did the Sunningdale experiment fail?

- The main reason for the failure was that a clear majority of unionists opposed the Agreement and supported the UWC strike.
- They feared the Council of Ireland would force them into a united Ireland. The Boland case in Dublin strengthened these fears as did unwise speeches about Irish re-unification from some nationalist politicians.
- Some unionists also opposed it because of power-sharing. They could not accept men like Gerry Fitt whom they blamed for the fall of Stormont, being part of their government.
- Nationalists blamed Merlyn Rees for not using the police and army against the strikers. This might have worked if he had acted quickly but he hesitated and once the strike was fully under way it is unlikely it would have been any good.
- He hesitated for several reasons:
  ○ The result of the general election showed a majority of unionists were against the Agreement.
  ○ Army commanders did not want to take on the loyalists while they were still fighting the IRA.
  ○ The fact that the Agreement was put in place by the Conservatives made Labour leaders less concerned about its fate.

The 'double veto' leads to stalemate

- Rees made another attempt to get power-sharing in 1975. He held elections to a **Constitutional Convention** in which anti-power-sharing unionists, including Craig and Paisley won a clear majority.
- The SDLP boycotted the Convention and the unionists demanded a return to the Stormont system. The British turned this down.
- The failure of the Sunningdale Agreement and the Convention showed what people called 'the double veto'.
  ○ Nationalists could stop unionists getting the majority rule they wanted.
  ○ Unionists could stop nationalists getting the power-sharing they wanted.
- As a result, the rest of the 1970s was a period of stalemate. Direct rule, which the British hoped would be temporary, continued and there was little political action.

Roy Mason

- In September 1976 **Roy Mason**, a tough former miner, replaced Merlyn Rees as Northern Ireland Secretary.
- Aware of the 'double veto' he did not look for a political solution.
- Instead he planned to strengthen security and develop the North's economy in the hope that jobs might draw people away from violence.

Mason deals with the second loyalist strike

- In May 1977 Ian Paisley called another strike to demand a return of Stormont.
- Mason acted decisively. He sent soldiers into the power stations and told the RUC to remove barricades as soon as they were built.
- After a few days the strike collapsed. This was partly because of Mason's action, but also because fewer unionists supported this strike.

Mason's anti-terrorism policies

- After IRA bombs in England killed 28 people in 1973–4, Westminster passed the **Prevention of Terrorism Act**. It allowed the police to question suspected terrorists for seven days before they were charged.
- Northern Ireland police questioned suspects at Castlereagh in Belfast and Gough Barracks in Armagh. They used the information they got to bring people before the Diplock courts. But there were rumours that suspects were beaten during interrogation.
- Mason continued to free internees but he ended '**special category status**' for anyone sentenced by the Diplock courts. They were to be treated like ordinary criminals. IRA prisoners objected to this and it led eventually to the hunger strikes.
- The deaths of young soldiers in Northern Ireland led to a 'troops out' movement in Britain. To counter it, Mason gave the RUC and the Ulster Defence Regiment (UDR) a bigger part in combating violence. This was called '**Ulsterisation**'. From then on the army was mainly involved in patrolling the border areas.
- By 1979 Mason could claim some success. More IRA people were in jail and the level of violence had fallen. Only about 100 people died violently in 1977 and in 1978, compared with over 500 in 1972.

Mason's economic policy

- The North's economy did badly in the 1970s. Unemployment averaged 10 per cent, though in some Catholic areas 50 per cent of the men had no job.
- Many multinational firms closed and the violence discouraged others from starting up. In 1974 British government had to take over the shipbuilders Harland and Wolfe to stop them closing.
- Mason increased government spending and gave generous grants to community groups and local leisure centres. He protected Harland and Wolfe and tried to bring in foreign firms.
- One apparent success was the plan by an American, **John DeLorean** to build a new type of car in Belfast. But after the government had spent millions, the plan collapsed when DeLorean was charged with embezzling the funds.

Unionist power struggles

- After the UUUC defeated Sunningdale, it soon fell apart as Craig, West and Paisley competed for the leadership of the unionist community.
- **Craig's Vanguard Party** was quickly discredited by its links to loyalist paramilitaries and Craig's poor leadership.
- **West** led the traditionally strong **Ulster Unionist Party** (UUP) but he too was a poor leader and was hampered by the party's weak organisation. In the first direct elections to the European Parliament in 1979, he lost out to Paisley.
- He then resigned and was replaced by **James Molyneaux**. He thought Northern Ireland should be more fully integrated into Britain and spent much of his time in Westminster.
- **Ian Paisley** quickly recovered from the defeat of the second loyalist strike and his party gained support in local elections at the expense of the UUP. His victory over West in the European elections saw him emerge as an important unionist spokesman.

James Molyneaux (1920–)

- Molyneaux served in the RAF in World War II, then became a farmer in Co. Antrim. An active member of the Orange Order and the Ulster Unionist Party (UUP), he was elected to Westminster in 1970.
- He opposed the Sunningdale Agreement and the power-sharing Executive.
- While Harry West was leader of the UUP in Northern Ireland, Molyneaux led the Ulster Unionist MPs at Westminster.
- When the Labour government needed extra votes in the late '70s he supported them in return for a number of concessions to Unionists. The main one was to increase the number of Northern Ireland seats at Westminster from 12 to 17.
- In 1979 he replaced West as UUUP leader. The party was under threat from Paisley's DUP and divided about what policy to follow. Should it work for

Northern Ireland to be further integrated into Britain or look for a return to devolved government?

- Molyneaux favoured integration to Britain but most of his followers wanted to restore Stormont.
- He opposed power-sharing and any involvement with the republic and he trusted **Margaret Thatcher** to defend the unionists.
- Because of this he did not to take part in the talks that led to the 1985 **Anglo-Irish Agreement** which took him completely by surprise.
- He joined with Ian Paisley in opposing it. As part of the protest he resigned his seat in Westminster but won it back in the subsequent by-election. He drew back from the protests when the DUP seemed to be working with loyalist paramilitaries.
- In the early 1990s he led the UUP delegation to the all-party talks with the main political parties in Northern Ireland, (apart from Sinn Féin) and the London and Dublin governments. When these ended in failure the British and Irish governments pursued an alternative strategy which led to the Downing Street Declaration of 15 December 1993.
- Though sceptical, Molyneaux gave it a guarded welcome. Discontent with his leadership began to emerge and in 1995 he resigned.
- He remained active in politics, opposing the Good Friday Agreement and power-sharing.
- A quiet, rather grey man, Molyneaux led the UUP for 16 years but his desire to integrate Northern Ireland into Britain was not shared by the majority of his followers.

The SDLP after Sunningdale

- On the nationalist side, Gerry Fitt resigned from the SDLP in 1979 because he felt it had become too nationalist. **John Hume** then became leader. He was also elected to the Westminster and European parliaments.
- He used these positions to win influence over political leaders in Britain, the EU and the United States. He wanted them to support a political settlement in Northern Ireland which would involve:
  - nationalists accepting that a united Ireland could only come with the consent of the unionists in Northern Ireland and
  - the British saying that they would do nothing to stop a united Ireland if the unionists agreed to it.
- This he thought would open the way to another power-sharing Executive.

Gerry Adams and the reorganisation of the Provisional IRA

- In the early 1970s most IRA leaders were based in Dublin. This changed after they agreed to a ceasefire in 1975. Northern republicans disapproved and they took over the leadership.
- The most significant of the new leaders were **Gerry Adams** and **Martin McGuinness**. They thought that republicans must engage in a 'long war' to force the British to leave Northern Ireland.

- They reorganised the Provisionals. Small **Active Service Units** (ASU), which engaged in bombing, murder and bank raids, replaced bigger battalions. It was harder for the police to infiltrate the smaller units and captured members could only give information about their own ASU.
- Adams also believed in political action. He encouraged the IRA's political wing, **Sinn Féin** to become active in local politics, helping nationalists with issues like housing and jobs.

Gerry Adams (1948–)

- Belfast-born Adams was working as a barman when violence broke out in 1969.
- He became involved in the IRA and was interned in 1971 because the RUC believed he was the local commander.
- He was freed in 1972 to take part in secret talks with William Whitelaw. They failed when the republicans demanded that the British withdraw from Northern Ireland.
- The Provisionals resumed their violence. Adams was re-arrested in 1973 and spent four years in the Maze prison. While there he developed the idea that republicans should have a political programme as well as the 'armed struggle'.
- Released in 1977, he remained at the centre of the republican movement though he denied that he was in the IRA. In 1978 he became Vice-President of Sinn Féin and was elected President in 1983.
- Bobby Sands' election to Westminster won over more republicans to his idea of political action. In 1982 Adams and four other Sinn Féin candidates won seats in the Northern Ireland Assembly elections and others won seats in Dáil Éireann. In 1983 Adams took Gerry Fitt's seat in Westminster.
- The Sinn Féin candidates refused to take their seats in any of these assemblies (**abstention**). Adams believed that abstention prevented further Sinn Féin success and in 1986 he got the party to end it in relation to Dáil Éireann. Although more traditional republicans left Sinn Féin, the majority stayed with Adams.
- In the later 1980s talks between Adams and John Hume helped to convince republicans that they could gain more from peace than violence.
- That led to an IRA ceasefire in August 1994 and opened the way for talks between all the parties in Northern Ireland and the British and Irish governments.
- As leaders of Sinn Féin Adams and McGuinness were careful to move slowly in the direction of peace and they skillfully kept the majority of republicans united behind them in spite of abandoning traditional republican ideas and policies.

The Peace People

- Opposition to the Provisionals' brutal bombings and killings led to the emergence of the **Peace People**.
- After an IRA getaway car killed three children, their aunt, **Mairead Corrigan** and **Betty Williams** set up the Peace People to campaign against violence.
- They organised marches in both communities and the two women won the Nobel Peace Prize but the movement fizzled out after quarrels about future policy.

Margaret Thatcher

- In 1979, the Labour Party lost the British general election and **Margaret Thatcher**, leader of the Conservative Party became Prime Minister. Known as the *Iron Lady*, she dominated British politics until she retired in 1990.
- On Northern Ireland she:
  - ○ supported the unionists' desire to remain part of the United Kingdom
  - ○ rejected the idea that the republic should have any role in the North and
  - ○ was determined to defeat terrorism.
- Her opposition to the IRA was strengthened in 1979 when they killed her advisor on Northern Ireland, Airey Neave. In 1984 the Provisionals almost killed her too when they set off a bomb in Brighton during the Conservative Party conference.
- At first Thatcher continued the Labour government's policy towards Northern Ireland. But in 1980–81 she had to deal with the IRA hunger strikes.

Protests at criminalisation

- These were due to Roy Mason's decision to treat paramilitary prisoners like ordinary criminals (**criminalisation**).
- After being sentenced in the Diplock courts, paramilitary prisoners were put into the newly built **H-Blocks** in the Maze prison where they had to wear prison clothes and obey prison rules.
- When IRA prisoners refused to wear prison clothes they were left in their cells with only a blanket for covering. When this failed to change anything, they refused to clean the cells, then began to smear the walls with excrement.
- By 1978 over 300 prisoners were involved in the 'dirty protest'. To support them, the IRA killed prison officers.

Bobby Sands and the hunger strike

- Not many people outside the republican movement were aware of these protests, although Bernadette Devlin stood in the 1979 European election to draw attention to them.
- Finally the prisoners decided to go on hunger strike in October 1980, although republican leaders opposed this. The strike ended after 53 days because they thought the government promised concessions.

- But nothing changed so the IRA leader in the Maze, **Bobby Sands**, began a second hunger strike on 1 March 1981. After two weeks another prisoner joined him, then a week later a third and so on. They hoped the propaganda impact would grow as, one by one, the men approached death.
- When the Nationalist MP for Fermanagh-South Tyrone died suddenly, the republicans nominated Sands to replace him. No other nationalist stood and he won by 30,492 votes to 29,046. This put Bobby Sands and the hunger strike on news bulletins around the world.
- Thatcher saw the hunger strikers as terrorists and was determined not to give in to them. By August ten were dead.
- In the end the strikers' families persuaded doctors to treat men who became unconscious. The strike ended in October.
- The strikers believed they had failed but afterwards the government quietly granted many of their demands.

The impact of the hunger strikes

- The hunger strikes had a huge impact on Northern Ireland.
- They strengthened the Provisionals by bringing in new recruits. This let them to continue their campaign of bombing and destruction into the 1980s and 1990s.
- But Sands' election victory also showed republican leaders the value of political activity. Sinn Féin began to fight elections. In the republic they got several TDs elected to the Dáil and in Northern Ireland, Adams won Gerry Fitt's Westminster seat, although he refused to enter the Commons.
- The way Britain handled the hunger strikes damaged its reputation around the world.
- It also appalled the Irish government which knew it would strengthen republicans at the expense of the moderate SDLP.

Thatcher looks for power-sharing

- The hunger strikes made Thatcher think again about her Northern Ireland policy.
- She knew that the conflict there damaged Britain's international reputation, drained its economic resources and killed its soldiers.
- William Whitelaw persuaded her that power sharing was the best way to achieve peace, but she knew that would not be possible if the hunger strikes destroyed the moderate SDLP.
- She encouraged her Northern Ireland Secretaries to look for agreement among the northern parties. But various attempts ended in failure as unionists refused to accept power-sharing and demanded a return of Stormont.

Agreement with the South

- Thatcher also changed her attitude towards the republic because:
  - ○ She hoped that this would improve security along the border and make it easier to control the IRA.
  - ○ US President Regan, influenced by important Irish Americans like Edward Kennedy, urged her to talk to the Dublin government.
- Soon after Thatcher came to power she met Taoiseach **Charles Haughey**. They got on well but relations grew frosty when he announced that a united Ireland was coming soon.
- She got on better with the next Taoiseach, **Garret FitzGerald**, who led a Fine Gael/Labour Coalition between 1982 and 1987.

Garret FitzGerald and the New Ireland Forum

- FitzGerald feared the hunger strike would undermine support for the SDLP. To help nationalists decide on their aims he set up the **New Ireland Forum** in 1983.
- Representatives of all the Dáil parties met in Dublin Castle and interviewed many people including Catholic bishops, Protestant clergymen and individual unionists about the future of Ireland.
- The discussions at the Forum encouraged nationalists to re-examine their attitudes to the northern conflict.

The 1985 Anglo-Irish ('Hillsborough') Agreement

- Thatcher rejected the Forum's proposal for a united Ireland but soon afterwards talks began between the two governments.
- There were several reasons for this:
  - ○ Thatcher liked and trusted Garret FitzGerald. He convinced her that only co-operation between the two governments would make northern Catholics trust the RUC and the British army.
  - ○ She hoped that he would do more to control the border and extradite IRA people to Northern Ireland to stand trial.
  - ○ In the European Union, Irish and British politicians and civil servants had worked together and had learnt to trust each other.
- The talks led to the Anglo-Irish Agreement which the two leaders signed at Hillsborough, Co. Down on 15 November 1985. It contained several important parts:
  1. To reassure unionists, the Irish government accepted that Northern Ireland was part of the United Kingdom and that could only change with the consent of the majority of the people in Northern Ireland. (This is called *the principle of consent*).
  2. But to protect nationalists, an **Inter-Governmental Conference** was set up.

- ❏ It would meet regularly and be jointly chaired by the Northern Ireland Secretary and the Irish Foreign Minister.
- ❏ It would discuss issues that concerned the Catholic community such as job discrimination or the teaching of Irish. A '*determined effort*' would be made to sort out differences.
- ❏ To support the Conference, civil servants from London and Dublin would be permanently based in **Maryfield**, near Belfast.

Nationalist reactions to the Agreement

- The IRA and Sinn Féin denounced the Agreement.
- So did Charles Haughey, saying it 'copper-fastened partition'. He later amended this attitude when it became clear that a majority of people in the republic supported the Agreement.

Unionists resist the Agreement

- Unionists were caught off guard by the Agreement. The UUP leader, James Molyneaux had refused to join in the talks because he was sure Thatcher would not do a deal with Dublin.
- They were horrified to realise that officials and ministers from the republic would be at the heart of Northern Ireland's government. They felt the British had betrayed them.
- Molyneaux and Paisley led a huge '*Ulster says no*' rally in central Belfast. Loyalist workers called a one day strike and loyalist paramilitaries threatened to kill the civil servants and ministers at Maryfield.
- Fifteen unionist MPs resigned their Westminster seats and stood again in the by-elections as anti-Agreement candidates. Their aim was to stage a kind of referendum on the Agreement but they lost one of the seats to the SDLP.
- In the end, unionist resistance proved futile. Margaret Thatcher again lived up to her reputation and refused to bend.

Margaret Thatcher (1925–)

- Margaret Thatcher joined the Conservative Party while a student in Oxford and was elected an MP in 1959.
- In 1970 Edward Heath appointed her as Education Secretary. After the Conservatives lost to Labour in 1974, she was elected party leader of the party in 1975. She won the 1979 general election, mainly because of Britain's economic decline under the Labour government.
- Thatcher supported the unionists' place in the United Kingdom and was committed to defeating the IRA, which had assassinated her Northern Ireland advisor, Airey Neave, shortly before the election.
- She refused to negotiate with the republican hunger strikers, ignoring pleas from the Dublin government.

- But her friend, William Whitelaw, persuaded her that power-sharing between Protestants and Catholics was the best way to get peace. She allowed her Northern Ireland Secretaries to organise talks between the leaders of the two communities. But she did little to encourage them and was not too surprised when they failed.
- She hoped that better relations with the republic would improve security by sealing the border and extraditing republicans to Northern Ireland for trial.
- She got on well with Charles Haughey at first but that changed after he claimed a united Ireland was near.
- She had a better relationship with Garret FitzGerald, whom she trusted but she bluntly rejected the proposals of his New Ireland Forum.
- In spite of that, talks continued, leading to the signing of the **Anglo-Irish Agreement** at **Hillsborough**, Co Down in November 1985.
- To the fury of unionists the Agreement gave the Irish government a say in Northern Ireland affairs and created a permanent Secretariat of civil servants from both governments in Maryfield near Belfast.
- Thatcher withstood the unionist '*Ulster Says No*' campaign but grew disillusioned with the Agreement because it failed to deliver the better security she had hoped for.
- In 1990 she resigned as Conservative leader. Later she expressed doubts about the 'peace process' and criticised the 1998 Good Friday Agreement for allowing the early release of paramilitary prisoners.

Questions

For Examination questions on Later Modern Ireland, Topic 5 see page 274.

Your revision notes

Libyan arms and Provisional murders

- Northern violence increased in the late 1980s. Part of the reason for this was three ship-loads of arms and semtex explosives sent by the Libyan dictator **Colonel Gaddafi**, to the Provisionals.
- To damage the economy and make it too expensive for the British to remain in Northern Ireland, the Provisional used the semtex to set off large explosions in town centres.
- Although their main targets were buildings not people, people were killed. On 11 November 1987 an IRA bomb at a **Remembrance Day** ceremony in Enniskillen killed eleven Protestants.
- The IRA also announced that anyone providing a service to the British army was a '*legitimate target*' and they murdered people like civil servants, caterers and builders.
- Some of their victims were Catholics but most were Protestants. This increased the bitterness between the two communities.

'Shoot to kill' and 'supergrasses'

- In response to IRA violence the British brought in their counter-terrorism agents, the **SAS**. They succeeded in intercepting some IRA actions.
- At Loughgall in Co Armagh on 8 May 1987 they killed eight IRA men as they attacked an RUC barracks. Guns they captured had been used in 33 raids or murders. Republicans complained about a British 'shoot to kill' policy.
- The British also used '**super-grasses**', i.e. IRA people who informed on their comrades.

Loyalist tit-for-tat killing

- Loyalist violence also increased in response to IRA activity. Between 1986 and 1989 the UDA killed over 40 Catholics.
- In the early 1990s they succeeded in killing a number of IRA men and Sinn Féin councillors. Republicans claimed that the security forces showed them who to kill.

The impact of the violence

- The violence made life difficult for people in Northern Ireland. There was always fear of a bomb or a shooting. Town centres were sealed off and people were searched when they went shopping.

- The economy was damaged. Businesses closed after bombs went off and no new ones wanted to open, so unemployment remained high. Only a large British subsidy kept the economy from collapsing.

A new departure in Sinn Féin policy

- But behind scenes, changes were taking place. The most important was a gradual shift in Provisional thinking.
- Gerry Adams was impressed by Sinn Féin's success in winning seats in Northern Ireland and the republic during the hunger strike. But when the impact of the hunger strikes wore off, they lost these seats.
- Adams thought that one reason for that was the Sinn Féin policy of **abstention**. Ever since the Treaty in 1922, Sinn Féin TDs had refused to take their seats in Dáil Éireann. In 1986 he got the Sinn Féin Ard Fheis to end abstention.
- He also encouraged Sinn Féin people to get elected to local councils where they helped local people with issues like unemployment, vandalism and drugs.
- But this led to tension within the republican movement.
- How could Sinn Féin councillors get jobs for people when IRA bombs were destroying them?
- And would more people vote for Sinn Féin if IRA violence stopped?
- These issues started a debate among republicans. What was the best way forward? Could they win the war? If not, might it not be better to cease fire so that talks could begin?

'Talks about talks'

- Alongside the violence in the late 1980s, there was a complex web of secret 'talks about talks' to try to get the Provisionals to agree to a ceasefire.
- There were secret contacts between Gerry Adams and John Hume, and between Adams and Taoiseach, Charles Haughey.
- They all told Adams that if the IRA called a ceasefire, a '**pan-nationalist**' alliance could be formed to negotiate with the British.
- The British held talks with the unionists hoping for agreement on power-sharing but these failed when Molyneaux wanted to get rid of the Maryfield Secretariat.
- The British also had informers within the leadership of Sinn Féin and were aware of the debates among republicans about future policy. They held secret talks with Provisionals, hoping to encourage a more peaceful approach.
- Republicans wanted the British to promise to leave Ireland if an agreement was reached between nationalists and unionists. This led the Northern Secretary, Peter Brooke to make an important speech

Remember...

Pan-nationalist = including all nationalists, i.e. the SDLP, Sinn Féin and the Irish government.

EDCO REVISE WISE POINTS TO NOTE

in November 1990. In it he said that '... *the British government has no selfish strategic or economic interest in Northern Ireland*'.

The IRA bombs England

- But even as the secret 'talks about talks' were going on, the IRA set off bombs in England. In 1992 it fired mortars into the garden of 10 Downing Street while the British Cabinet was meeting and set off a huge bomb in the financial district of London, causing millions of pounds worth of damage.
- This may have been intended to show that the IRA was still strong, even if it did call a ceasefire.

Three new leaders

- Three new leaders who appeared on the scene in the early 1990s helped to achieve peace. They were:
  1. **John Major** who replaced Margaret Thatcher as Prime Minister in 1990. He had formed a personal friendship with Albert Reynolds, when they met at EU meetings.
  2. In 1992 **Reynolds** replaced Haughey as Taoiseach. A practical businessman, he was eager to achieve peace in Northern Ireland. His friendship with Major made it easier to persuade the British to deal with the republicans.
  3. In 1992 **Bill Clinton** became President of the United States. He was influenced by a group of wealthy and powerful Irish Americans and promised to seek peace in Northern Ireland.
- Progress towards peace was interrupted in October 1993 when an IRA bomb exploded in the Protestant Shankill Road area of Belfast, killing nine Protestants as well as the IRA bomber. To keep the trust of his followers Adams carried the coffin of the bomber at his funeral.
- Outrage at this nearly ended all negotiations but Reynolds convinced Major that it was important to go on talking.

15 December 1993: The Downing Street Declaration

- On 27 October 1993 the Irish government issued '*six principles*' which must underlie any peace settlement. They included:
  - ❍ no talking to people who used violence and
  - ❍ no change in the status of Northern Ireland without the clear consent of the majority there.
- Major accepted these principles.
- On 15 December Reynolds met Major in Downing Street and they issued the **Downing Street Declaration**.
- A short document with just eleven paragraphs, stated firmly that it was up to '*the people of the island alone*' to decide their future and that a united Ireland could only come '*on the basis of consent, freely given, North and South*'.

Tempting the republicans

- Some hard-line IRA people wanted to ignore the Declaration but Adams and McGuinness thought it could form the basis of talks.
- Reynolds then offered concessions to Sinn Féin. He let them appear on TV and radio and set up a **Forum for Peace and Reconciliation** to discuss the way forward.
- In America, Clinton agreed to let Adams attend a conference on Northern Ireland in New York but only if there was a permanent IRA ceasefire.
- The republican leaders hesitated and in London the IRA fired mortar bombs at Heathrow airport.
- This produced an angry reaction from Reynolds and the Americans. So did the announcement of a limited ceasefire in March 1994.
- Finally on 31 August, 1994 the IRA announced an unconditional ceasefire.
- At last the way was open to a full peace process.

Questions

For Examination questions on Later Modern Ireland, Topic 5 see page 274.

Your revision notes

Later Modern History of Europe and the Wider World   Topic 3
Dictatorship and Democracy 1920-1945

1.1 Lenin's regime

Tsarist Russia

- Up to 1917, Russia was an **autocracy**. Just one man, **Tsar Nicholas II**, made laws, levied taxes and appointed Ministers, generals, etc
- After a revolution in 1905, Nicholas agreed to an elected parliament, the **Duma**, but gave it no real power
- Eighty per cent of Russians were **peasants** (farmers). They had very small farms and their farming methods were old-fashioned and inefficient. They envied wealthy nobles who owned great tracts of land, and wanted to acquire it
- In the 1880s, the Tsar had begun to **industrialise** Russia. Its economy had grown rapidly before 1914, but it was still behind the more powerful countries of western Europe, like Germany or Britain
- Many people in Russia were unhappy with the Tsarist government and wanted to replace it. One of them was Lenin. But because political parties were banned, the only way open to them was to plot a violent revolution.

The ideas of Karl Marx (1818–1883)

- Lenin was sent into exile for plotting against the Tsar. He joined the Social Democratic Party which believed in the ideas of **Karl Marx**
- In his book, *Das Kapital* (1867), Marx claimed to have discovered **the scientific laws** that governed how societies developed
- He wrote that all societies change because of "**a struggle between the different classes for control of the means of production**" (i.e. ways of making money)
- Marx forecast that factory workers would stage a revolution against factory owners (**capitalists**) and take over all property
- That would end the class struggle. After that there would be a '**classless society**', all property would be held in common and there would be equality and justice for all.

Lenin adapts Marx's ideas

- Many people were impressed by Marx's claim to have discovered the **scientific laws** which controlled social change
- Even socialists who did not want violent revolution, believed his claim that a classless society was certain to come about. The only problem was how to achieve it

- In 1900, Lenin wrote a pamphlet called *"What is to be done?"* In it he suggested that a **small body of dedicated revolutionaries** would start the revolution. They would then lead the workers to the classless society. He called the transition period "**the dictatorship of the proletariat**".

Bolsheviks and Mensheviks

- Lenin's ideas caused a big debate in the Russian Social Democrats. In 1903, they divided into the **Bolsheviks**, who supported Lenin, and the **Mensheviks**, who opposed him
- Lenin and most Bolsheviks lived in exile, moving from country to country just ahead of the police
- When revolution finally came to Russia in 1917, Lenin was far away in Switzerland.

The fall of Tsarist Russia

- In 1914, Tsar Nicholas declared war on Germany. At first Russians rallied to the defence of their country, but their armies were defeated by the better-organised Germans
- By the end of 1916, discontent was growing:
  - The Germans had invaded Russia and the army was not getting enough guns or ammunition to fight them
  - In the cities, prices had risen by 400% since 1914, and shortages of food and fuel made life miserable for most Russians
- In January 1917, strikes and food riots began. In March, Nicholas abdicated and the Duma elected a 'Provisional Government' and declared a republic.

The failure of the Provisional Government

- The Provisional Government decided to keep Russia in the war and began to organise elections for a new Assembly. It also tried to stop the peasants taking the nobles' land
- These decisions did little to help ordinary Russians. To meet their needs they began to form **soviets** (committees) to distribute food, keep order, run factories, etc
- In Petrograd, soldiers and workers formed the **Petrograd soviet** led by **Leon Trotsky**. He organised its members into an armed group, the **Red Guards**
- As ordinary Russians grew disillusioned with the Provisional Government they put their trust in the soviets, which became an alternative government.

Lenin seizes power

- In April 1917, the Germans helped Lenin to return from Switzerland, hoping he would undermine the Provisional Government
- He saw it was unpopular and ordered the Bolsheviks not to co-operate with it. He told his followers to **infiltrate and take over the soviets**
- In his *April Theses*, he called for "*All power to the soviets*", promised to end the war and allow the peasants to take the nobles' land. These ideas, summed up in the slogan *Peace, Bread, Land*, were designed to appeal to soldiers, peasants and workers
- Lenin won the backing of Trotsky and the Red Guards. In July, they tried to seize power, but were defeated. Lenin fled to Finland but returned after the Red Guards prevented the Russian army from overthrowing the Provisional Government
- Lenin now told the Bolsheviks they must seize power at once. They chose **24 October**, the day before a **Congress of Soviets** (with many Bolsheviks in it) was due to meet
- On that day, the **Red Guards** took over the **Winter Palace** where the Provisional Government's offices were. The Russian army refused to intervene and Lenin became the new ruler of Russia.

Lenin's government

- On 25 October, Lenin formed a **Politburo** (Cabinet) with **Commissars** (Ministers) in change of different areas of government. **Trotsky** was Commissar for War and **Stalin** Commissar for Nationalities
- The Congress of Soviets recognised Lenin's Politburo as the new Russian government. It was the first Marxist government in history
- Lenin and his followers faced huge problems. They had to (1) end the war with Germany, (2) set up a Marxist-style state (no one knew what that might look like in 1917), and (3) hold on to power against all their opponents.

Peace: The Treaty of Brest Litovsk

- Lenin knew they must end the war if they were to survive. He sent **Trotsky** to hold peace talks with the Germans
- They demanded large areas of Russia. Some Bolsheviks wanted to refuse, but Lenin insisted that peace was essential
- In March 1918, the Bolsheviks signed the **Treaty of Brest Litovsk**. Russia lost Poland, Ukraine, the Baltic states, 30% of its population, 50% of its industry and 30% of its good agricultural land. Russia re-conquered Ukraine during the civil war.

Changing Russia

- The Bolsheviks (who changed their name to **Communists** in 1918) **nationalised** banks, mines and factories, **abolished** private property, **ended the privileges** of the Church and took over its property, gave women the vote and abolished the Tsarist secret police

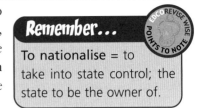

Remember...

To nationalise = to take into state control; the state to be the owner of.

- They also let the peasants seize the nobles' land. This was not really Marxist, but they needed to please the peasants
- Lenin let elections for the Assembly, promised by the Provisional Government, go ahead. The Bolsheviks won 175 seats out of 700
- The Assembly met in January 1918, but Lenin closed it after one day. This showed he did not want democracy.

Growing opposition to Lenin

- After this, opposition to the Communists grew, even among other socialists
- In August 1918, Lenin was shot and badly wounded. The Communists then launched a reign of terror (the '**red terror**') on their critics
- A new secret police, the **CHEKA** arrested and executed thousands, including any Bolshevik who criticised Lenin's policies. The Tsar and his family were murdered at this time.

Civil War, 1918–1920

- Tsarists, Social Revolutionaries, Mensheviks and others ('**the Whites**') joined together to fight the Communists ('**the Reds**')
- Britain, France, the US and Japan sent help to the White armies
- The Reds seemed weak at first. They only controlled the area around Moscow and Petrograd. But that was the industrial area where the arms factories were
- Lenin imposed a harsh economic system called '**War Communism**'. It suited his Marxist ideas and also ensured food for soldiers and factory workers
- Red Guards went into the country and seized grain from peasants without paying. It was rationed out to soldiers and workers in the arms factories. Other classes got little or nothing
- At first this worked, but the peasants stopped growing food and this brought famine in 1920, in which millions died
- By then, the Reds had won the civil war. Their victory was due to (1) their unity, (2) the military skill of Trotsky who built up the Red Army, (3) War Communism which ensured the soldiers had food and guns, and (4) the passive support of the peasants, grateful for being allowed to take the nobles' land
- The Whites lost the civil war because (1) they were divided in their aims (return the Tsar? a liberal democracy? socialism?) and fought among themselves (2) the peasants did not trust them and (3) having foreign allies made them seem anti-Russian.

Problems caused by War Communism

- But by 1920, War Communism had produced an economic disaster. A severe drought in 1919–1920 made things worse. In 1920–1921, millions died in a famine
- In 1921, riots and mutinies broke out. The worst one was in **Kronstadt Naval Base** where sailors demanded an end to the Communist dictatorship
- Lenin recognised that his government was in danger and acted swiftly. He ordered the brutal suppression of the mutinies. The CHEKA shot thousands of mutineers without a trial.

The NEP (New Economic Policy) 1921–1928

- But Lenin also changed his economic policy. At the **10th Party Congress**, he announced that War Communism was to be replaced by a **New Economic Policy (NEP)**:
  - ○ Peasants had to give 10% of their crops to the state as a tax, but could sell any surplus they had after that
  - ○ Banks, railways and large industries remained in state control, but small shops and private businesses, with fewer than 20 workers, could be set up
  - ○ When some Communists protested that this was going back to capitalism, Lenin replied that sometimes it was necessary to take one step back in order to take two forward
- The NEP was successful. By 1928, the Russian economy had recovered. This gave the Communist regime time to establish itself firmly in power.

The Soviet Union

- In 1923, a new Constitution was introduced. The name of the country was changed from Russia to the **Union of Soviet Socialist Republics (USSR or Soviet Union)**
- Officially, the **Congress of Soviets** was the governing body that elected the government. But since only one party – the Communist Party – was allowed to exist, the leaders of the Communist Party were the true rulers of the USSR.

1924: The death of Lenin

- Lenin never really recovered from the attempt to assassinate him in 1918. From 1922, he suffered from a series of strokes which prevented him from taking part in the government
- In 1923, suspecting the end was near, he wrote his *Testament*. In it, he voiced his fears for the future of the communist revolution and criticised the members of the Politburo. He was especially harsh in criticising **Stalin**, suggesting that he be removed from his job as Secretary of the Party
- Lenin died shortly after writing the *Testament* in January 1924, at the age of 53.

Assessing Lenin

- Lenin set up the world's first Marxist state and steered it though its first difficult years with a mixture of political skill and ruthless brutality
- Lenin was a **pragmatist** – for while he believed in Marxism, he was willing to adopt non-Marxist policies (peasant ownership of land, the NEP) in order to stay in power
- He introduced many necessary reforms into Russia but ruthlessly used force to suppress anyone who dared to criticise him or his policies
- He opened the way for the even more brutal dictatorship of Stalin.

Remember...

Pragmatist: a person who changes his ideals when faced with difficult realities.

Lenin (Vladimir Ilyich Ulyanov) (1870 – 1924)

- Lenin was born in 1870 into a prosperous family
- He became involved in plotting a revolution after his brother was executed. Arrested, he was exiled to Siberia and then forced to live outside Russia
- He joined the Marxist **Social Democratic Party**. In a pamphlet, *What is to be done?*, he suggested important changes to Karl Marx's ideas. This split the Social Democrats into Mensheviks and **Bolsheviks**, who were Lenin's supporters
- In 1917, he returned to Russia after the Tsar fell
- He and the Bolsheviks seized power in October 1917
- He set up the world's first **Communist** (Marxist) government, nationalised all property, abolished the power of the Church and established a secret police
- With the help of Leon **Trotsky**, he won a civil war against his opponents, the **Whites**, by a ruthless use of terror and **War Communism**
- When his policies caused a famine and made the Communists unpopular, he changed to the **New Economic Policy** (**NEP**)
- He died in 1924 at the age of 53.

1.2 Stalin's regime

Power struggle 1924 – 1928

- Lenin died in 1924 without saying who should take over. This led to a power struggle among members of the Politburo, **Trotsky**, **Stalin**, **Kamenev**, **Zinoviev** and **Bakunin**
- Many people thought Trotsky would win because he controlled the Red Army. But he was unpopular with the other Politburo members who feared a military dictatorship
- They did not fear Stalin, who was just the Party Secretary, and agreed to suppress the criticism of him in Lenin's *Testament*
- Stalin spoke at Lenin's funeral, while Trotsky was absent. This made Stalin look like Lenin's favourite.

Debating the future of Communism

- In the struggle for power, Stalin used debates about the future of communism to outmanoeuvre his opponents
- The first debate was about how to protect communism in Russia. *Should they encourage communist revolutions in other countries or concentrate on strengthening communism in Russia first?*
  - ○ **Trotsky argued** that the communism in Russia was not safe until other countries became communist. He wanted to '*export*' a '*permanent revolution*' to other countries
  - ○ **Stalin argued** that they should first build up communism in Russia ('*socialism in one country*') and then it could be spread
- Stalin's view was more popular with Russians, weary of war. In 1925, the **Party Congress** adopted it and removed Trotsky from his army command
- A second debate then developed over economic policy. Should they keep the NEP, which mixed capitalism with communism, or should they move to full communism?
  - ○ **Kamenev and Zinoviev** wanted to end the NEP and have full communism
  - ○ **Bakunin** wanted to keep it and Stalin backed him, because this was popular.

Stalin becomes the sole ruler of the Soviet Union

- By this time **Kamenev** and **Zinoviev** realised that Stalin was dangerous. In 1927 they joined **Trotsky** and planned a workers' revolt. Stalin found out and had them expelled from the Party. Trotsky was sent to Siberia and in 1929 was exiled from USSR
- Stalin then changed policy. He dropped the NEP and went for full communism. **Bakunin** too was expelled, and by 1928 Stalin was the only 'Old Bolshevik' (comrade of Lenin) still in power.

Stalin's economic policies

- Stalin wanted to make the USSR into a great military power through **rapid industrialisation**. In 1928, he said: *We are fifty years behind the capitalists; we have ten years to catch them up*
- The NEP had improved the Russian economy since 1922, but too slowly to satisfy Stalin. To achieve his aims he developed economic policies that were very different from the policies of any other country at that time.

What Stalin needed for industrialisation

To industrialise Russia, Stalin needed:
- **Capital** to start industry, but foreign banks would not lend him money because Lenin had repudiated earlier loans made to the Tsar's government and the communists took over foreign owned businesses

- **Factory workers**, but most Russians were peasant farmers who preferred to work on their own farms
- **Some way of feeding the factory workers**. Russian agriculture was very backward. There were about 25 million tiny farms, which produced barely enough to feed the peasants themselves, leaving very little over to feed people living in towns.

Reasons for collectivisation of agriculture

- Stalin decided the solution to his problems was to **collectivise agriculture**. That meant **combining millions of tiny, peasant-owned farms into big, state-owned 'collective' farms (kolkhoz)**
- For Stalin collectivisation had many advantages:
  - Peasants who lost their farms would go to work in the new industries
  - The big collective farms would be more efficient because they could use modern machinery. Therefore, they would produce enough food to feed the workers in the towns
  - The money the state earned by selling food from the collective farms could be invested in industrialisation.

Enforcing collectivisation

- At first Stalin thought collectivisation could be voluntary, but by 1929, when peasants would not give up their land, it was brutally enforced
- Peasants resisted collectivisation. They killed animals and destroyed equipment rather than give them to the state. Between **1929** and **1933**, crops were not sown and 53% of horses, 45% of cattle and 67% of sheep were destroyed
- Most resistance came from the slightly richer peasants, the **kulaks**. Communist officials called kulaks *'enemies of the workers'* and encouraged poorer peasants to turn on them
- The secret police rounded up kulaks. About five million were deported to labour camps where many of them died
- This helped overcome peasant resistance, as anyone who resisted could be labelled a "kulak" and arrested
- The conflict over collectivisation caused a man-made famine in 1931–1932, in which millions died. It was particularly severe in Ukraine, where it amounted to genocide
- In 1931, Stalin pulled back a little, blaming officials for being 'over-zealous'. He agreed to let peasants keep a small plot to grow vegetables for their own use.

Results of collectivisation

- At least 10 million peasants disappeared during collectivisation – dead from famine or in labour camps

- By 1937, over 90% of Russian land was in state-owned **collective farms**. As resistance diminished, food production rose and animal numbers had recovered
- On each collective farm, 75 peasant families (on average) worked using modern machinery, like tractors. Each family was paid a wage to work a fixed number of days per year (between 100–150). The rest of the year they worked on their own plots
- Peasants worked hardest on their private plots. More food was produced on these plots than on the collective farms.

Industrialisation through Five-Year Plans

- Industrialisation accompanied collectivisation. It was based on the idea of **central state planning** of all industry. The state planning body, **Gosplan**, drew up targets and saw that they were met
- The **first Five-Year Plan** was drawn up in 1928. It **set targets** for the expansion of heavy industry. In five years electric power was to grow by 335%, iron production by 200%, coal production by 111%, etc. Little attention was paid to consumer goods like shoes, furniture, etc
- Targets were not met but results were still impressive: Electric output grew by 160%; iron by 100%; coal by 80%
- The **second Plan** (1932–1937) was more successful with many sectors doubling production. Under it railways, canals and airports were built. It placed more emphasis on consumer goods like shoes and clothes. With Hitler strengthening Germany and threatening the USSR, tank factories were set up beyond the Urals, out of German reach
- The **third Plan** began in 1937, but was interrupted by purges, then by the German invasion in 1941. It continued to emphase military expansion.

Workers

- Workers were set individual targets. There were **prizes** for those who exceeded their targets and **punishment** for those who failed. Absentees got no rations
- **Propaganda** about building a better world or making the Soviet Union great also encouraged workers to try harder
- A big problem was shortage of skilled workers. It was solved by giving extra pay and prizes for good workers. **Internal passports** were introduced to stop skilled workers moving from job to job. Some skilled workers were recruited from abroad
- Living conditions were poor. Huge apartment complexes were built with just one room for each family. They shared kitchens and bathrooms. But rents were low, cheap entertainment was provided and education and health care were free

- In remote and difficult areas like Siberia, where workers were reluctant to go, the state had hundreds of **slave labour camps**, where millions of '*enemies of the people*' worked in mines or built roads, railways and canals, etc, without pay.

Results

- The Five Year Plans produced spectacular results. By 1939, the USSR had become Europe's second industrial power after Germany
- Industrialisation produced **urbanisation**. In 1926, only 15% of Russians lived in cities; by 1940 30% did
- The development of industry helped the USSR to defeat Hitler in the second World War.

> **NB.** Stalin's economic policies had three main features: (1) There was no private property. Everything: farms, houses, shops, factories, mines, banks, etc, belonged to the state. (2) Farming was on huge state-owned collective farms. (3) All industrial development was planned by the central government. This was very different from the rest of the world in the 1930s, where most property and industries belonged to private individuals or companies and the state did not interfere much in economic decisions.

Education and the arts

- Education expanded to meet the needs of industry. By 1940, only 15% of Russians were still illiterate and over one million were university graduates
- Access to university was controlled by exam success and the right political views. Students had no choice of career, but studied what the state told them to study
- Artists were told to produce 'socialist realism' celebrating the achievements of socialism. Art, literature, film and music were heavily censored and many artists suffered in the purges.

Stalin's totalitarian State

- In 1936, Stalin introduced what he called '*the only thoroughly democratic **Constitution** in the world*'
- Everyone over 18 could to vote for Congress every four years (though only the Communist Party was allowed to put up candidates)
- The right to work, education, free medicine, freedom of speech and freedom from unlawful arrest, were guaranteed, '*in conformity with the interests of the working people*'. That phrase meant that none of these freedoms operated in reality

- In fact, Stalin's Russia was a **totalitarian state** where the government controlled every aspect of people's lives
- The secret police, the **NKVD** spied on everyone, could arrest, torture or execute anyone it suspected of dissent and controlled the labour camps where millions of Soviet citizens ended up
- Stalin cultivated a **cult of personality**. History books were re-written to emphasise Stalin's role in the 1917 revolution, while Trotsky was left out. His name and image were everywhere and propaganda encouraged Russians to see him as their protector and revere him almost as a god.

●●●Case study

1.3 Stalin's Purges and the Show Trials

The start of the Purges

- In 1931–1932 some Communist Party members criticised Stalin's brutal collectivisation policy, and his wife committed suicide perhaps for the same reason. This increased his isolation and paranoia
- At the 1934 Party Conference, there was considerable support for **Sergei Kirov**, the Party's leader in Leningrad. Later that year, Kirov was assassinated
- Stalin (who may have ordered the assassination) claimed it was evidence of a '**Trotskyite plot**' and used it as an excuse to purge the Party. He wanted to rid it of all '**Old Bolsheviks**' whose membership went back to Lenin's time and leave only those who owed their position to him.

Purging the Communist Party

- The NKVD rounded up thousands of Party members, along with their relatives, neighbours and acquaintances. Some were tortured or shot, most were sent to work in slave labour camps
- State propaganda insisted that all those arrested were '*enemies of the people*' or '*Trotskyites*' who were plotting with the exiled Trotsky and even with Hitler, to kill Stalin, overthrow the revolution and destroy the Soviet Union.

The first Show Trial, August 1936

- As part of this propaganda, Stalin organised '**Show Trials**' in Moscow. The purpose of these trials was not to see if the accused were guilty or innocent, but to show their guilt to the world
- In August 1936, 16 senior Party members, including Stalin's old rivals, **Zinoviev** and **Kamenev** went on trial
- The state prosecutor, **Vyshinsky**, accused them of killing Kirov, plotting to kill Stalin and Lenin and conspiring with Trotsky and foreign governments against the Soviet Union

- For months before, the accused had been subjected to physical and psychological torture and their families had been threatened. As a result, they all pleaded guilty to all the charges, reciting confessions that had been written for them by the authorities. They were sentenced to death and executed at once
- One hundred and fifty Soviet citizens and 30 foreign journalists and diplomats were invited to attend the trial. Amazingly, many of the foreign observers were convinced that the men received a fair trial and a just sentence for their crimes.

The second Show Trial, January 1937

- On 23 January, 1937, another 17 Old Bolsheviks were put on trial. They included men who had supported Trotsky in the leadership struggle like **Karl Radek**
- Again all confessed. Thirteen were sentenced to death. Radek whose confession implicated others, was sent to a labour camp, where he died soon after.

Purging the Red Army

- Stalin feared the power of the Red Army and decided to purge it too. In 1937, **Marshal Tukhachevsky**, the army commander was arrested, tried in secret and shot
- After that, half of the 35,000 officers in the army were either executed or sent to labour camps. This seriously weakened the Red Army at a time when Hitler was threatening to attack the USSR.

The Great Show Trial

- The final Show Trial took place in March 1938. Among the accused were **Bukharin**, one of Lenin's close associates who had criticised Stalin's collectivisation and **Yagoda**, who as head of the NKVD had been responsible for the earlier purges
- They were accused of spying, sabotage, and working with Trotsky and Hitler to destroy the Soviet Union
- Bukharin insisted on his innocence until his wife and baby were threatened. In return for Stalin's promise that they would be safe, he confessed. Stalin later sent his wife to a labour camp
- All were found guilty and executed.

The results of Stalin's purges

- Fifty four men were brought up before the Show Trials, of whom 47 were executed
- But at the same time, about **five million people** were arrested. Nearly a million of them were sentenced to death, with Stalin personally signing thousands of execution warrants

- The rest were sentenced to labour camps where an estimated 90% died of over-work, malnutrition, cold or casual violence
- After the second World War Stalin re-opened the labour camps and continued his purges. In all it is estimated that by the time he died in 1953, he was largely responsible for the death of **at least 20 million** Soviet citizens.

● ● ●

1.4 Russian Foreign Policy: 1917 - 1941

1917 - 1920: Communism fails to spread

- After 1917, Lenin hoped communist revolutions would break out elsewhere in Europe. In 1918, he set up the **Communist International (Comintern)** to support and encourage them
- He and Stalin used it to give orders and money to communist parties across Europe
- After the first World War, there were communist uprisings in Germany and other countries, but they all failed.

1920 - 1933: Isolation

- This left USSR isolated. Britain, France and the US distrusted it because they feared communism, and because Lenin had let them down by pulling out of the war and making peace with Germany
- The Soviet Union was not invited to attend Paris Peace Conference (1919) or join the League of Nations
- In 1922, Lenin made the **Treaty of Rapallo** with the other 'outcast' nation, Germany. Germany was to train its army in Russia and build arms factories. This suited Lenin, as it divided his enemies and made an anti-communist alliance between Germany and its former enemies less likely
- The succession struggle after Lenin's death, collectivisation and industrialisation kept Stalin too busy for foreign policy.

Stalin and the rise of Hitler

- After the Great Depression began in 1929, communist parties in the West grew rapidly
- This convinced Stalin that capitalism was dying as Marx had forecast. He ordered the Communist Parties he controlled through Comintern not to prop up democracy by co-operating with socialist or liberal parties. He thought communists would come out on top if there was a revolution
- Ironically, in Germany this policy helped Hitler, with his anti-communist and anti-Russian policies, to gain power.

Stalin seeks alliances against Hitler

- Realising the threat from fascism, Stalin changed his foreign policy
- He ended Soviet isolation by joining the **League of Nations** in 1934. He hoped that 'collective security' would protect him against Hitler
- He also encouraged Communist Parties in France and Spain to resist fascism by forming '**popular fronts**' with socialists and others
- He sought alliances with capitalist governments against Hitler
- But Britain and France were too anti-communist to accept his overtures. They appeased Hitler instead and did not consult Stalin during the Munich Crisis in 1938
- In August 1939, when Hitler suggested a "**non-aggression pact**" between them, Stalin eagerly accepted
- The secret clauses in it allowed Stalin to invade Poland, the Baltic states and Finland to recover the land Russia lost in 1918 at Brest-Litovsk. It also gave time to rebuild the Red Army, weakened by the purges
- Stalin seems to have believed in the pact, but Hitler never did. He always intended to invade Russia when it suited him to do so. He finally did in June 1941.

Stalin (Joseph Dzugashvili) (1879 – 1953)

- Born into a poor family in Georgia, Stalin briefly studied to be a priest, but was expelled for spreading Marxist ideas
- He supported the Bolsheviks and organised bank robberies to fund them. In 1912, Lenin made him a member of the Party's Central Committee and he edited their paper *Pravda* (Truth)
- He was in prison in Siberia when the Tsar fell in 1917, but returned to Petrograd and led the Party until Lenin returned from Switzerland
- After the Bolsheviks seized power, Lenin made him **Commissar of Nationalities**, responsible for the 65 million non-Russians in the new Soviet Union. He brutally crushed independence movements, even in his native Georgia
- In 1922, he became **Secretary of the Communist Party**. After the Reds won the civil war, he appointed the Party officials who ran the re-conquered areas. These officials who owed their jobs to him, later supported him in the leadership struggle after Lenin's death
- By 1928, Stalin was undisputed ruler of the Soviet Union. He (**1**) brutally collectivised agriculture, (**2**) forced the country to industrialise at breakneck speed, (**3**) ruthlessly purged all opponents and (**4**) led Russia during the second World War
- After the war he (**1**) resumed the policies he followed in the 1930s, (**2**) extended Soviet control over Eastern Europe, and (**3**) fought the **Cold War** with Western democracies led by the United States
- He died in 1953.

CHAPTER 2
The Democracies

Introduction

The first World War ended in November 1918 and the peace treaties were signed at Paris (Versailles) in 1919. After that, most people hoped that life could go back to what it had been before 1914. But this could not be. The war had changed Europe too much.

The economic problems left by the first World War

- Until 1914, Europe was the most industrialised and prosperous part of the world. The first World War changed that

- Most governments had borrowed heavily to pay for the war and after it these **debts** had to be repaid. The German government faced the added the cost of **reparations** imposed on it by the Treaty of Versailles (see page 170). These debts made it difficult to restart the European economy

- Before the war, other parts of the world bought industrial goods from Europe. During the war, when Europe was no longer producing these goods, these countries began to develop their own industries. When the war ended, they wanted to keep their new industries going, so they imposed tariffs on European goods (**protection**). This (a) reduced world trade and (b) made economic recovery more difficult

- These circumstances left the European economy depressed in the early 1920s. After a brief recovery in the late-1920s, the **Wall Street Crash** in 1929 began a global Depression that lasted into the 1930s

- In industrialised countries weak economies produced mass unemployment, misery and hunger. This led to social unrest and political instability, as well as the growth of both **communism** and **fascism**. In some countries democracy was strong enough to survive these tensions and where it was not, dictators took over.

2.1 France: the Third Republic 1920 – 1940

The Third Republic

- The Third French Republic was set up in 1870 after Germany invaded France. It was a **democratic state** that guaranteed the freedom of its citizens

- Its parliament consisted of a **Chamber of Deputies**, elected by all men over 21, and a **Senate** elected by French local councils

- The government, headed by the **Prime Minister**, was answerable to parliament, which also had to approve all laws

- The **President of the Republic** was elected by the members of the Chamber and the Senate.

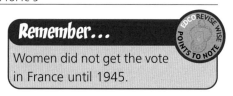

Remember…

Women did not get the vote in France until 1945.

The cost of the first World War

- In 1914, Germany invaded France again, starting the first World War. Although France and its allies won, the French paid a very high price for victory
- Much of the fighting on the Western Front took place in the north-east of France. By 1919, large areas of farmland were scarred by trenches and filled with unexploded bombs. Towns and villages were flattened and mines and factories destroyed
- About 1.3 million French men were dead and another million were permanently disabled. Almost all of them were young men in their 20s and 30s (the most productive section in society)
- Their loss and the loss of the children they might have had, left France seriously short of workers and soldiers for the next 20 years
- The French government had borrowed heavily to pay for the war and these debts would make it difficult to rebuild or to develop its economy.

French political parties

- France had many political parties. This led to a series of weak coalition governments (18 between 1920 and 1940). They found it hard to deal with the country's economic and social problems
- French parties can be divided into:
  - **Right-wing** (conservatives) who represented business men, devout Catholics, wealthy landowners and (later) fascist sympathisers. They were often anti-semitic
  - **Left-wing** parties who mainly represented industrial workers. After the Russian revolution they split into;
    - **Socialists** who wanted to improve workers' conditions through democratic action
    - **Communists** who wanted to imitate Lenin and belonged to **Comintern**
  - The **Radicals** of the centre. They represented the middle classes of small businessmen and farmers
- All of the French coalitions of this period contained Radicals in alliance with either right-wing or left-wing parties.

1919 - 1924: The Bloc National

- The first post-war governments were centre-right coalitions called the **Bloc National**. They were nationalistic, anti-German and anti-communist
- Their main achievement was to reconstruct to war-torn areas of France. To make up for the manpower shortages caused by the war, they allowed two million immigrants from Italy, Spain and Poland to come to France
- They planned to use **German reparations** to pay for the reconstruction, partly to avoid higher French taxes and partly to keep Germany weak
- When Germany stopped paying reparations in 1923, the Prime Minister **Poincaré**, sent French troops into the German industrial area of the **Ruhr**
- The policy was a disaster. No reparations were collected and the cost of the troops forced taxes up
- In 1924, a compromise was reached with the **Dawes Plan**. Germany agreed to pay reduced reparations and the French troops withdrew.

1924 - 1926: the Cartel des Gauches

- Dissatisfaction with this outcome led to the victory of the left-wing parties in the 1924 election. The Radicals formed a government with the support of the Socialists
- They faced a major financial crisis. The government had to increase borrowings to pay for reconstruction and the Ruhr occupation. Prices went up and the franc fell in value, making imports more expensive
- Failure to deal with these problems led to fall of the left and its replacement by a government of national unity led by Poincaré and with some socialist members.

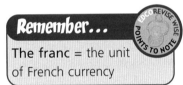

Remember...

The franc = the unit of French currency

1926 - 1932: the Union National

- World economic conditions improved after 1925, and this helped Poincaré deal with the main economic problems. From 1926 to 1930, France enjoyed economic prosperity. Unemployment fell and industrial output increased. By 1930, new industries like electricity, steel and car-making had been developed.

1932 - 1936: The impact of the Depression

- Because France was an agricultural rather than an industrial country, the Great Depression did not affect it until 1931. But then overseas trade fell and a large gap appeared between imports and exports. Investment in industry declined, prices rose and the real value of wages fell
- Governments tried to deal with the Depression by cutting spending on wages, but that led to protests and strikes

- A number of semi-fascist 'Leagues' appeared. They included;
  - **Action Française**, an anti-democratic group set up in 1905. It was very nationalistic, anti-semitic and anti-communist. Its youth wing, **Camelots du Roi**, often engaged in riots with communists
  - **Croix de Feu**, made up of ex-soldiers, was very anti-communist and adopted a paramilitary style
  - **Solidarité Française**, who wore blue shirts, was financed by the millionaire perfume maker, Coty.

1934: The Stavisky Affair

- In 1927, Serge **Stavisky**, a Russian Jew, was charged with fraud but his trial was postponed nine times
- In January 1934, the police wanted to question him about another fraud, but he was found dead before they could
- It looked like suicide, but soon the press began to suggest that he was murdered to cover up his links to certain politicians, including the Prime Minister, who had to resign
- The Leagues used the fact that Stavisky was Jewish to stir up anti-semitism, and his links with politicians to attack democratic government
- In February 1934, they staged riots in which several people were killed and hundreds injured. Trade unionists responded with strikes and protests.

1936–1938: The Popular Front

- The riots and the existence of the Leagues, aroused fears of a fascist coup. This helped to unite the left
- Stalin ordered French communists to co-operate with the Socialists to block a fascist takeover
- In 1936, Radicals, Socialists and Communists formed a coalition called the **Popular Front**. The Socialist leader, **Leon Blum** became Prime Minister
- They promised social reform, the abolition of the Leagues and '*Bread, Peace and Liberty*'
- Trade unionists expected immediate victory. They occupied factories and organised strikes
- Blum met with trade unions and employers and produced the **Matignon Agreements** promising pay rises, a 40-hour week and two weeks paid holidays a year. He also outlawed the Leagues and raised the school leaving age to 14
- But prices continued to rise and there were still a million out of work. Blum had to end his reforms and was forced to resign in 1937
- The **Popular Front** survived until 1938, but achieved little more. The right constantly attacked it, both because it was supported by the communists and because Blum was Jewish.

1938–1940: the Government of National Defence

- A coalition, led by **Edouard Daladier**, took power in 1938. Though mainly concerned with the growing threat from Hitler, Daladier was able to restore economic stability by devaluing the franc and increasing government spending to create jobs
- Daladier was still in power when the second World War began in 1939.

French foreign policy, 1920–1926

- The main aim of French foreign policy after 1918 was **security against Germany**, which had invaded France twice in 50 years
- At the **Paris Peace Conference** in 1919 they got (1) the reduction of the German army to 100,000 men, (2) the demilitarisation of the Rhineland, and (3) the German promise to pay reparations
- **Britain** and the **United States** also promised to defend France against German aggression, but in 1920 the American Senate refused to ratify the relevant Treaties and the United States went into isolation. That left **Britain** as France's major ally, but the British were more inclined to **appease Germany** than to challenge it
- The French tried to keep Germany weak by demanding high reparations payments and invading the Ruhr in 1923
- They also tried to isolate Germany by making alliances with Poland, Czechoslovakia, Yugoslavia and Romania. Known as the '**Little Entente**', this system of alliances was weakened by quarrels among the members
- The French also began to build a huge line of trenches, known as the **Maginot Line**, along the border with Germany. They hoped it would protect them against another German invasion.

> **Remember...**
>
> **To appease:** to try to win someone over by giving them what they want.

1926–1932: Briand and reconciliation with Germany

- **Aristide Briand** was Foreign Minister from 1926. He sought reconciliation with Germany and was helped by the German Foreign Minister, **Gustav Stresemann**
- In 1925, in the **Locarno Pact**, both countries accepted the borders between them set by the Versailles Treaty. Britain and Italy agreed to act as guarantors of the Pact
- In 1926, France agreed to Germany joining the **League of Nations**. The two countries also participated in talks about disarmament and signed the **Kellogg-Briand Pact** (1928) outlawing war as a means of settling disputes
- In 1929, with the **Young Plan**, they reached a final agreement on reparations.

1933 – 1939: France and Hitler

- At first the French did not realise how dangerous Hitler was. As the threat became clearer, they began work again on the Maginot Line, which had been abandoned in the late-1920s
- Because of their loss of manpower in the first World War, they did not feel strong enough to take on Germany alone, so they depended for security on their alliances with **Britain**, **Italy** and the countries of the **Little Entente**
- For this reason they were willing to let Mussolini conquer **Abyssinia** (see page 168). But many French people supported the League of Nations, and that forced the French government to agree to sanctions on Italy
- When Hitler's troops entered the **Rhineland** in 1936, in open violation of the Treaty of Versailles, the French did nothing because the British would not act with them
- The French and British also let Hitler take over **Austria** in 1938 without protest
- But when he threatened **Czechoslovakia** later that year, the Czechs appealed for help to their French ally. Daladier wanted to help, but felt it was impossible because the British Prime Minister **Chamberlain** was determined to appease Hitler
- The result was the **Munich Agreement** (September 1938) in which Hitler got the **Sudetenland**, but promised not to touch the rest of Czechoslovakia. When Hitler broke that promise six months later, Daladier followed the British example and gave a guarantee to protect **Poland**
- When Hitler ignored them and invaded Poland in September 1939, France and Britain declared war.

The 'phoney war' and the fall of France

- Through the winter of 1939, Hitler concentrated on conquering Poland while the French and British waited for him behind the Maginot Line
- During this '**phoney war**', divisions appeared among French politicians, with some wanting peace with Hitler
- In May 1940, the German tanks bypassed the Maginot Line, entering France through the Ardennes. The British army retreated towards the sea at **Dunkirk**. The French army fell back towards Paris, which surrendered to the Germans on 14 June.

France surrenders

- On 22 June, the 84-year-old **Marshall Pétain**, France's most famous soldier, became Prime Minister and agreed to an **armistice** (truce) with the Germans
- France was divided into two zones:
  - ❑ The Germans occupied two-thirds of France to the north and west, including the whole Atlantic coast

○ The south-east remained under the control of Marshall Pétain. Because he had his headquarters at Vichy, it is usually known as '**Vichy France**'. It was independent in name but in reality it only existed as long as Hitler let it

- The 1.5 million French soldiers captured by the Germans remained in prison camps, the French army was reduced to 100,000 men and France had to pay the cost of the German conquest

- At first Pétain's surrender was popular. Many French people were glad to be spared the slaughter of another war.

Why did France fall?

The sudden collapse of France shocked many. It happened because:

- Hitler's pact with Stalin allowed him to send all his armies into France without worrying about Russia
- French generals placed too much faith in the Maginot Line, which did not even extend along the whole frontier
- The French tanks were spread thinly along the front, rather than in massed battalions like the Germans
- There were many pro-fascist elements in France who welcomed a deal with Hitler and they were joined by the communists after the Nazi-Soviet pact of 1939.

2.2 British economic and social problems: 1920–1939

Britain: The cost of victory

- Although Britain was one of the winners in the first World War, the cost of victory was high
- Seven hundred and fifty thousand soldiers were dead and over a million badly wounded
- To pay for the war Britain had sold off 20% of its foreign investments, its **national debt** was ten times higher than in 1914, and taxes had risen substantially
- Prices doubled between 1914 and 1918 and went on rising after the war, making life difficult for the poor.

The British economy

- Before the war, Britain had the second biggest economy in Europe
- Its prosperity was based on exports of **coal**, **textiles** (cotton, wool and linen), **steel** and **ships**. Most of these industries were situated in the north and west
- Even before the war, these British exports were losing out to foreign competition because:
  - ○ British industrialists had not invested in new machinery and processes so their goods were more expensive
  - ○ American and European manufacturers were more up to date and productive.

The economy after the war

- When the war ended, many British people expected that life would get better but in fact it got worse. After a brief boom in 1919, the economy began to decline from 1920
- Soldiers returning from the war found it hard to get jobs. Unemployment rose to two million by 1921, and did not fall much below that level until the second World War
- The post-war depression was due to a decline in exports:
  - ○ American, Polish and German **coal**, produced with modern machinery, was cheaper than British coal dug out with pick and shovel
  - ○ China, India and other areas, which used to buy British textiles before the war, now made their own or bought from the Americans or the Japanese
  - ○ World trade declined after the war, cutting the demand for ships
  - ○ In 1925, **Winston Churchill**, the Chancellor of the Exchequer (Finance Minister) restored the link between Britain's currency, the **pound** (sterling), and gold. The **gold standard** raised the cost of British exports by 10%
- To reduce costs and improve exports, employers cut jobs and wages. Workers joined trade unions to resist this and strikes became common.

The coal industry and the General Strike

- Coal mining was Britain's greatest industry. Over one million miners produced coal to power other industries, drive trains and heat people's homes
- Many coalmines were small and privately owned. The owners lacked the money to invest in new machinery
- After the war demand for British coal declined, especially after the return to the gold standard. In 1925, the mine owners announced that they would have to cut miners' wages

- When the miners went on strike in protest on 1 May 1926, the **Trade Union Congress (TUC)** called a **general strike** to support them. About three million workers, mainly in transport, the docks and electricity, joined it, paralysing the country
- The government overreacted. Claiming it was the start of a **communist take-over**, they sent in troops and tanks. Middle-class people volunteered to replace striking workers by driving buses, lorries, etc
- Realising they had little public support, the TUC called off the general strike after only nine days
- The miners remained out until October, but at last hardship forced them back to work on the employers' terms
- After the strike, membership of trade unions fell. In 1927, the government passed the **Trades Disputes Act**, which made a future general strike impossible.

The Great Depression

- The **Great Depression** hit Britain in 1930. Exports fell by 50% and unemployment rose, reaching a peak of three million in 1932
- The government found its income from taxes falling, while the cost of helping the unemployed rose
- The Labour Party, led by **Ramsay McDonald**, was in power. In 1931, it was advised to cut wages and spending on welfare to avoid a **budget deficit** (spending more than it earned)
- The Labour Party split on the issue and McDonald joined the Conservatives to form a **National Government**
- They cut wages and unemployment pay by 10% and increased income tax. This policy only made things worse by reducing what people had to spend on goods.

The recovery begins

- Late in 1931, the government had to **abandon the gold standard**. This did some good because value of the pound fell by 25% and exports became more competitive
- The government also imposed a **tariff on imports**, which **protected** industries from foreign competitors
- These measures led to a gradual improvement in the economy. This accelerated after 1936, when the threat from Nazi Germany forced Britain to **rearm**.

The social impact of the Depression

- The effect of the Depression varied from place to place. In areas with the old industries people suffered badly, but in areas where new industries were developing living standards went up.

Poverty in the old industrial areas

- Where the old industries existed – **south Wales, western Scotland and northern England** – unemployment was well above 30% and people suffered from extreme poverty
- When a worker had a job, he paid **insurance** which gave him an income if he was unemployed. But the payment only lasted for 26 weeks. After that workers had to rely on handouts from local councils
- In 1934 the government replaced the insurance system with unemployment pay based on need, but payments were subject to a strict **means test**
- Inspectors visited people's homes to check that no one in the house was working and that they had no hidden savings. Workers hated means testing because it was humiliating
- Unemployment pay was never enough to cover food, clothing and rent. In Liverpool, a survey found almost half of unemployed workers had less than the minimum needed for a decent life
- In many places people depended on charity-run **soup kitchens** for food. Hunger and malnutrition were common, leaving children undersized and sickly.

●●●Case study

2.3 The Jarrow March

- **Jarrow** on the river **Tyne** was one of the worst affected areas. When the local shipbuilding company, Palmer's, closed in 1935, unemployment rose to at least 70% of the workforce
- The local council and the local Labour MP, **Ellen Wilkinson**, decided to organise a march to London to draw attention to their plight
- The marchers were to carry a petition to parliament asking for the establishment of new industry in Jarrow
- On 5 October, 1936, 200 men set out to march the 300 miles to London. They covered around 15 miles a day
- Well-wishers from all parties greeted them along the way and gave them food and shelter each night
- They reached London after 25 days, and presented their petition to parliament on 1 November. The Prime Minister, **Stanley Baldwin**, refused to meet them
- In spite of that, the march attracted a lot of attention. In 1938, an engineering works and a ship-breaking yard were set up in Jarrow as part of Britain's rearmament programme before the second World War.

Prosperity in the new industrial areas

- Life in the **English midlands** and **around London** was very different from the poverty of the north and west
- The economy there was based on making new consumer goods like motorcycles, cars, electric cookers and radios
- Jobs in these industries were plentiful. The number of people working in the car and electrical industries doubled between 1919 and 1939
- These jobs were relatively well paid, so people could afford better houses and house building also created jobs
- New techniques of mass production reduced the price of goods, so workers had more money to spend on them. They could afford better food and housing, while some were able to enjoy luxuries like radios, frequent visits to the cinema and even annual holidays.

Fascism in Britain

- Britain in the 1930s, like most European countries, had its fascist movement – the **British Union of Fascists** (BUF). Its leader was **Sir Oswald Mosley**, a wealthy landowner
- The BUF was anti-communist, anti-semitic and in favour of tariffs to protect British industry. At the start it had over 50,000 members. Mosley formed some of his followers into a paramilitary bodyguard who were dressed in **blackshirts**
- The BUF was most active in London where there was a large Jewish population. Blackshirts intimidated them and riots were common through 1933 and 1934
- But as the nature of Hitler's regime became obvious, the BUF lost support and never won more than a few council seats
- In 1936, the government banned the wearing of uniforms, and when war began it interned Mosley and his wife.

Why did democracy survive in France and Britain?

Democracy survived in France and Britain because:
- There was a tradition of democratic government in both countries
- The fascist movements lacked skilful and charismatic leaders like Mussolini and Hitler
- Economic conditions never got as bad as they did in Germany.

John Maynard Keynes (1883–1946)

- The reasons for the Great Depression and the best way to deal with it were hotly debated by economists in the 1930s. The man who suggested the best remedy was **John Maynard Keynes**, the greatest economist of the 20th century
- Born in England, he studied economics and during the Paris Peace Conference was economic advisor to the Prime Minister, **David Lloyd George**
- He disagreed strongly with the way the Allied leaders handled the peace settlement, especially their demand for huge **reparations** from Germany, which would make it difficult for the German economy to recover
- He resigned and wrote a book called *The Economic Consequences of the Peace*, in which he made his criticisms public
- In 1925 he criticised Churchill's decision to take Britain back on the gold standard
- In 1936 he published his greatest work, *The General Theory of Employment, Interest and Money*
- In it he argued against two ideas that were popular at the time:
  - That governments should not meddle in the economy
  - That the way to treat a depression was to cut government spending and keep the budget balanced
- Keynes said that governments must **manage the economy**. In a depression, they should invest in the economy, even if they had to borrow to do so. Their investment would stimulate economic activity and speed up the recovery. After that they could pay back the money they borrowed
- During the second World War, Keynes worked on plans for a post-war economic system that would avoid the depression and misery which followed the first World War and which helped fascists to power
- In 1944, he led the British delegation to the Bretton Woods Conference in the United States, where plans were laid for a new economic order after the war
- It succeeded in creating prosperity in the 1950s rather than the depression that followed the first World War, but Keynes died in 1946 before he could see the result of his ideas.

3.1 Why democracies failed

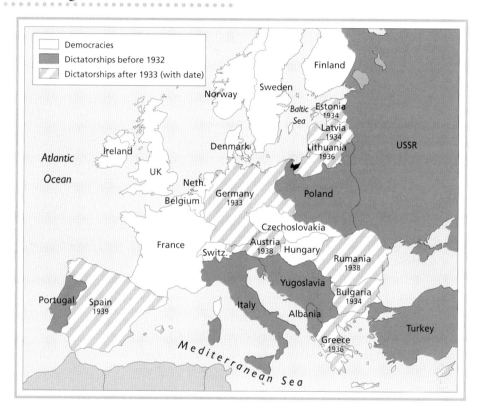

Map legend:
- Democracies
- Dictatorships before 1932
- Dictatorships after 1933 (with date)

Map labels: Finland, Sweden, Norway, Baltic Sea, Estonia 1934, Latvia 1934, Denmark, Lithuania 1936, USSR, Atlantic Ocean, Ireland, UK, Neth., Belgium, Germany 1933, Poland, France, Switz., Czechoslovakia, Austria 1938, Hungary, Rumania 1938, Yugoslavia, Bulgaria 1934, Portugal, Spain 1939, Italy, Albania, Greece 1936, Turkey, Mediterranean Sea

The new states of Europe

- One important result of the first World War was the emergence of new states in Central and Eastern Europe
- In 1914, **four empires** (Austria-Hungary, Turkey, Russia and Germany) had ruled there. At the end of the war they collapsed and were replaced by 11 **successor states**
- The new states were **Poland**, the three **Baltic states, Czechoslovakia, Yugoslavia, Austria, Hungary**, the **Soviet Union** (Russia), the **Weimar Republic** (Germany) and **Turkey**
- These states were weaker and more unstable than the empires they replaced
- All the new states (apart from Lenin's Russia) became **liberal democracies** with:
  ○ **Written Constitutions** which guaranteed freedom of speech, assembly, religion and the press
  ○ **Freely elected parliaments** which passed laws, decided on taxes and elected the governments.

The failure of democracy

- But by 1939, many European countries had abandoned democracy and become **dictatorships** (see map). This was due to (1) the economic problems left by the first World War, (2) the weakness of democratic governments, and (3) the fear of communism
- The war damaged the European economy and through the 1920s and 1930s unemployment was high and most people were poor. They suffered from bad housing, poor health and limited access to education
- Poor economic conditions made many people feel that **democracy was failing to give them what they wanted**. What use was the right to vote if there were no jobs? What use was free speech if the children were hungry?
- Some turned to anti-democratic parties – **communist** or **fascist** – whose leaders promised to create a better society.

Who was afraid of communism?

- After 1917 communist parties gained support from unemployed industrial workers and landless labourers who admired what Lenin did in Russia
- But the growth of communism terrified many people:
  - ○ **Rich landlords, bankers** and **factory owners** feared they would lose their wealth and power
  - ○ **People who owned a little property** (e.g. small farmers, shopkeepers) feared communists would confiscate it as they had in Russia
  - ○ The **clergy** and **devout Christians** feared the Church would be persecuted as it was in the Soviet Union
  - ○ **Nationalists** feared that 'international communism' would undermine respect for their nation
- These groups felt liberal democracy was too weak to protect them because 'free speech' left communists free to spread their ideas
- These groups wanted a '**strong leader**' to protect them from communism, even if that meant giving up the freedoms guaranteed by democracy
- They looked for an alternative to liberalism and communism. They found it in Italy, where, **Mussolini** and his **Fascist Party** won power in 1922, and by 1925 had destroyed Italy's democratic Constitution.

> **Remember...**
>
> **Communists** wanted **international co-operation** among workers to overthrow capitalists.
> **Nationalists** hated this idea. They wanted their nation to be powerful and respected.

3.2 Italy 1919 – 1926: the emergence of fascism

Italian Dissatisfaction with the Results of the first World War

- When the first World War began in 1914, Italians stayed neutral. They joined in on the Allies side in 1915 after France and Britain promised them Tyrol and Dalmatia (parts of the Austria-Hungarian empire)
- But at the **Paris Peace Conference** in 1919, the Allies would only give Italy the South Tyrol and the north of Dalmatia. They also refused to give the Italians any German or Turkish colonies
- Italian nationalists resented Italy's limited gains. They demanded '*Italia irredenta*' (unrecovered Italy). Some nationalists, led by the poet, **Gabriele D'Annunzio**, took over **Fiume** (an Italian-speaking city in Dalmatia) and declared a republic. An embarrassed Italian government had to expel them.

1919 – 1922: Economic and social problems

- After the war, Italy faced major economic and social problems:
  - **Inflation** was high (prices up by 600% since 1914), but wages stayed low and the poor were often hungry
  - **Unemployment** grew as arms factories closed and millions of demobilised soldiers returned from the war
- Workers and landless peasants, inspired by Lenin's example, joined the Communist Party. They formed 'red guards', and from 1919 to 1922 organised strikes and set up 'soviets' to take over factories
- Nationalists and ex-soldiers like **Benito Mussolini**, formed gangs to fight the communists;
  - Wealthy landowners and businessmen (e.g. Agnelli of Fiat) paid them to break up strikes and recover the factories
  - Small businessmen (e.g. shopkeepers) and more prosperous farmers joined in to defend themselves against a communist take-over
- Between 1919 and 1922, over 300 people were killed in riots between red guards and right-wing gangs
- Italians longed for peace and stability – there were five coalition governments within four years, none of which could take any hard decisions
- This encouraged Italians to look for a 'strong' leader who could restore order.

Mussolini's Fascist Party

- Benito Mussolini was a former socialist who fought in the war. After it, he gained a reputation as an Italian nationalist opposed to communism
- He organised ex-soldiers into gangs he called the *Fascio di Combattimento*. He gave them a uniform of **black shirts**. Similar groups appeared in other parts of Italy
- Wealthy businessmen backed him as a barrier against communism, and his **Blackshirts** regularly attacked trade unionists and broke up strikes

- In 1921, Mussolini linked up with similar groups and set up the **Fascist Party**
- He appealed to Italian nationalists by calling for *Italia irredenta*. At first, he opposed the Catholic Church and aimed for a republic but when he realised this was not very popular, he switched to supporting the Church and the monarchy
- In the 1921 election, the Fascist Party won 35 seats
- In 1922, when trade unions called a general strike, Fascist gangs terrorised workers and destroyed communists' and socialists' offices and newspapers. This made them popular with Italians who feared communism.

Remember...

The **fasces** was a bundle of rods with an axe in the centre, used by the Romans as a symbol of unity and power. Mussolini chose it as his emblem and named his Party after it.

The March on Rome

- Mussolini hoped that he would be invited to join in a coalition, but the old established politicians despised him
- In October 1922, he threatened that **50,000 Blackshirts** would '**march on Rome**' to demand that Fascist Party be included in the government
- The Prime Minister, **Facta**, asked King **Victor Emmanuel** to call out the army and stop them, but the King, who feared communism, refused. Instead, he invited Mussolini to form a coalition and become Prime Minister
- Only then did the Fascists march into Rome.

1922 – 1926: Steps to dictatorship

- Between 1922 and 1926, Mussolini destroyed Italian democracy
- He incorporated the Blackshirts into the police, and banned the Communist Party. This was popular with many people
- In 1923, he brought in the **Acerbo Law** to change the electoral system. The party with most votes would automatically get 66% of the seats in the Assembly (parliament). He claimed this would provide stability
- In the 1924 election, the Fascists used brutal tactics to intimidate other parties, especially the Socialists. They broke up their meetings, burned their offices and destroyed their newspapers
- When a leading Socialist, **Giacomo Matteotti**, protested he was murdered by fascist thugs. The scandal nearly destroyed Mussolini, but he was saved when the Socialists walked out of the Assembly in protest
- Not surprisingly, the Fascists got most votes and with his 66% majority, Mussolini could change system of government from democracy to dictatorship.

3.3 1926 – 1945: the Fascist dictatorship

Imposing Fascism

- Parliament gave Mussolini power to rule by decree, making laws and approving taxes. In theory, he was advised by the Fascist Grand Council, but in reality, he acted alone. He became know as **Il Duce** (the Leader)
- All parties except the Fascists were banned. Trade unions were declared illegal. Newspapers and radio were censored and had to carry the Fascist message or be closed down
- Fascist officials replaced elected local councils and a secret police, the OVRA was set up
- Although it could be brutal, Mussolini's regime was not as bad as Hitler's or Stalin's. By 1940, about 4,000 opposition politicians were in exile in remote villages or on islands off the coast and about ten had been executed.

Propaganda

- Mussolini made skilful use of **propaganda** to develop a personality cult
- Newspapers and radio carried Mussolini's speeches in full. Photographs of Mussolini flying planes, riding horses, working on building sites or saving the harvest, appeared every day
- Slogans like '*Il Duce is always right*' covered the walls of public buildings. The light was left on all night in Mussolini's Roman office to show he was working for the Italian people. In fact, he was seldom there
- The Fascists staged marches and demonstrations, with bands, music and flags, to whip up popular enthusiasm.

Education and youth policy

- Education improved, with more children going to school, but schools were expected to teach the Fascist message
- Teachers had to belong to the Fascist Party. Schoolbooks encouraged boys to be good fascist soldiers and girls to be good fascist mothers
- History was re-written to emphasise the glories of the Roman Empire, which Mussolini intended to repeat
- Young people were expected to belong to fascist youth movements. Boys aged 8 to 14 belonged to the **Balilla**, where they trained to be soldiers who would fight to create a new Roman Empire.

The Corporate State

- Mussolini claimed to have invented a middle way between liberal democracy and communism. He called it the **Corporate State**
- To avoid class conflict, all economic activity was divided into 32 **corporations**. There were corporations for mining, agriculture, fishing,

etc. In each corporation, worker and employer representatives set wages and working conditions

- But since the Fascists appointed the various representatives, the decisions made usually favoured employers
- Workers were not allowed to form trade unions to defend their interests, so wages and working conditions got worse during the Fascist period
- In 1938, an Assembly of Corporations nominated by Mussolini, was supposed to replace parliament
- Although largely a sham, the idea of the Corporate State appealed to many people in Europe (e.g. Winston Churchill/de Valera).

Economic policy

- Unlike the communists, the Fascists did not confiscate private property, but they interfered a great deal in the economy, especially after the depression began in 1930
- Up to 1925, **Albert de Stefani** was Minister for Finance. He reduced taxes and borrowing. Employment rose and the economy began to recover. This was also due to the improvement in the world economy
- But Mussolini sacked de Stefani because he wanted to follow a policy of 'self-sufficiently' (**autarky**) – i.e. that Italy should produce all the food and raw materials it needed and not have to depend on imports
- This led to a series of propaganda 'battles':
  - ❍ The '**battle for grain**' encouraged farmers to grow more grain. It worked in northern Italy, but not in the south where the land and climate was more suitable for olives and fruit. High tariffs (taxes) on grain imports pushed up the price of food for ordinary Italians
  - ❍ The '**battle for land**' aimed at keeping more Italians in farming. Its main achievement was the draining of the mosquito-infested **Pontine Marshes** near Rome. The land was divided among landless peasants
  - ❍ The '**battle for the lire**' set the exchange rate for Italy's currency (the lire) very high. This hit exports and damaged the economy
  - ❍ The '**battle for births**' tried to increase the population by giving bounties for babies and taxing bachelors. It did not work
- To create jobs, the government poured money into big building projects, improving the railways and building motorways
- In the 1930s, Mussolini, as part of his imperial policy, increased spending on armaments which took money away from more socially useful projects.

Mussolini and the Catholic Church

- Up to 1860, the Pope ruled Rome and a large part of central Italy. The Italian government took over his territories when the country was unified. This caused a quarrel with the Catholic Church which lasted from 1870 to the 1920s

- Mussolini was personally hostile to the Church, but realised this was pointless in a country where over 90% of people were Catholic. He tried to win favour with the Church by allowing Catholicism to be taught in schools
- Pope **Pius XI** (1922–1939) feared communism more than he valued democracy. He did not protest when Mussolini outlawed the Catholic People's Party and he accepted his dictatorship
- In 1926, negotiations opened between the two sides. This led to the **Lateran Treaty**, signed in **1929**. Its terms were:
  - Italy recognised the independence of the Pope's **Vatican state** and the Pope recognised the Italian state
  - Italy paid **compensation** to the Pope for the property it took in 1860–70
  - It recognised the Catholic Church as **the official Church of Italy**. This gave it control of religious education in the schools and banned divorce and contraception
- Later relations between Church and state deteriorated when Mussolini tried to close down the independent Catholic organisation **Catholic Action**
- The Pope also opposed Mussolini's introduction of anti-Jewish laws after his alliance with Hitler.

3.4 1922–1945: Mussolini's foreign policy

Early success

- When Mussolini came to power, he talked about re-establishing the old Roman Empire in the Mediterranean, especially in the **Balkans**. Up to 1936, he was also Foreign Minister and kept foreign policy in his own hands
- He had success in 1923, when he negotiated with the Yugoslav government to let the Italians take the city of **Fiume**.

1923: The Corfu incident

- Two Italians who were working for the League of Nations on the Greek-Albanian border, were killed in 1923
- Mussolini saw a chance to move into the Balkans. He demanded compensation from Greece and sent his army into the Greek island of **Corfu** to enforce the claim
- Britain and France did not want a war in the Mediterranean. They backed a League of Nations compromise: the Greeks would pay compensation, but Mussolini must withdraw his troops
- This showed Italy was not strong enough to defy the great powers, Britain and France, when they took a united stand.

The international statesman

- After this Mussolini adopted the role of international statesman, while secretly meddling in the Balkans and Abyssinia with the intention of seizing territory there later
- He was active in the **League of Nations** and helped to negotiate the Locarno Pact and other international agreements
- In 1934, he successfully opposed Hitler's move against Austria and organised the **Stresa Front** to take a stand against Hitler's expansion plans.

The Abyssinian Crisis

- But Mussolini still wanted an empire, and during the Depression years he needed a way of distracting Italians from their economic problems
- In 1935, he invaded **Abyssinia**. He was sure Britain and France would not object because they needed him on their side against Hitler
- But the Emperor of Abyssinia appealed to the League and public opinion in France and Britain forced their governments to agree to impose sanctions on Italy in 1936
- Sanctions did not stop the Italians, but they persuaded Mussolini to abandon his alliance with Britain and France and move towards Hitler.

The Rome-Berlin Axis

- In July 1936, a **civil war** broke out in **Spain**. Mussolini sent 70,000 troops to help **Franco** (who had fascist support) because he saw this as a way of building up Italian influence in Spain. Hitler too helped the fascists
- This drew the two dictators together. In October 1936, they signed **the Rome-Berlin Axis**
- As a result, Mussolini agreed to Hitler taking Austria in March 1938
- During the **Munich crisis** in September 1938, Mussolini, who was not ready for war, acted as a peacemaker
- In 1939, he signed a military alliance, the **Pact of Steel**, with Hitler.

Mussolini in the second World War

- Mussolini did not enter the war until 1940, when Germany had beaten France. He then sent the Italian army into southern France and gained some territory there
- In October 1940 he invaded **Greece**, but the Italian army did so badly the Germans had to intervene
- In North Africa, the Italians were defeated in Libya and Hitler had to send **Rommel** to rescue them
- After the German army was defeated, the Allies invaded the south of Italy in 1943
- Mussolini was ousted and the new Italian government joined the Allies

- But the Germans rescued Mussolini and set him up with a puppet state in northern Italy. When they lost, he was captured by anti-fascist partisans and killed in 1945.

Benito Mussolini (1883–1945)

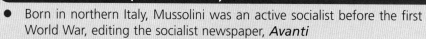

- Born in northern Italy, Mussolini was an active socialist before the first World War, editing the socialist newspaper, *Avanti*
- But when he supported Italy entering the war, the socialists expelled him
- He joined the army in 1915, but was badly wounded and invalided out in 1917
- After the war he became an **extreme nationalist**, opposed to communism
- He got ex-soldiers to join a uniformed gang, the **Fascisti** (**Blackshirts**), and later joined with similar groups to form the **Fascist Party**
- In 1922, he became Prime Minister and by 1926 had turned Italy from a democracy into a fascist dictatorship
- A master of **propaganda**, he ruled by decree, outlawed opponents, advocated economic self-sufficiency and formed the **Corporate State**
- His main achievement was the **Lateran Treaty** which solved the long-standing the quarrel between Italy and the Pope
- In the 1930s, he allied with Hitler, introduced anti-semitism, brought Italy into the second World War and was killed by communists in 1945.

Questions

For Examination questions on Later Modern History of Europe and the Wider World, Topic 3 see page 277.

Your revision notes

4.1 The Weimar Republic 1919–1933

- As the first World War came to an end the German Kaiser (emperor) fled and the German government declared a republic
- Its democratic Constitution was drawn up in the city of Weimar, so it was called the '**Weimar Republic**'
- But the Weimar Republic faced major political, economic and social problems which it could not solve. This enabled Hitler to rise to power in 1933 and destroy German democracy.

Founded in defeat

- The first act of the new republican government was to sign Germany's surrender in **November 1918**. Many Germans considered this an act of treachery, ('a stab in the back' by the 'November criminals') even though the German army could not have continued fighting
- The **Peace Conference** began in **Paris** in January 1919
- The Germans were not invited to take part in the negotiations. The victorious Allies simply agreed the terms of the **Treaty of Versailles** among themselves, then presented them to the German government who were forced to accept them.

The terms of the Treaty of Versailles

- In the west, Germany lost territory to France, Belgium and Denmark. It was also forbidden to have any soldiers in the Rhineland on the border with France (**demilitarisation of the Rhineland**)
- In the east, West Prussia went to Poland (**the Polish Corridor**) cutting East Prussia off from the rest of Germany. The German city of **Danzig**, was made a free city under League of Nations control
- Germany was forbidden to unite with Austria
- Germany lost all its colonies
- Germany was **disarmed**. Its army was limited to 100,000 men and it was to have no military aircraft, no submarines, and only six small warships
- Germany was forced to accept the blame for starting the war ('the **guilt clause**')
- Because of its 'guilt', Germany was to pay **reparations** to other states. No agreement on the amount was reached in Paris, so a commission was set up to consider it. It reported in 1921, with a bill for £6,000 million.

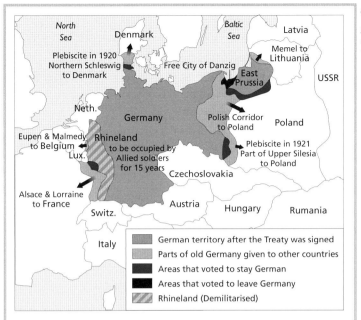

German losses in the Versailles Treaty

Impact of the Versailles Treaty on Germany

- Germans were shattered by severity of the Versailles terms. They deeply resented having no part in the negotiations, calling it '*a diktat*'
- They also resented disarmament, the loss of territory and above all the 'guilt clause' with the reparations
- Many, like Hitler, blamed the Weimar politicians who signed it. They thought that these democratic politicians were too weak to stand up for the interests of Germany.

Political weaknesses of the Weimar Republic

- The Weimar Republic had a very democratic Constitution. It had a **Reichstag** (parliament) elected by all men and women using proportional representation (PR), and a President elected by all voters every seven years
- But the President had power to **declare an emergency** when he could **rule by decree** without consulting the Reichstag. This was used many times in the Weimar Republic and undermined respect for democracy
- PR voting produced many political parties ranging from extreme left (**Communist**) to extreme right (**anti-democratic Nationalists** and **Nazi**)
- That resulted in all governments being short-lived coalitions – there were 19 between 1919 and 1933. This made it impossible for them to deal with the problems the Weimar Republic faced
- From 1930, as the crisis caused by the Great Depression grew, the President used his emergency powers to nominate governments that did not have the backing of the Reichstag.

1919–1921: Post-war instability overcome

- After the war Germany was very unsettled. The Allied navies blockaded the country until mid-1919, causing starvation
- Strikes and bread riots grew common as prices rose, but wages did not keep pace. Many factories closed. Unemployed workers imitated Lenin by setting up 'soviets' to take them over
- In several parts of Germany, communists or right-wing groups attempted to take power, but by the end of 1920, all had been defeated.

1921–1924: The Great Inflation

- The German economy was just beginning to recover in 1921 when it was hit by the bill for £6,000 million in **reparations**
- Germany made a few payments then stopped in January 1923
- France and Belgium sent troops into **Ruhr** to collect reparations
- German workers went on strike and the government paid them for doing nothing. It printed money to do so
- This created **hyper-inflation** which made the German currency worthless (see box)
- Inflation wiped out the savings of middle-class Germans and increased support for anti-democratic parties.

Hyper-inflation:	
In 1914 $1	= 4 marks
Jan '22	= 200 marks
July '22	= 500 marks
Jan '23	= 18,000 marks
July '23	= 4.2 million
Oct '23	= 4,000,000,000,000,000 marks

Stresemann and the recovery of the German economy 1924–1929

- **Gustav Stresemann** who was Chancellor (Prime Minister) briefly in 1923, and then Foreign Minister until his death in 1929, is given credit for Germany's economic recovery
- An ardent nationalist, he hated the Versailles Treaty, but knew that Germany must compromise with its neighbours if it was to grow strong again
- He restored economic stability with new currency
- In 1924, he negotiated a deal on reparations, the **Dawes Plan**, with France and Britain, who at last realised it was not in their interests to destroy the German economy
  - Reparation payments were suspended until Germany could afford to pay and US loans were arranged to help the Germany economic recovery
- In 1925, Stresemann ended German isolation by signing the **Locarno Pact** with France. In it Germany promised to respect the western borders set at Versailles
- Germany joined **League of Nations** in 1926

- In 1929, Stresemann negotiated the **Young Plan**: reparations were reduced and Germany would pay them over 50 years
- But Stresemann was also a German nationalist who hoped to restore German greatness:
  - He refused to accept the loss of the Polish Corridor (East Prussia) and talked of taking it by force when Germany regained its strength
  - He turned a blind eye to the German army's secret re-armament
- In the '**Stresemann years**' the German economy recovered, unemployment fell to 500,000 and Weimar seemed secure
- Stresemann died in October 1929, just before the **Wall Street Crash** began the Great Depression.

The Great Depression in Germany

- After the Wall Street Crash, US banks which were on the brink of collapse, recalled their loans to Germany
- **Brüning**, the leader of the Centre Party was Chancellor from 1930 to 1932. He made things worse by following the economists' advice to reduce government spending and cut wages
- German factories closed and unemployment rose quickly (three million in 1930; six million by 1932)
- Despairing Germans were very afraid. They saw their livelihood being destroyed for **a second time in ten years** and many blamed the weakness of the democratic Weimar system
- In growing numbers they voted for the **extreme anti-democratic parties** – Communists on the left, Nazis on the right
- The Great Depression gave Hitler his chance to seize power.

4.2 The rise of Hitler and the fall of the Weimar Republic

1919 – 1923: Start of the Nazi Party

- Adolph Hitler was an Austrian who joined the German army in 1914. When the war ended in 1918 he went to Munich where he joined a small right-wing party
- He quickly became their leader (**Führer**) and renamed them the **National Socialist German Workers' Party** (**Nazis**). Like Mussolini, he also set up a uniformed (brown shirts) private army, the Storm Troopers (SA), led by **Ernst Röhm**
- In November 1923, during **great inflation**, Hitler tried to seize power in Munich (the **Munich Putsch**). The Nazis were defeated by the army, which stayed loyal to Weimar.

Hitler's ideas

- Hitler was sent to jail for a year where he wrote *Mein Kampf*. This book showed:
  - ○ His hatred of Jews, communists, democrats and the Versailles Treaty
  - ○ His belief that Germans were a 'master race', designed by nature to rule 'lesser people' like the Slavs (Poles, Czechs, Russians, etc)
  - ○ His plans: (1) to destroy the Versailles Treaty, (2) to unite all Germans into a great **Third Reich** (empire) and (3) to conquer Slav lands in Eastern Europe for Germans to live in (**Lebensraum**).

1925–1929: spread of the Nazis

- By the time Hitler was freed in 1925, Mussolini had shown that democracy could be destroyed from within. This influenced Hitler who set out to copy him
- He linked the Nazis up with similar groups around Germany
- He set up an elite group, the SS (**Schutzstaffel**) to act as his bodyguard. It was led by **Heinrich Himmler**
- **Joseph Goebbels**, a genius at propaganda, organised colourful demonstrations and marches to attract attention to their ideas
- In 1928, the Nazis fought the general election, but only won 12 seats (out of 608) due to the improved economic situation
- In 1929, Hitler got nationwide publicity with his campaign against the **Young Plan** in which Germany agreed to pay reduced reparations.

1929–1932: The Great Depression helps the Nazis

- The Depression convinced many Germans that democracy had failed to protect them. They turned to the anti-democratic parties that promised quick solutions
- In the 1930 election, the Nazi Party got five million votes and the Communists got one million
- Brüning, the Chancellor, wanted to cut wages and government spending on welfare, but he could not persuade the Reichstag to agree. He got **President Hindenburg** to impose the cuts by decree
- Hitler toured Germany, making speeches attacking Brüning. He offered simple explanations for the depression: it was all the fault of the Versailles Treaty, of bankers, of communists, of Jews and of weak democratic politicians. Only a 'strong government' (i.e. a Nazi dictatorship) would solve economic problems and restore German self-respect and power
- At meetings, SS and SA thugs beat up opponents and rioted with communist 'red guards'. Germans longed for order.

1932: The year of three elections

Three elections in 1932 helped Hitler to power

- In **March**, Hitler stood for President against the 80-year old **Hindenburg**. Amid violence from the SS and the SA, he got 37% of votes
- Afterwards, Brüning wanted to ban the SA, but Hindenburg sacked him instead and invited a right-wing noble, **Von Papen**, to be Chancellor although he had little support in the Reichstag
- In **July**, von Papen called a general election. The Nazis won 230 seats; the Communists won 89 (out of 608)
- Now two anti-democratic parties had more than half the seats in the Reichstag. Throughout the summer, they refused to work with other parties to form a coalition government to deal with the country's economic crisis:
  - ❍ **Hitler** would not talk to other parties unless he was made Chancellor, but Hindenburg would not appoint him
  - ❍ **Stalin** thought the Depression would kill capitalism and ordered German communists not to prop up democracy by forming a coalition with the socialists
- When no government was formed by **November**, von Papen called another election. Some voters deserted the Nazis because they had failed to provide a government and they won only 186 seats.

January 1933: Hitler becomes Chancellor

- After the Nazis lost seats, von Papen felt he could control Hitler. In January 1933, he persuaded Hindenburg to let him become Chancellor
- It seemed to be a safe strategy, as only two other Nazis were made Ministers. But one of those Ministers was in charge of the police, and he enrolled members of the SS and SA in the police force.

January–April, 1933: ending democracy

- Hitler at once called another election for **March**. The SA and SS were now free to attack communists and socialists
- In February the **Reichstag building burnt down**. Communists were blamed (possibly unjustly) and banned
- In spite of considerable violence and intimidation, the Nazis only got 44% of votes
- Hitler then asked the Reichstag to pass the **Enabling Act**. It declared that Germany was in danger and gave the government special **emergency powers** to save it
- All parties, except the Social Democrats, voted for it. It was the end of Weimar democracy.

4.3 The Nazi State: Setting up a Dictatorship

- Under the Enabling Act, press and radio were censored and forced to publish Nazi propaganda
- All other political parties were banned and trade unions replaced by the Nazi-controlled '**labour front**' that fixed wages and working conditions
- A secret police, the **Gestapo**, was set up to hunt opponents of the Nazis. Thousands of communists, socialists and anti-Nazi Germans were rounded up and sent to concentration camps
- **Heinrich Himmler** and the SS controlled the concentration camps. In 1934, Himmler took control of the Gestapo too.

30 June, 1934: The 'Night of the Long Knives'

- Himmler and Röhm, the leader of the SA, were rivals for power
- Röhm really believed the Nazis planned a socialist revolution and was disappointed when Hitler changed very little in the economy
- He began to criticise Hitler. He also boasted that the SA, which had two million men by 1934, would replace the German army
- This worried Hitler. He needed army support to stay in power and he feared that Röhm was becoming too powerful
- He made a deal with the army and the SS to eliminate Röhm and the SA
- On **30 June 1934** (known as the '**Night of the Long Knives**'), the Gestapo murdered Röhm and about 400 leading SA men and others Hitler considered a threat
- In **August 1934**, President Hindenburg died. Hitler then combined the offices of President and Chancellor into a new one of **Führer**. From then on all soldiers had to take an oath of loyalty to *Der Führer* (The Leader).

The Nazi State: totalitarianism

- Like Mussolini's Italy, Nazi Germany was a **totalitarian state** which demanded the **total** loyalty and obedience of all citizens
- The **SS** and the **Gestapo** spied on everyone. People were encouraged to betray neighbours, friends, even family
- Special courts, with Nazi judges, were set up to try dissidents who were sent to concentration camps
- Germany was reorganised on the 'leadership principle', which Hitler claimed this was more efficient than democracy
- Elected councils were replaced by Nazi officials (**Gauleiter**) who were appointed by Hitler and answerable to him
- In operation, this was an inefficient, corrupt system. Nazi officials were either too afraid to make independent decisions or got away with corruption that people were too afraid to expose
- Long term this could have destroyed Germany, but the Nazi regime lasted too short a time for it to become a major problem.

4.4 Nazi propaganda and the Nuremberg Rallies
Goebbels and Nazi propaganda

- Propaganda was central to the Nazi system. From the 1920s this was run by **Joseph Goebbels**
- In 1933, Hitler made him **Minister for Propaganda**. He imposed censorship on the press and controlled all public meetings, as well as films and radio
- In 1933, he organised the **mass burning of books** by Jews and modern writers the Nazis disliked
- He saw the value of **radio** as a means of propaganda, arranging for the production of cheap radios so that Germans would get the Nazi message in their own homes
- He also used **film**, employing the best directors (like **Leni Riefenstahl** (see page 183)) and film stars to make propaganda films, praising Nazi achievements or attacking Jews, communists and other enemies of the Nazis
- He drove Jews out of public life and organised the propaganda against them, which made the holocaust possible
- He organised the **Nuremberg Rallies** as demonstrations of Nazi power.

The Nuremberg rallies

- The Nuremberg Rallies began as **Nazi Party Congresses** held in Nuremberg every year from 1927
- Nuremberg was chosen because it was in the centre of Germany and had a sympathetic local government
- The rallies involved the SA marching with their swastika banners, torchlight processions and Hitler's speeches
- After Hitler came to power in 1933, the rallies were renamed **Congresses of the German People** to symbolise how the Nazi Party represented all Germans
- They became huge, highly organised demonstrations of Nazi policies and power which lasted for several days
- Hitler had his architect, **Albert Speer**, design the rallies. He treated them like giant theatrical events intended to convey the Nazi message
- The rallies centred on Hitler's arrival, his appearances and his speeches. The SS, the SA, the army and the Hitler Youth marched in his honour and listened, awestruck, while he spoke
- Speer built a Congress Hall seating 60,000 and planned a stadium to hold 400,000, which Hitler hoped would be his monument to the future. It was never completed

- Each rally had a different theme, usually linked to some Nazi achievement, e.g. 1933 was the '*Rally for Victory*' because the Nazis had come to power and 1938 was the '*Rally for Greater Germany*' because Austria was taken over
- Important announcements of policy were made at the rallies. At the 1935 rally, the anti-semitic policy known as the '**Nuremberg Laws**' was announced. It stripped German Jews of citizenship and forbade inter-marriage between Jews and Germans
- Although hundreds of thousands of Germans attended the rallies, Hitler had documentary films made of them so that those who did not attend could still participate. The most famous of these films was the *Triumph of the Will*, made in 1934 by **Leni Riefenstahl**
- The last Nuremberg rally was planned for 1939 under the title, '*Rally for Peace*'. It was cancelled at short notice when Hitler started the second World War by invading Poland
- After the war, the Allies held the trials of leading Nazis for war crimes at Nuremberg (the **Nuremberg Trials**) to symbolise the defeat of the policies the Nazis had proclaimed there.

4.5 The Nazi State, 1933–1945
Art and literature under the Nazis

- The Nazis believed artists must serve the state. Artists were told to be "realistic" and "heroic" and experimental work was forbidden
- In 1933, Goebbels organised the **burning of books** by modernist or Jewish writers
- Paintings by modern masters like Picasso and Van Gogh, were destroyed, though some Nazi leaders secretly saved some for themselves
- **Albert Speer** (architect) designed huge buildings in the classical style to celebrate Nazi triumphs.

Education and youth

- Nazis targeted young people so as to ensure the future of their ideas
- Boys were enrolled in the **Hitler Youth** and trained as soldiers. They were taught to be unquestioningly loyal to the Führer. By 1935, 3.5 million boys were enrolled in the Hitler Youth
- Girls joined the **League of German Maidens**. They were taught domestic skills and encouraged to have children for Germany
- Teachers had to join the Nazi Party and teach loyalty to the Führer. Schoolbooks were rewritten and the Nazi version of German history (which was anti-semitic) became part of the curriculum.

Church and State in Nazi Germany

- Hitler and the Nazis despised Christianity because it encouraged people to love each other. They wanted to replace it with the kind of paganism that they imagined ancient Germans practised
- Despite this, the leaders of the main Christian churches accepted Nazi rule, fearing communism more.

The Protestant Churches and the Nazis

- German Protestants were divided into 28 different churches. They had a tradition of obedience to the state, and in 1933 agreed to unite into Nazi-controlled state Church, the *Reichskirche*
- Some Protestants refused to accept the *Reichskirche*. In 1934, **Martin Niemöller** and **Karl Barth** helped to form the *Confessional Church* which was independent of Nazi control
- When they protested about anti-semitism in 1936, the Gestapo arrested Niemöller and many other clergymen. Some were executed, most sent to concentration camps. Niemöller remained in Dachau until 1945
- **Dietrich Bonhoeffer**, a Protestant theologian, returned to Germany from the US at the start of the war. He linked up with anti-Nazi groups, was arrested and executed in 1943.

The Catholic Church and the Nazis

- Although the Catholic Church, with the Pope outside Germany, was in a stronger position to resist the Nazis, it did little to oppose their policies
- In July 1933, the Vatican made a **Concordat** (treaty) with the Nazis. In return for keeping control of its schools, the Church agreed to keep out of politics
- As the Nazis tightened their grip, the Church became alarmed about their youth policies, their interference in education and their creation of the Reichskirche. Individual bishops and priests protested
- Pope **Pius XI** also became concerned about Hitler's anti-semitism, which he attacked in an encyclical (letter) *Mit Brennender Sorge* (*With Burning Anger*) in 1937
- Pius XI died in 1939. His successor, **Pius XII**, was Papal Ambassador in Berlin in the 1930s and saw the ruthlessness of the Nazis. He did not attack them, fearing the effect it would have on German Catholics
- In fact, the Nazis did not arrest the bishops who protested when they had popular support and Pius's failure to condemn the treatment of the Jews has damaged his reputation
- Individual Catholics did protest and many were executed or sent to concentration camps.

The Nazi economy

- The poor state of the German economy with six million unemployed was the main reason the Nazis came to power
- Hitler appointed a banker, **Hjalmar Schacht** as Finance Minister. Private companies were left alone, but they had to follow orders from the state
- To create jobs the Nazis organised big **public works projects**, building schools, hospitals and motorways. Young people enrolled in **Labour Battalions** to work on them
- Hitler's rearmament of Germany also created work in arms factories, and when conscription was re-introduced in 1935 many men were enrolled in the army
- The removal of Jews and trade unionists also increased the number of jobs available to those Germans who accepted Hitler
- Unemployment fell fast, wages rose, and by 1939 most Germans felt much better off under Hitler than under Weimar.

Unemployment in Nazi Germany in the 1930s					
1933	1934	1935	1936	1937	1938
25%	13%	10%	7.4%	4.1%	1.9%

'Self-sufficiency' (autarky)

- From the start Hitler planned a war. He knew that to win, Germany must be **self-sufficient** in food and raw materials
- He dismissed Hjalmar Schacht (Reich Finance Minister) in 1937 because he had not achieved this. A committee chaired by **Herman Goering** drew up a four-year plan for 'self-sufficiency' (autarky)
- Huge investments were made in research and development as scientists tried to find substitutes for petrol, wool, rubber, etc
- These researches were only partially successful, and by 1939 Germany was still importing a fifth of its food and a third of its raw materials
- Hitler's invasion of the Soviet Union in 1941 was partly an attempt to gain control of its oil and other raw materials
- In 1942, **Albert Speer** re-organised the arms industry using slave labour and raw materials from the countries Germany conquered. This enabled Germany to fight on until 1945
- The Nazis achieved a limited success with their economic policies, but it was based on high state spending that could not have continued over a long period
- Other countries, like the US and Britain, also solved the economic problems of the Depression, but without destroying democracy.

Anti-semitism in Nazi Germany

- In 1933, there were only about 500,000 Jews in Germany (out of 80 million Germans), but Hitler claimed they were a threat to his 'master race'
- From 1933, anti-semitism became official state policy and the pressure against Jewish people increased step by step
- At first Nazis beat up individual Jews, organised boycotts of Jewish businesses and expelled them from schools, universities and the civil service
- In 1935, the **Nuremberg Laws** took away their German citizenship and forbade intermarriage with non-Jews
- Hitler seems to have hoped Jews would emigrate under pressure, but only rich or famous Jews (e.g. Freud/Einstein) were welcome elsewhere. Most Jewish people were not well off, some were old, others children. Other countries did not want a flood of penniless refugees in the middle of the Depression.

The 'final solution'

- In **November 1938**, a French Jew assassinated a German official in Paris. This gave Nazi-led mobs in Germany an excuse to attack synagogues and vandalise Jewish shops (**Kristallnacht** – translates as 'broken-glass night')
- Jewish people were then herded into special areas of cities (**ghettos**), 'for own their protection' according to the Nazis, but really it was so they could be controlled and used as slave labour
- They were forced to wear a yellow **Star of David** whenever they left the ghetto
- Between 1938 and 1941, Germany took over Austria, Czechoslovakia, Poland, France, etc. About eight million Jews in these countries were now at their mercy
- In 1942, top Nazis decided on a '**final solution**' to the 'Jewish problem': bring all Jews in Europe to certain camps where they would be killed. At first they were shot, but when this turned out to be too expensive as a means of disposal, gas was used
- About six million Jewish people were killed in these camps
- 500,000 gypsies, homosexuals and disabled people, whom the Nazis believed also threatened the purity of the master race, were also killed
- The discovery of the camps when the war ended in 1945 horrified the world. Up to then, many people had refused to believe reports about the gas chambers and other horrific information which Jewish groups had managed to get out.

Adolph Hitler (1889–1945)

- Born in Austria in 1889, Hitler studied art in Vienna and was influenced by the anti-semitic and German 'master-race' theories which were wide-spread there before 1914
- He joined the German army in the first World War and was decorated for bravery. Like many soldiers, he felt betrayed by the surrender in 1918
- After the war he joined a group of ex-soldiers (**Freikorps**) and went to Munich
- He took over the leadership of the **National Socialist German Workers' Party** (Nazis) and set up private army, the Storm Troopers (**SA**), dressed in **brown shirts**
- After a failed attempt to seize power in Munich (**Munich Putsch**), he was sent to prison where he wrote *Mein Kampf*. In it, he set out his anti-semitic and 'master race' ideas and his aims for Germany
- Once released, he began to build up the Nazi Party. He took part in elections to the Reichstag, hoping to take over legally as Mussolini had in Italy
- The Great Depression increased support for the Nazis. They became the biggest party in 1932, and Hitler became Chancellor in January 1933
- He quickly destroyed democracy, created a dictatorship and purged his opponents on the '**Night of the Long Knives**'
- He enforced his anti-semitic programme (**Nuremberg Laws**) against German Jews. After Nazi conquest of much of Europe in 1940, eight million Jewish people were rounded up and six million died in the gas chambers (the '**Final Solution**')
- He took advantage of divisions among his opponents and **appeasement** to [1] break the terms of Versailles Treaty, [2] rearm Germany, [3] re-militarise the Rhineland (1936), [4] take over Austria (1938), and [5] the Sudetenland (1938) without firing a shot
- After he invaded Czechoslovakia (1939) Britain and France threatened war if he went into Poland
- In August 1939, he made a '**Non-Aggression Pact**' with Stalin, then sent German armies into Poland on 1 September, thus starting the second **World War**
- Germans conquered much of western Europe in 1940. After losing the **Battle of Britain**, Hitler invaded the Soviet Union in 1941. In December, after **Pearl Harbour**, he declared war on the United States
- Defeat at **Stalingrad** and in **North Africa** in 1942–1943 turned the tide of war against him. By 1945, Allied armies were invading Germany from all sides
- Hitler committed suicide in his bunker in Berlin on 30 April, 1945.

Joseph Goebbels (1897–1945)

- Born in the Rhineland in 1897, he was lame as a result of a childhood disease and could not fight in the first World War
- He joined the Nazi party in 1924, and after some initial doubts became an admirer of Hitler, whose anti-semitism he shared
- Goebbels was a **skilful propagandist** and is credited with developing many techniques of modern propaganda and advertising
- He believed that if something (even a blatant lie) is repeated often enough, people will come to believe it
- From 1933, he was **Minister for Propaganda**, able to censor newspapers, magazines, books, public meetings, art, music, films, and radio
- During the second World War he continued to claim victory, even when defeat was inevitable
- Just before Hitler committed suicide, he appointed Goebbels as Chancellor, but he refused to accept and committed suicide with his wife and children in the Berlin bunker.

Leni Riefenstahl (1902–2003)

- After an early career as a dancer and actress, Riefenstahl began to work as a film director
- After hearing Hitler speak in 1932, she came to admire him and agreed to make a short documentary on the 1933 Nuremberg rally
- She first turned down a request to film the 1934 rally, and only agreed when she was given unlimited control over how it was made
- With a generous budget and a large film crew, she produced *The Triumph of the Will*
- It is both an original and innovative piece of film-making and a brilliant example of Nazi propaganda. It won many international awards, but was banned for many years after the second World War
- In 1936, she filmed the **Berlin Olympic Games**. She was the first to put cameras on rails and the film, *Olympics*, was a major influence on the way modern sporting events are shown
- After the second World War she was cleared of war crimes but her connection with the Nazis made it impossible for her to work as a film director again

5.1   International Relations 1920 – 1933

The League of Nations

- After the first World War, the victors hoped to avoid another war. At the Paris Peace Conference, they set up the **League of Nations** to keep the peace:
  - The League was to act a **mediator** when countries quarrelled
  - The League was to organise all other countries to resist an aggressor. This was called '**collective security**'
- But the League was weak because from the start several important countries were not in it:
  - **Germany** was not a member until 1926 and Germans always disliked it because it was set up by the victors of the first World War. Hitler pulled Germany out in 1933
  - The **Soviet Union** was not invited to join at first because it was communist. Stalin always despised the League, but joined in 1934 hoping for support if Hitler threatened the USSR
  - The **United States Senate** refused to approve the treaty setting up the League, so the Americans never joined it
- The League also lacked an army of its own to enforce its decisions. Only Britain and France among its members had large armies, and they were not willing to use them to stop aggression unless their own interests were involved.

1919 – 1929: Growing hope of peace

- Immediately after the war, tension was high in Europe, with issues like reparations causing ill-feeling between Germany and France
- But once these were settled in the **Locarno Pact** (1925) and the **Young Plan** (1929), people began to believe that peace was possible
- The Wall Street Crash in 1929 and the Great Depression which followed changed that.

The impact of the Depression

- Some undemocratic governments tried to take their people's minds off their economic problems with foreign conquests. **Japan** invaded **Manchuria** in 1931. **Italy** invaded **Abyssinia** in 1935
- In democratic countries, voters began to support more extreme parties (either communist or nationalist/fascist) that seemed to offer solutions to the economic mess

Europe in 1933

- In Germany, the Depression led to the rise of **Hitler**. His aims, which he set out in *Mein Kampf*, were:
  - To destroy the Versailles Treaty
  - To unite all Germans into a new **Reich**, i.e. take over countries in which there were Germans – **Austria**, **Czechoslovakia** and **Poland**
  - To conquer living space (*lebensraum*) for Germans in Eastern Europe i.e. **Russia**
- These aims could only be achieved by war.

How did other countries react to Hitler's rise?

- The **French** were horrified when Hitler came to power. They strengthened the **Maginot line** but felt too weak to take him on unless they were sure that their British ally would support them
- At first the **British** were not too concerned about Hitler:
  - They did not really believe what he wrote in *Mein Kampf* and thought it was better to have a fascist dictator than a communist in Germany
  - They also believed that the **Versailles Treaty** had been unfair to Germany and were willing to let him dismantle it
  - Finally, they were growing more worried about **Japan**'s threat to their Asian empire and did not want a conflict in Europe at the same time
- For all these reasons and because of a genuine horror at the idea of another war, British leaders were willing to give Hitler some of what he wanted in

the hope that it would satisfy him. This led to the policy known as **appeasement**

- **Mussolini**'s attitude to Hitler was ambiguous:
  - ❏ He was flattered because Hitler claimed to admire him as the first fascist ruler
  - ❏ But he also feared that Hitler might try to take the **South Tyrol**, which Italy got from Austria after the first World War. For that reason, he was willing at first to stand up to Hitler
  - ❏ Later he changed sides because he saw that France and Britain were more likely to block his plans for a Mediterranean empire than Hitler
- **Stalin** indirectly helped Hitler to power in 1932:
  - ❏ When he realised what he had done, he told communist parties in other countries to co-operate with democrats to keep fascists out
  - ❏ He also sought alliances with western governments, and in 1934 joined the League of Nations to get the protection of "collective security".

5.2 The steps to war

1933-1934: Hitler moves cautiously

- Once in power, Hitler set out to achieve his aims. He skilfully exploited the divisions among his opponents, especially France, Britain and the Soviet Union
- He took Germany out of the League of Nations in 1933, and began to **rearm secretly**. But he had to move carefully because the German army was still weak and he did not want to provoke an attack until he was ready
- In January 1934, he signed a **ten year non-aggression pact** with **Poland**, even though he planned to take over the **Polish Corridor**. This gave other countries the impression that Hitler's intentions were peaceful
- **Austria** was a small republic whose five million people were German speaking. The Versailles Treaty forbade it to unite with Germany (*Anschluss*)
- Hitler encouraged the growth of an Austrian Nazi Party. It campaigned for *Anschluss*. In July 1934, Nazis murdered the Austrian Chancellor **Dollfuss** and planned to seize power
- **Mussolini** moved his troops to the border and Hitler had to back down.

1935: Hitler openly breaks the Versailles Treaty

- The **Saarland** was a rich coalmining area which the Versailles Treaty put under French control for 15 years. In **March** 1935, in a referendum there, the Saarlanders voted overwhelmingly to return to Germany
- Hitler then announced conscription. This was his first open breach of the Versailles Treaty

- In **April**, Italy, Britain and France formed the **Stresa Front** to resist him. They promised to uphold international treaties, but they did not remain united for long
- In **June**, the British, who feared a naval race with Germany, which they could not afford, signed a **Naval Pact** with Hitler. This allowed him to increase the size of the German navy and seemed to give British approval to Hitler breaking the Treaty of Versailles
- In **October**, Mussolini sent his troops into **Abyssinia**. He believed that Britain and France would approve because they needed him on their side against Hitler.

1935–1936: The Abyssinian Crisis: Mussolini changes sides

- Abyssinia was a member of the **League of Nations** and appealed to the League for help
- The League condemned Italian aggression against another member and forbade its members to trade with Italy (**trade sanctions**)
- But Britain and France did not want to annoy Mussolini, so they made **the Hoare-Laval Pact**. It let Italy keep most of its conquests
- When this became public, people in both countries were outraged. They forced their governments to withdraw the Pact and accept League of Nations sanctions on Italy
- The sanctions did not help Abyssinia, however, because Britain and France saw that they did not include oil and they left the Suez Canal open to the Italian navy
- Mussolini kept Abyssinia, but he was annoyed by the British and French actions and began to consider an alliance with Hitler.

March 1936: Hitler sends his troops into the Rhineland

- While the other countries were pre-occupied with Abyssinia, Hitler sent his army into the **Rhineland**. This was also forbidden by the Versailles Treaty
- The German army had orders to retreat if the French opposed them, as it was still relatively weak
- The French wanted to send their army to stop them, but the British preferred to appease Hitler, claiming the Treaty was too harsh
- The French would not act alone, so Hitler got away with it.

1936–1939: The Spanish civil war

- Civil war began in Spain in July when **General Franco** led a rebellion against the republican government. The League urged its members to remain neutral and Britain and France obeyed
- Hitler and Mussolini sent troops to help Franco who was backed by the Spanish fascist Party, the **Falange**
- Stalin sent some arms to communists fighting on the republican side

- Many people in Britain and France saw Spain as a **dress rehearsal** for a greater war between the two rival ideologies, **fascism and communism**. They passionately supported one side or the other
- About 18,000 people went to Spain to fight for the side they believed in.

The alliance of the fascist dictators

- Abyssinia and Spain drew the fascist dictators together
- Mussolini dreamed of dividing Europe between them, with him creating a Mediterranean empire (Spain through Franco, Greece and the Balkans) in the south, while Hitler expanded east into Russia
- This suited Hitler as it divided his enemies. He recognised Italian conquests in Abyssinia, and in **October** 1936, made the **Rome-Berlin Axis** with Mussolini
- In **November 1936**, Hitler made the **Anti-Comintern Pact** with Japan, which Italy joined in 1937. This threatened Russia with war from two sides.

March 1938: Hitler unites Germany and Austria (Anschluss)

- By 1938, Hitler felt strong enough to begin expanding into other countries, but he still hoped to do so without a fight. His first target was **Austria**, where the Nazi Party was now very strong
- Early in 1938 he summoned the Austrian Chancellor, **Schuschnigg** to Berlin and demanded that Nazis be included in his coalition government
- When he went home, Schuschnigg organised a referendum to forestall a German invasion, but the German army moved in before it could take place
- *Anschluss* was popular with Austrians and France and Britain did not feel there was anything they could do about it.

September 1938: The Munich Crisis

- Hitler's next target was **Czechoslovakia** (see map on p. 185), a small democratic country with a large German-speaking minority in the **Sudetenland**
- Hitler funded a **Sudeten Nazi Party**, led by **Konrad Heinlein**. It stirred up discontent among the Sudeten Germans and demanded unification with Germany
- The Czechs had a modern, well-equipped army and their frontier with Germany was well defended. They also had guarantees of help from France and Stalin
- But when Hitler took over Austria, the German army could go into Czechoslovakia from the Austrian side (see map on p. 189)
- In **August 1938**, Hitler threatened to invade Czechoslovakia to "protect" the Sudeten Germans. The Czechs appealed for help to their Allies, France and the Soviet Union

- There was little France could do because it was on the far side of Germany. Stalin offered to help if France would too, but they would only act with British support
- **Neville Chamberlain**, the British Prime Minister, was desperate to avoid a war and determined to **appease** Hitler. He flew to Munich to meet him at his summer home. At first Hitler refused to compromise and around Europe people prepared for war
- But on **29 September**, a final meeting was arranged between the French Prime Minister, **Daladier**, Chamberlain and Hitler, with Mussolini acting as mediator. Neither the Czech leader **Benes** nor Stalin was invited to attend
- They produced the **Munich Pact**:
  - All areas of Czechoslovakia with **German majorities** were to go to Germany. This deal gave most of Czech industry, including its modern tank factories to the Nazis
  - Hitler promised not to touch the rest of Czechoslovakia
- After Munich, Chamberlain returned home saying he had secured 'peace in our time'.

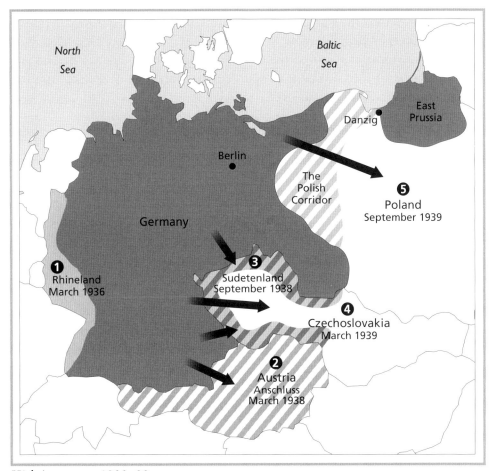

Hitler's conquests 1933–39

1939: The end of appeasement

- But Hitler was not satisfied. In **March 1939**, he sent his army into the rest of Czechoslovakia. This finally showed that appeasement had failed and that it was impossible to trust Hitler
- Hitler then began to use the same tactics against Poland, demanding the Polish Corridor and the city of Danzig
- Britain and France declared they would go to war to defend the Poles. They also reluctantly opened talks with Stalin about an alliance against Hitler
- But the talks dragged on because Stalin wanted to send his army into Poland to defend it, and the Poles feared him as much as they feared Hitler.

August 1939: The Nazi-Soviet Pact

- Stalin then turned to Hitler, who seized his chance. On 23 August the two arch-enemies agreed to a **Ten-year Non-aggression Pact**
- Publicly it only promised that neither side would attack the other for ten years
- But **secret clauses** allowed Stalin to invade Finland, Eastern Poland and the Baltic States (all lost to Russia during the first World War) and supply Germany with oil:
  - For Stalin, the Pact bought time to rebuild the Red Army, seriously weakened by his purges
  - For Hitler, it removed the fear of having to fight France, Britain and Russia at the same time (a 'war on two-fronts'), while leaving him free to invade Russia whenever it suited him.

September 1939: the second World War begins

- On 1 September, Hitler invaded Poland
- On 3 September, Britain and France declared war on Germany.

5.3 War in Europe: 1939 – 1945

War-time alliances

- There were two sets of alliances in the second World War: the **Allied powers** (the **Allies**) and the **Axis** powers:
  - At first **Poland**, **France** and **Britain** (with its empire), were **the Allies**, but after the defeat of Poland and France, Britain fought alone. In June 1941 Hitler's invasion of the **Soviet Union** brought Stalin in on the Allied side. The **Americans** joined in December after Pearl Harbour
  - **Italy** and **Germany** were called the **Axis powers** after they formed the **Rome-Berlin Axis** in 1936. They were later joined by **Japan** in the **Anti-Comintern Pact**, and later by Hungary, Romania, Slovakia and Bulgaria.

September 1939 – March 1940: war in Eastern Europe

- On 1 September, 1939, Hitler invaded **Poland**, using a new military tactic called **blitzkrieg** ('lightening war'). The planes of the **Luftwaffe** bombed the Polish army and then great numbers of tanks (**panzers**) and soldiers poured over the border
- The Poles fought bravely but were quickly overwhelmed, especially after **Stalin**, as part of the **Nazi-Soviet Pact**, invaded eastern Poland and the **Baltic states** on 17 September
- The Germans and Russians divided Poland between them
- In October, Stalin also invaded **Finland**. Strong Finnish resistance delayed the Soviet victory until March 1940. Hitler believed this showed the Red Army was weak and could easily be beaten.

April – June 1940: German conquests in western Europe

- In the west, Britain and France declared war on Germany on 3 September, but their armies waited behind the **Maginot Line** through the winter of 1939–1940 (the 'phoney war')
- On **9 April**, 1940, Hitler launched a blitzkrieg against **Denmark** and **Norway**. British and French troops tried to help Norway but had to withdraw in June
- On **10 May**, the German army entered the neutral **Netherlands** and **Belgium** which were overwhelmed in days
- The French and British expected an invasion through Belgium and moved their armies north to stop it
- But Hitler sent his armies through the **Ardennes**, which the French thought impassable for tanks. The Germans split the French and British armies:
- Most of the British and some French troops retreated to the sea at **Dunkirk** where the Royal Navy and many small boats rescued over 300,000 of them
- The French and some British moved south, to defend Paris, but it fell to the Germans on 14 **June**
- On 22 **June**, **Pétain** signed an **armistice** with Hitler, taking France out of the war. (see **France**, 2.1).

Why were the Germans so successful?

- German success was due to (1) a bigger army and air force than Britain and France combined, (2) more skilful tactics, especially in the use of tanks and the blitzkrieg, (3) disagreement about tactics between the British and French armies, and (4) the defeatist attitude of the French leaders.

The Battle of Britain (July – September 1940)

- As the German armies rolled across Europe in May 1940, the British parliament elected **Winston Churchill** as Prime Minister, in place of

Chamberlain who was associated with the failed policy of appeasement

- When France fell, Hitler assumed that Britain would make peace, but Churchill was determined to continue the war
- Hitler then ordered the Luftwaffe, which had 1,300 bombers and 1,000 fighter planes, to destroy the RAF, so that he could invade Britain (**Operation Sealion**)
- In July and August, the Germans sent wave after wave of planes against RAF airfields in southern England
- British **Spitfires** and **Hurricanes** retaliated, inflicting considerable losses on the Germans. Their main problem was a shortage of trained pilots
- In September, after the British bombed Berlin, Hitler sent the Luftwaffe to bomb London (the **Blitz**). He hoped to break the British people's will to resist. This was a mistake as it took the pressure off the RAF, which had been close to collapse
- The RAF continued to inflict heavy losses on the Luftwaffe. By October, it was clear they had not gained control of the air. Hitler then called off his invasion plans.

Why did Hitler lose the Battle of Britain?

- The Battle of Britain was Hitler's first defeat. He lost it despite having a larger air force because (1) British planes were superior to the German **Messerschmitts** and **Stukas**, (2) German planes had further to travel, which limited what they could do, while British planes were near home, and (3) the British developed **radar** which gave them advance warning of Luftwaffe attacks.

The Battle of the Atlantic, 1939–1945

- Churchill wrote: *'the only thing that ever really frightened me during the war was the U-boat peril'*. Britain imported a large proportion of its food, raw materials and weapons across the Atlantic. If Hitler could cut off these supplies he could starve Britain into submission
- From the start of the war, German surface ships like the *Graf Spee* attacked British ships. The **Royal Navy** dealt with this threat which ended in May 1941 with the sinking of the battleship *Bismarck*
- Germans also used submarines (**U-boats**). They became more dangerous from the summer of 1940 because they could set out from bases in France and Norway
- They destroyed three million tons of Allied shipping between June and December 1940 alone. In 1941 they formed '**wolf packs**', i.e. groups of U-boats attacking ships at night
- From 1942 the Allies turned the tide against the U-boats. Their counter-measures included (1) bigger convoys, (2) the use of **sonar** and **radar**, (3) the development of long-range aircraft and (4) the cracking of the **Enigma code**, which allowed them to track submarines' movements

- In the **Battle of the Atlantic**, the Allies lost almost about 80,000 seamen and 4,000 ships but the vital supply lines remained open.

Italy in the war (1940–1945)

- In spite of Mussolini's alliance with Hitler, he stayed neutral until he was sure the Germans were going to win
- On **5 June, 1940**, he declared war on France and acquired some French territory after the armistice
- In **October**, he invaded Greece, but was defeated. Hitler had to come to his aid, occupying most of the Balkans
- In North Africa, Italy had an army in **Libya**. It attacked Egypt, intending to capture the British-controlled **Suez Canal**
- After the British defeated the Italians, Hitler sent his best general, **Rommel**, with troops and tanks, to support them
- Rommel succeeded at first, but General **Montgomery** defeated him at the battle of **El Alamein** in October 1942
- After the US entered the war, American, British and French armies occupied Morocco and Algeria, which had belonged to Vichy France
- This trapped the Axis forces and they surrendered in May 1943
- The Allies then invaded **Sicily**. In Rome, the King dismissed Mussolini and the new government made peace
- But Hitler rescued Mussolini and set up a puppet Italian state in northern Italy to continue the war. Fighting lasted until the collapse of Germany
- In April 1945, Mussolini was captured by partisans (anti-fascist fighters) and killed.

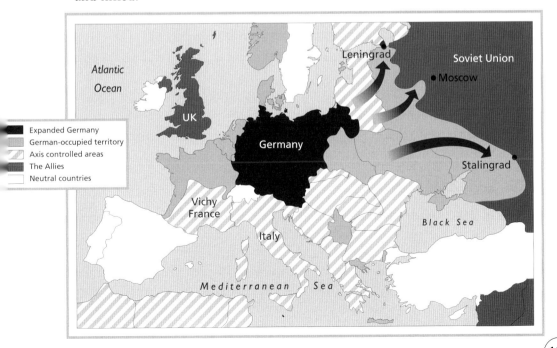

Europe in 1942

The Soviet Union at war (1941–1945)

- Although Hitler made a ten-year **Non-Aggression Pact** with Stalin, he always intended to invade the Soviet Union
- He wanted to destroy communism, gain *lebensraum* for Germans and get control of Russia's oil and raw materials
- The German invasion plan was called **Operation Barbarossa**. It was delayed from May to June 1941, because Hitler had to send troops to help Mussolini in the Balkans
- On 22 June, 1941, Hitler sent 2,000 planes, 3,500 tanks and 3.5 million men into the Soviet Union:
  - To the north their target was **Leningrad**
  - To the centre it was **Moscow**
  - To the south they wanted to capture the **oil-fields of the Caucasus**
- The Germans advanced rapidly. **General Zhukov**, the Red Army commander, told his men to retreat before them. They were also to destroy air-fields, railways, animals, crops and factories – anything that might be used by the Germans. This would force them to bring food, fuel and whatever else they needed all the way from Germany
- The Russians also moved thousands of factories and a million factory workers beyond the **Ural Mountains**, out of reach of the German bombers. Tanks from these factories helped the Soviet Union win the war
- Zhukov's main hope lay in the fierce Russian winter. In 1941, it came early. The Germans, expecting a quick victory, were not prepared for it. Soldiers in light clothing died in their thousands, fuel froze and Russian resistance fighters stopped fresh supplies reaching them.

The Siege of Leningrad (September 1941 – January 1944)

- On 8 September, 1941, the German army surrounded Leningrad, Russia's second city, but the people refused to surrender
- For 900 days they endured constant bombing and shelling as well as hunger, cold and thirst
- One third of the people lost their lives, but on 27 January, 1944, the Germans finally acknowledged defeat.

The Battle of Stalingrad

- In 1942, with Germany short of fuel, Hitler decided to concentrate on conquering the oil-rich Caucasus region. He also sent part of his army to take the nearby city of **Stalingrad**
- Stalin ordered the Red Army to defend it to the last man. Fighting fiercely, street by street and house by house, the Russians resisted the Germans
- In November Zhukov sent fresh troops to encircle the exhausted Germans, trapping them in Stalingrad. The German general, **von Paulus**, wanted to retreat, but Hitler ordered him to fight on

- In February 1943, he was forced to surrender with 250,000 men. It was the greatest defeat in German history.

The Battle of Kursk (July 1943)

- The Germans attempted to recover in July 1943 by launching 2,700 tanks against the Russians at **Kursk**
- Russian tanks were not as good as the Germans', but they had an endless supply arriving from factories across the Urals
- They counter-attacked, and for seven days 6,000 tanks fought the biggest tank battle in history. The Germans had to retreat.

The German retreat

- After that, the Red Army drove the Germans out of Russia and eastern Europe, back into Germany
- By spring 1945, they were approaching Berlin.

Why did the Soviet Union defeat Nazi Germany?

- Hitler thought the Red Army was weak and expected a quick victory. When that did not happen, the Germans were unable to cope with the extreme Russian weather and did not have the manpower and raw materials, especially oil, to fight a long war
- Stalin's industrialisation in the 1930s gave the Red Army the guns, tanks and aircraft to fight the Germans and the arms factories were located where the Germans could not reach them. The US also poured equipment into the Soviet Union to help it withstand the Nazis
- Stalin's wartime propaganda played down communism and emphasised **Russian patriotism** and **religion** to encourage Russians to resist the invaders. In Russia the second World War was called '*the Great Patriotic War*'.

The United States and Britain: the war-time alliance

- After the first World War, the United States went back to its traditional policy of **isolation** (i.e. keeping out of European quarrels)
- **Isolationism** was popular, but some Americans, including **President Roosevelt**, grew concerned about the growth of undemocratic fascist regimes in Europe
- When the war began, America remained neutral, but Roosevelt supported the **Lend-Lease Program** which allowed Britain to get large quantities of armaments from the US
- On **7 December, 1941**, Japanese planes attacked the US Pacific fleet in **Pearl Harbour**. Hitler then declared was on the US
- This allowed Roosevelt to decide that defeating Hitler was his main priority. American troops arrived in Europe and the US sent supplies to Britain and the Soviet Union.

The war in the air

- After the RAF won the Battle of Britain they attacked targets in Germany. The US air force joined in from 1942
- The RAF commander, Sir Arthur ('**Bomber**') **Harris** first attacked military or industrial targets
- Then he switched to bombing cities, which were reduced to ruins. Hundreds of thousands of Germans were killed.

D-Day and the Normandy Landings, June 1944

- Stalin wanted his allies to invade France in 1943 to take German troops away from the Russian front but Churchill and Roosevelt preferred to attack Italy first
- Plans to invade France (**Operation Overlord**) were finally drawn up for June 1944
- On **D-Day**, **6 June**, 400,000 troops and 60,000 vehicles, under the command of the American general, **Dwight Eisenhower**, landed in **Normandy**
- The Germans, deceived into expecting them to land near Calais, were caught unprepared. The Allied troops swept across northern France and, in August, liberated Paris.

The end of the war

- The Allied advance was slowed in December 1944 by a last desperate counter-attack by the Germans (**Battle of the Bulge**)
- In January 1945, the Russians entered Germany. Hitler sent most of his remaining troops against them, letting the western Allies cross the Rhine into Germany
- By April, British, Americans and French troops had reached the **Elbe** and the Russians entered **Berlin**
- On 30 April, Hitler committed suicide in his bunker, and on **5 May** the Germans surrendered.

The meetings of the Allied leaders

- Throughout the war Roosevelt, Churchill and Stalin met to discuss military progress and make plans
- In **November 1943** they met at **Teheran**:
  - Stalin wanted the US and Britain to invade France and they agreed on May 1944
  - They agreed to divide Europe between Russian and western armies. Because Russia was still weak, the western leaders did not realise how much power this would give Stalin after the war
  - They failed to agree on how to treat Germany after the war
- In **February 1945**, they met in **Yalta**. By then the war was almost won and

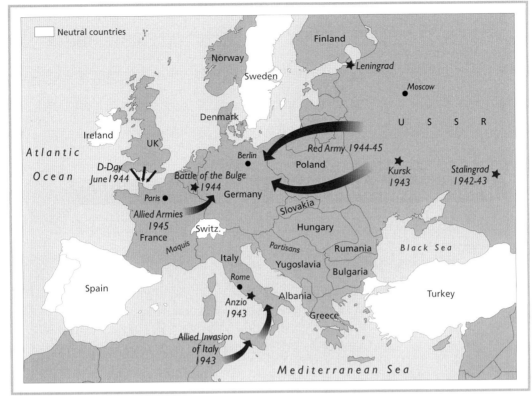

Europe 1943–45: Allied victories

Stalin's army controlled much of eastern Europe. Roosevelt was ill – he died in April – and he needed Stalin's help against Japan:

❍ They agreed Germany would be divided into **zones** occupied by the Allied armies, but failed to agree on its future treatment

❍ They could not agree on which kind of government – communist or capitalist – eastern Europe countries would have after the war

● The last conference was held in **Potsdam**, near Berlin, in July 1945. By then Germany was defeated and **Harry Truman** was President of the US. During the Conference, Churchill lost the British election and was replaced by **Clement Atlee**:

❍ The differences between Stalin and his war-time allies, hidden while they fought Hitler, emerged, especially over the future of eastern Europe

❍ They agreed to try Nazi leaders for war crimes

❍ During the conference, Truman heard about the successful explosion of the first **atom bomb**.

Why did the Allies win the war?

● Hitler planned for a short war. When he failed to beat Britain and then Russia quickly, Germany lacked the manpower, oil, minerals and other resources to fight a long war against overwhelming odds

- The entry of the United States, with its large population, big and efficient industries and huge supplies of raw materials made a German victory impossible
- The massive Allied bombing of German industry in 1944–1945 greatly reduced the resources available to the German armies
- The brutal racist policies of the Nazis made it impossible for them to win support from the people they conquered.

Winston Churchill (1874–1965)

- Born into an aristocratic family, Winston Churchill was elected a Conservative MP in 1900, but later moved to the Liberals. He served as a Liberal Minister from 1906 to 1917 and again from 1920–1922
- He then rejoined the Conservatives and was **Chancellor of the Exchequer** from 1924–1929. His decision to return Britain to the **Gold Standard** was economically disastrous. He lost office, and during the 1930s was seen as a failure
- He admired Mussolini, but feared **Hitler** from the start. He vigorously opposed the British government's policy of **appeasing** him and urged them to re-arm to meet the threat from Germany
- When appeasement failed, Churchill's reputation rose. At the start of the war, Chamberlain made him **First Lord of the Admiralty** (Naval Minister)
- When Chamberlain resigned in May 1940, all parties agreed to back Churchill as **Prime Minister** of a coalition government. In his first speech he said his only policy was *'to wage war by sea, land and air, with all our might and with all the strength that God can give us, against a monstrous tyranny'*
- After **Dunkirk**, some of his colleagues considered peace with Hitler but Churchill always insisted that they must fight on
- During **the Battle of Britain** he used the BBC to speak to the British people and his skill as a speaker (orator) was important in keeping them united and hopeful against what seemed like impossible odds
- He interfered, not always successfully, in military decisions during the war
- He developed a personal relationship with American President **Roosevelt**. In 1941, they met secretly to sign the **Atlantic Charter**, setting out their war aims. In January 1942, they met at **Casablanca** in North Africa and agreed to invade Italy and seek the **unconditional surrender** of Germany
- Although very anti-communist, Churchill welcomed **Stalin** as an ally after the German invasion of the Soviet Union, travelling to Russia to meet him
- Churchill, Roosevelt and Stalin held **three conferences** during the war – at **Yalta** (1943) **Teheran** (February 1945) and **Potsdam** (July 1945) at which they decided on war strategy and post-war plans
- Churchill was more sceptical than the Americans about Stalin's intentions once the war was over
- In the first post-war general election (July 1945) the Labour Party, led by **Clement Atlee**, unexpectedly beat Churchill's Conservative Party, so Churchill ceased to be Prime Minister during the Potsdam Conference
- Churchill became Prime Minister again in 1951–1954. He died in 1965.

5.4 Society during the second World War

France: The Vichy regime

- After the fall of France in 1940 (see page 154), the south-east, known as 'Vichy France' remained semi-independent, under the control of **Marshall Pétain**
- He wrote a new Constitution, creating a Corporate State like Mussolini's, with Pétain having dictatorial powers
- The Catholic Church's control of education was increased, trade unions were outlawed and the state was run in the interests of business.

Collaboration with the Germans

- Pétain and his main political ally, **Pierre Laval**, believed the Nazis were going to win the war and that it would be good for France to help them
- They sent supplies of food and raw materials to Germany
- They agreed to let French workers be conscripted to work in German factories
- They brought in **anti-semitic laws** and rounded up Jews. 75,000 were deported to the gas chambers in Germany
- But none of this satisfied Hitler. When the Allies occupied French colonies in North Africa in November 1941, he ended the independence of the Vichy government
- Collaboration was not confined to the Vichy area. Elsewhere many French people worked for the Germans. Most did so out of fear or necessity
- A few joined the *Milice*, set up in 1943 as a French equivalent to the Gestapo. It rounded up Jews, fought the resistance and was notorious for its brutality.

Resistance: General de Gaulle and the Free French

- Not everyone in France was content to collaborate with the Germans. In 1940 **General Charles de Gaulle**, escaped to London just ahead of the German armies
- On 18 June, he broadcasted from the BBC, calling on all French people to resist the Germans
- He set up the '**Free French**' movement, but got little support from either Churchill or Roosevelt who distrusted him.

The resistance in France

- In France, resistance to the Germans developed slowly. It increased after Hitler invaded Russia in 1941, when the communists joined in
- When the Germans began to conscript French workers to Germany, many young men chose to join the resistance instead

- At first, the resistance consisted of many groups, mostly operating independently. Later some of them formed an underground army, the **Maquis**
- They spied on the Germans, sending reports of their movements to London
- They rescued Allied airmen and helped them to get home
- Occasionally they sabotaged German installations but that was very risky. The Germans and the Milice retaliated very savagely, often killing many innocent civilians
- It is doubtful if the resistance made much difference to the war but they restored French self-respect.

De Gaulle gains control

- De Gaulle wanted to unite the various resistance groups under his leadership
- He sent **Jean Moulin** to France to talk to them. Moulin succeeded, though he was later captured, tortured and killed by the Germans
- The Allies did not tell de Gaulle about the **D-Day landings** in France in June 1944, but the resistance helped them by attacking the Germans
- When Paris was liberated, the Allies feared the communists might claim credit for the resistance, so they arranged for de Gaulle to lead the victory march into the city
- Around France people turned on those who collaborated with the Germans. About 9,000 were killed, many of them innocent
- De Gaulle insisted on proper trials for 100,000 'traitors'. Pétain and Laval were sentenced to death, but Pétain's sentence was reduced to life in prison because of his great age (89 at the time). Altogether about 750 people were executed.

Britain: the 'home front': 1939-1945

- Early in the war, thousands of refugees from the Nazis escaped to Britain. Political leaders like de Gaulle set up '**governments in exile**' to inspire resistance to Nazi rule. Others joined the British armed forces
- British men under 40 were conscripted unless they belonged to a **reserved occupation** vital to the survival of the country
- Those who were not fighting joined the **Home Guard** ('Dad's Army') to defend the country if the Germans invaded. Others served as **air-raid wardens** or **auxiliary firemen** during the Blitz
- Single women were also conscripted:
  - Some joined the women's branches of the armed forces such as the **WAAF** (air force) or **WRNS** (navy). They did not fight but worked as clerks, mechanics, etc
  - Others worked in the Women's Voluntary Services (**WVS**), organising evacuations, supervising shelters, etc
- Women, married as well as single, worked in arms factories, on building sites or on the land, replacing the men who were in the forces.

Rationing

- Food, clothing and petrol were strictly rationed. Foreign fruit like oranges and bananas disappeared, but the government made sure there were always supplies of tea and cigarettes
- People got **ration books** with 'points' that entitled them to a certain minimum of food. The amount they got was carefully estimated to ensure a healthy diet
- Slogans like *'Dig for Victory'* encouraged people to grow food in their back gardens or on their allotments to supplement their rations
- Those who had money could buy unrationed food or clothes on the illegal '**black market**'.

Evacuating the children

- In the 1930s, the British thought that millions would die when their cities were bombed, so it was decided to evacuate all children
- When war began in 1939, three million people, mostly school children and their escorts, were sent into the country
- Bewildered children went to live with strangers. Many were lucky in their hosts, being treated like members of the family. Some were exploited as cheap labour or abused
- When there was no bombing during the 'phoney war', many returned to their parents and remained throughout the Blitz.

Cities during the Blitz

- The Blitz continued from July 1940 to May 1941. London, Manchester, Liverpool, Coventry, Glasgow, Belfast and many other towns were bombed
- At first the bombers came in daylight but after the RAF inflicted heavy casualties, bombing was at night, usually when there was a full moon
- Cities were defended by hundreds of **barrage balloons** and **anti-aircraft guns**, as well as by **RAF fighter planes**
- **Air-raid wardens** enforced a strict **blackout** in case any light might guide enemy aircraft to a target
- **Air-raid shelters** were built, some in people's gardens, others in streets for the whole community. In London many people took refuge in Underground (urban rail) stations
- Some people left the cities each evening to sleep in the surrounding countryside where they felt safer
- In the Blitz about 50,000 people were killed and many more injured. Cities were badly damaged with over one million people made homeless
- During 1944 and 1945, the German rockets, the V1s and V2s ('**doodlebugs**'), caused panic because they were so unexpected and unpredictable. Over one million people left London and about 10,000 were killed.

Propaganda and entertainment

- The British government used censorship and propaganda to manage news about the war. The number of people killed in the Blitz was covered up, the number of British planes lost was understated, while German losses were exaggerated
- The decision of the King and his family to stay in London during the Blitz was designed to reassure people and strengthen their will to fight
- Films and news-reels celebrated British heroism and people still went to the cinema in spite of the danger of bombs
- The BBC played an important part in inspiring people, keeping them informed and entertaining them with music, comedy and plays.

Germany: the 'home front', 1939–1945

- In Germany **men** were conscripted into the army. **Women** were not because of Nazi views about the place of women, but in practice many women worked in war industries
- By 1942, Germany had a **labour shortage**. The Nazis solved it by forcing seven million prisoners of war and workers from Poland, France, and other conquered countries to work in mines and factories. Most were fed poorly and treated harshly
- **Rationing** was introduced in 1939. Most common foods were rationed. People received ration books showing how much they were entitled to. Men in vital industries got most, Poles and Jews got nothing
- Substitutes like roasted barley for coffee were common. People with gardens grew extra food or kept rabbits to supply meat.

German resistance to the Nazis

- Not all Germans supported the Nazis. Some were horrified by the treatment of Jewish people (see page 181) and risked imprisonment and torture to help them
- Students belonging to the **White Rose** group in Munich secretly produced anti-Nazi leaflets. They were betrayed to the Gestapo and executed
- In **July 1944**, some army officers, seeing that Germany was about to be beaten, planned to overthrow Hitler. **Von Stauffenberg** placed a bomb near Hitler, but he escaped with only minor injuries. The plotters were executed.

Bombing and refugees

- Towards the end of the war the relentless **bombing** by the Allies reduced most German cities to rubble and destroyed roads and railways. This left millions of people homeless and made food distribution difficult
- The worst raid was on **Dresden** in February 1945. It was filled with

civilian refugees when the RAF dropped 2,500 tons of explosives. This created a **firestorm** in which at least 50,000 died

- By 1945, Germany contained over nine million homeless **refugees**, who fled from eastern Europe before the advancing Red Army.

5.5 The Technology of War

Improving existing technology

- Before and during the war, each side had scientists and engineers working to improve existing technologies or develop new ones which would give them an advantage over the enemy
- **Tanks**, which were invented during the first World War, were much faster and easier to manoeuvre by 1939. German **Panzer** tanks were central to Hitler's early successes. As the war went on, bigger tanks with stronger armour like the **Soviet T-34**, the American **Sherman** or the German **Panther** were developed
- **Planes** were only used for reconnaissance during the first World War, but all countries believed control of the air would be vital in the next war. Through the 1920s and 1930s work went on to develop new aircraft, like the Luftwaffe's **Messerschmitt** or the RAF's **Hurricanes**. During the war, bombers like the American **Flying Fortress**, got bigger and could fly further. Fighter planes like the **Mustang** and the **Hawker Tempest** became faster, more agile and could stay in the air much longer
- **Radar** was vital to Britain's survival in the Battle of Britain. Discovered in the 1930s, the British secretly improved it while the Germans failed to realise its value
- **Sonar**, developed in the first World War, was improved by the Royal Navy, enabling it to detect German U-boats
- The British used a special interception device, known as **Ultra**, to break the German's **Enigma** code. They gave them advance warning of German attacks.

New weapons

- The main new weapons developed during the war were the **V1 flying bombs** and **V2 rockets** and the **atomic bomb**. They came too late to make much difference to the outcome of the war.

The V1 and V2

- Hitler hoped the **V1** (a **pilotless aircraft** carrying a large bomb) and the **V2** (a **rocket**, the ancestor of modern ballistic missiles) might save him from defeat. The Nazis poured enormous resources into their development
- About 10,000 V1s were launched at the south-east of England between June 1944 and March 1945. Early attempts to stop them using planes had

only limited success, but the development of **electronically guided anti-aircraft guns** reduced their impact from August

- Starting in September 1944, over 3,000 V2s were launched. Because they travelled at **supersonic speed** they came silently, dropping death and destruction unheralded from the sky. They had killed about 7,000 civilians by March 1945. Too fast for anti-aircraft guns or aircraft, the only way to deal with them was to bomb the launch sites.

The atom bomb

- British scientists were working on nuclear fission from the 1920s, but after the US entered the war they were moved to America to work on the **Manhattan Project** with Americans and Canadians
- The first atom bomb was tested in New Mexico in **July 1945**. President Truman decided to use it against Japan, which was still at war. Two bombs were dropped on **Hiroshima** and **Nagasaki** in August. The Japanese surrendered and the second World War came to an end.

How the war changed Europe

- The war killed between 40 and 50 million Europeans, most of them civilians. When it ended towns and cities were in ruins, roads and railways were destroyed and about 20 million people were homeless refugees
- Fascists and Nazis were discredited but communists gained respect because of their role in resisting Hitler
- France, Britain and Germany – the great powers of the past – were damaged by the war. After it only two countries mattered – the **United States** and the **Soviet Union**. They became known as the **superpowers**
- The line where their armies met in 1945 became a line – **the iron curtain** – that divided Europe until 1990
- Rivalry between the superpowers and their ideas – **capitalism** and **communism** – led to a new conflict, **the Cold War**
- In western Europe, leaders looked for a way of avoiding another war between France and Germany. This led eventually to the foundation of the **European Union**.

The emergence of popular culture

- Popular culture is culture that is available to the majority of the people and not just to the rich and privileged
- Popular culture emerged in the 1920s as a result of new technologies, invented before the first World War. These were **moving pictures**, **radio** and **gramophone records**. TV began at the end of the 1930s but made little impact until after the second World War.

6.1   Film
The 'Silent Era': 1895–1927

- The **Lumière brothers** invented moving pictures in 1895
- Within a few years, film was being used to tell stories and cinemas had opened in many cities and towns
- Film-making was mostly developed in France and Italy before 1914, but the disruption of the first World War opened the way for American filmmakers. By the 1920s, over 80% of the world's films were made in America
- During the 'silent era' film-makers developed many **genres of film** – comedy, romance, crime, adventure, horror and westerns
- Film historians estimate that over 80% of silent films have been lost, so it is difficult to appreciate their quality.

Hollywood, studios and stars

- From the 1920s, **Hollywood** in California, with its reliable sunshine, became the centre of the American film industry
- The success of Hollywood was based on the **studio system**. In the 1920s, five major and some minor studios produced 800 films a year in a ruthless multi-billion-dollar business
- The bosses of studios like **MGM** or **Warner Brothers**, sought to maximise profits by controlling the stories, directors, actors and, in many cases, cinemas too
- They developed the '**star system**' in which a few actors and actresses were promoted as 'stars'. There was **Mary Pickford** who was '*America's sweetheart*', **Clara Bow**, '*the IT girl*' ('IT' was slang for 'sex appeal'), and **Rudolf Valentino** whose death at 31 produced hysteria among his fans
- Stars had to sign contracts to work for only one studio. Their films received

extensive publicity, **fan clubs** were encouraged and stories about their private lives were leaked to the press

- Another promotional idea was the **Academy Awards** for best film and best actors, better known as the **Oscars**, which began in 1928.

Charlie Chaplin (1889 – 1977)

- One of the most important stars of the silent era was **Charlie Chaplin**
- Born in London in 1889, he had a poverty-stricken childhood. As a boy he worked in the music halls and on a tour of America, joined the Keystone Film Studio, famous for its comedies about the **Keystone Cops**
- Chaplin developed his own character of the **Tramp**, which he played in over 70 pictures. Small, vulnerable and brave, the Tramp won the hearts of cinema audiences everywhere, and by 1919 Chaplain was earning $10,000 a year
- In 1919, he joined several other film stars to set up a studio, **United Artists**. This allowed him to control his own films, which he wrote, acted in and directed
- His most famous films included *The Kid* (1919), his masterpiece, *The Gold Rush* (1925) and *The Circus* (1928)
- Even after talking-pictures came in he continued to make silent pictures like *City Lights* (1931) and *Modern Times* (1936)
- But he was strongly opposed to fascism, and in 1940 produced his first 'talkie', *The Great Dictator*. Mocking Hitler, Chaplin played **Adenoid Hynkel** ruler of (P)Tomania
- After the war, Chaplin was accused of being a communist and banned from America. He spent the rest of his life in Switzerland, making only a few, not very successful, films
- He died in 1977.

EDCO REVISE WISE KEY PERSONALITY

The start of the 'talkies'

- Talking pictures began with *The Jazz Singer* in 1927. It was so popular that all studios were making 'talkies' by 1929
- Because they cost more to make, talkies increased the power of the big studios
- Some stars (like Clara Bow) failed to make the transition but others flourished and new ones emerged like **Greta Garbo**, **Clark Gable** and **Shirley Temple**
- A new type of film, **the musical**, developed with new stars like **Bing Crosby**, **Fred Astaire** and **Ginger Rogers**
- Talkies increased the **influence of American culture**, with people around the world singing American songs, adopting American slang words like 'OK' or trying to speak with an America accent.

The British film industry

- Britain was slow to develop a film industry, and in the 1920s almost all films shown were American. To avoid complete American dominance, an

Act, passed 1927 and renewed in 1938, required 20% of films in British cinemas to be British

- This rescued the industry from extinction. British film-makers standardised production and created a studio system
- They made small budget films mainly crime, comedy, musicals, stories from British history and celebrations of the Empire
- A number of British stars appeared, notably **Gracie Fields** in *Sing As We Go* (1934). **Alfred Hitchcock** emerged as Britain's greatest director with films such as *The Thirty Nine Steps* (1935) and *The Lady Vanishes* (1938). He later went to Hollywood
- British audiences were too small for the industry to produce the kind of lavish films the Americans could afford, and few British films were successful in the US.

Cinemas

- From the 1920s to the 1950s, a majority of people on both sides of the Atlantic went to the cinema at least once a week
- To meet the demand, **huge cinemas** were built, often in the latest architectural style. Most were glamorous and luxurious
- Prices were kept low so that even during the Depression most people could afford a brief escape from the drabness of their everyday lives
- As well as the main picture, the show usually included a cheap B-rated film, a news-reel showing the latest events or a travelogue of exotic locations the audience could never hope to visit.

Censorship

- The popularity of films worried the older generation. This led demands for **censorship**
- To stop the state intervening, the Americans produced the **Hayes Code**. It set out what could or could not be dealt with in films and how various things were to be shown. For example, even married couples had to be shown sleeping in single beds
- In Britain, a system of grading developed with films defined as suitable for different age groups. Local councils could also ban a film from being shown in its locality
- Official censorship led to **self-censorship**. Studios did not make films showing social problems or the misery caused by the Depression.

Cinema during the second World War

- When war began, the British government closed cinemas for fear of bombs. But they quickly re-opened and played an important part in keeping people's spirits up during the war

- Many war-time films blended pro-Allied or anti-Nazi propaganda into their well-worn genres of romance, crime and adventure. Others like *In Which We Serve* (1942) or *Western Approaches* (1944) gave audiences an insight into the experience of war
- Many film stars joined the forces or went on tours entertaining the troops.

6.2 Radio

The early years

- 'Wireless telegraphy' was invented by **Marconi** in the 1890s and improved during the first World War. For the first 20 years it was used only for '**narrowcasting**' (i.e. sending messages directly from one person to another)
- '**Broadcasting**' (sending out a message to anyone who happens to be listening) began in the United States after the first World War.

Commercial broadcasting in the US

- From the start American radio stations were **commercial**, making their money by selling advertising
- There was little regulation so stations multiplied. By the 1930s, there were about 600
- Most were local, reporting local news and playing music. They also bought in drama programmes, sports reports and foreign news from larger radio companies, like NBC
- Politicians, both local and national, quickly realised the value of radio as a way of reaching the voters. In the depth of the Depression, **Roosevelt** broadcast his '*fire-side chats*' to win support for his economic policies
- After America joined the war, radio stations sent foreign correspondents overseas to report on events, encouraged support for the troops and sold war bonds.

Radio in Britain: Sir John Reith and the BBC

- Radio developed very differently in Britain. After a brief period of commercial broadcasting from 1922, the government set up a '**public service**' broadcasting company, the **BBC** in 1927
- The BBC was a **monopoly** (i.e. no competitors allowed). Its money came from a **licence fee** which anyone who owned a radio set had to pay. It was not allowed to broadcast advertisements
- The BBC's first Director General was **Sir John Reith**, an austere Scotsman
- He believed the BBC should **inform** and **educate** its audience as well as entertain them and he was determined to keep it independent of politicians and of commercial interests

- Reith's attitude meant that the BBC combined popular entertainment with high culture. Classical music was broadcast as well as popular songs; Shakespeare's plays as well as comedy; science as well as sports reports
- In 1932, Reith set up the **British Empire Service,** and in 1936 the world's first **TV service**. It closed during the war.

The importance of the BBC

- Because the BBC was Britain's only radio station, it played an important role in British life:
- King George V began the tradition of a royal broadcast to the people every Christmas
- When his son Edward VIII abdicated, he explained his reasons on the BBC
- On 3 September, 1939, everybody listened in, as **Chamberlain** told them they were at war with Germany.

The BBC during the second World War

- During the war, the BBC helped to create a sense of common purpose in the fight against Hitler by broadcasting Churchill's most inspiring speeches
- It doubled in size and made more popular programmes like '*Forces Favourites*' that linked people on the Home Front with those serving in the forces
- The **news services** expanded. War correspondents reported on battles and other events, like the discovery of the Nazi death camps. The BBC's reputation for independence meant that people believed what it told them
- The BBC expanded its **foreign language** broadcasts. In occupied Europe, people secretly listened to it to get reliable news about the progress of the war. Anyone found doing so was punished severely by the Gestapo. Some BBC broadcasts carried coded messages to the resistance.

The impact of films and radio

- Film and radio developed people's **interest in music**, both classical and popular. They bought records to play music they enjoyed in films or heard on the radio
- **New forms of music** were popularised. **Jazz**, from the American south, dances like **the Charleston**, the **big band sound** of Glen Miller, all became popular as a result of being in films and on the radio
- American radio and films helped to reinforce racial stereotypes with popular films like *The Jazz Singer* or *Gone With The Wind*, presenting unflattering images of black people
- By broadcasting commentaries on **sporting events** radio increased the number of people who were interested in sports.

Bing Crosby (1903–1977)

KEY PERSONALITY / EDCO REVISE WISE

- Harry Lillis '**Bing' Crosby** was born in the US in 1903. He dropped out of law school to become a singer in a band, the *Rhythm Boys*
- Crosby quickly emerged as the leading singer and in 1928 he had his first solo hit with *Ol' Man River*
- In 1932, he starred in his first full length feature film, *The Big Broadcast* and in the 1930s he made several successful musicals. His hit song 'White Christmas', from the 1942 film *Holiday Inn*, became the biggest hit song of all time, selling over 100,000 million copies
- During the war he teamed up with the comedian Bob Hope to make *The Road to Singapore*, the first of a series of light-hearted Road movies
- He also showed his talent as an actor in the 1944 film, *Going My Way*, for which he won an Oscar. Altogether he starred in 59 films
- Through the 1930s and 1940s, Crosby combined his film career with a **weekly radio show** in which he sang and presented other acts
- Through his films and radio he moulded the popular music of his time, singing jazz and rhythm and blues as well as popular romantic songs
- He developed a relaxed, conversational style of singing, known as '**crooning**' which looked easy, though he worked hard at it
- He spent a great deal of time entertaining the US forces during the second World War. In a poll in 1945, troops chose him as the person who did most to raise their morale during the war
- Crosby continued to work on his career as an entertainer until his death in 1977

Questions

REVISE WISE QUESTIONS

For Examination questions on Later Modern History of Europe and the Wider World, Topic 3 see page 277.

Your revision notes

Later Modern History of Europe and the Wider World   Topic 6

The United States and the World 1945–1989

1.1 The American Constitution and the 'Separation of Powers'

The American Constitution

- To understand American politics and history you have to understand the **Constitution of the United States**
- It was drawn up in 1787 by the '**Founding Fathers**', the men who led the American revolution against British rule
- They feared that their newly founded republic might be taken over by a tyrant (dictator). To stop that happening they wrote a Constitution that limited the government's power with an elaborate system of '**checks and balances**'
- The most important of the checks and balances is '**the separation of powers**'. This prevents any one part of the government getting so strong that it can over-rule the others
- Power is separated in two ways:
    1. Between the **States** and the **Federal** government
    2. Within the Federal government.

> **Remember...**
>
> In 1776, there were **13 states** e.g. Virginia and New York. As the US expanded into the West, new states like Texas and California were created. Today there are **50 states**.

State government

- The Founding Fathers left a great deal of power with the States that started the revolution against Britain:
    - Each State can write its own Constitution
    - It can elect its own **Legislature** (parliament) to make laws and its own **Governor** to enforce those laws
    - It can raise its own taxes and control its own education, health, welfare and transport system.

The Federal government

- To keep the States united and to deal with general issues, the Founding Fathers set up a **Federal Government**
- It controls foreign policy, trade, the armed forces, currency, banking, travel between the States, etc. It is located in **Washington, DC** (which is not in any of the States)
- If there is a conflict between State law and Federal law, Federal law wins.

How powers are separated within the Federal government

- The Founding Fathers also divided the Federal government into three parts. Each part was given a separate task:
    1. The **Congress** is the **Legislature** which makes the laws
    2. The **President** is the **Executive** which enforces the laws
    3. The **Supreme Court** is the **Judiciary**, which decides if the actions of Congress, the President and the States are in line with the Constitution and laws of the US.

The Congress

- The Congress has two Houses:
    1. **The House of Representatives**: Its members, called **Congressmen**, are elected for two years. Seats in the House of Representatives are given on a **population basis**, so a big state with a big population like California has more Congressmen than a state with a small population like Vermont
    2. **The Senate**: Each State, big or small, elects **two Senators** who must seek re-election after six years
- All Bills (proposed laws) must be accepted by both Houses and signed by the President. If he **vetoes** a Bill (i.e. refuses to sign), it will still pass if **two-thirds** of both Houses vote for it
- The President must get the approval of the Senate before he can appoint members of his Cabinet, Ambassadors and Judges of the Supreme Court.

The President

- The **President** is the most important person in the United States. He or she is elected for four years. All citizens may vote in the election. Voting is on a State-by-State basis, with the candidate who wins most votes in each State getting all the votes in that State
- A **Vice-President** is elected at the same time. If the President dies in office, the Vice-President takes over
- The President is elected in November and takes office in the following January. Since 1948, Presidents may only serve for two terms (i.e. eight years)
- The President is **Commander-in-Chief** of the armed forces and controls foreign policy, though the Senate must approve any treaties he makes
- He draws up the **annual budget** (taxes and what they will be spent on) and submits it to Congress, which has to approve it
- He draws up **Bills**, and submits them to Congress, which has to approve them before they become law
- He is responsible for collecting taxes and enforcing laws

- He is advised by a **Cabinet**, with members (called **Secretaries**) in charge of particular areas of government. The **Secretary of State** is responsible for foreign affairs, the **Secretary of Defence** is responsible for the armed forces, and so on
- Presidents also have many unelected advisers. Often they have more power than Cabinet members.

Amending the Constitution

- The Constitution can be **amended** (changed) when two-thirds of the Congress and two-thirds of the States agree
- Since 1789 the Constitution has been amended 27 times. The first ten Amendments were passed in 1791. They are called the **Bill of Rights** and guarantee freedom of speech, freedom of religion and the right to own guns, among other rights
- Later Amendments abolished slavery (14th) and gave women the right to vote (19th).

The importance of the Supreme Court

- The Constitution was written over 200 years ago when America was a small rural country
- It has not changed greatly since, yet it continues to work in a century when America is an urban, industrialised superpower
- The reason for this is the Supreme Court. As the United States changed, the Supreme Court interpreted the wording of the Constitution in ways which allowed it to deal with modern problems
- Federal and State courts are supposed to enforce the decisions of the Supreme Court
- People who want something in the law changed take cases to the Supreme Court, hoping it will support their point of view.

Parties

- Most Americans support one of the two major Parties, the **Republicans** and the **Democrats**:
  - ❍ Republicans usually represent business and favour low taxes and less power for the Federal government
  - ❍ Democrats usually represent poorer people and ethnic minorities, and want the Federal government to be involved in welfare and civil rights
- American parties are much less disciplined than Irish parties and Congressmen and Senators often vote independently of the party-line.

1.2 The Presidency from Roosevelt to Reagan 1945-1989

The growth of Presidential power: 1945-1990

- Since 1941, the United States has been involved in almost continuous warfare
- Because the President is Commander-in-Chief of the armed forces, war has greatly increased Presidential power at the expense of Congress
- Historians sometimes call this the 'Imperial Presidency'.

1933-1945: Franklin D Roosevelt (Democrat)

- Roosevelt led America during the Depression of the 1930s and most of the second World War. In dealing with these crises, he greatly expanded the powers of the President
- He was the only President in American history to be elected four times. After his death the Constitution was amended to make this impossible.

1945-1953: Harry Truman (Democrat)

Harry S Truman Democrat (1945-1953)

- Truman was Roosevelt's Vice President and became President when Roosevelt died on 12 April, 1945, shortly before Germany surrendered
- Fearing many American soldiers would die if the Allies had to invade Japan, he dropped the **atom bomb** on Hiroshima and Nagasaki in August. This forced a quick Japanese surrender
- Once Hitler was beaten, relations between the US and Soviet Union declined. Truman thought that Stalin planned to expand communism and conquer Europe. To stop him, Truman:
  - ○ Approved the investment of millions of dollars in Europe to help it recover from the effects of the war (**Marshall Aid**)
  - ○ Adopted the policy of '**containment**' to stop communist expansion
  - ○ Issued the **Truman Doctrine**, which promised American aid to any government opposing a communist take-over
- When Stalin blockaded **Berlin** in 1948, Truman ordered that supplies be airlifted into the city
- In 1949, he organised democratic European countries into the **North Atlantic Treaty Organisation** (NATO) to resist communist expansion
- When the communists under **Mao Zedong** took power in China 1949 Republicans accused Truman of '*losing China*'
- Truman sent US troops to defend **South Korea** in 1950 when it was invaded by the communist North. But he sacked **General McArthur** when he suggested using the atom bomb against China
- At home, the **GI Bill of Rights** gave special help to soldiers returning from the second World War. But the Republican-controlled Congress turned down Truman's proposal for a **Fair Deal** to provide more equal treatment for racial minorities and greater social security and housing for the poor
- His last years as President were dominated by the panic over communist infiltration (the '**red scare**') associated with **Senator Joseph McCarthy** (see page 223).

1953–1961: Dwight D Eisenhower (Republican)

- Eisenhower led the Allied armies to victory in the second World War and became a hero. In 1952, the Republicans chose him as their candidate and he won the Presidential election

- He arranged a truce which ended the Korean War in 1953, but continued Truman's policy of containing communists. This led him to begin America's involvement in Vietnam (see Section 2.5)

- Stalin's death in 1953 eased tension with the Soviet Union. Eisenhower held '**summit meetings**' with the new Soviet leader Nikita **Khrushchev**

- At home, he encouraged economic stability and saw the US enjoy eight years of economic growth

- He saw the start of the civil rights movement in the American South (see Section 5.2) and reluctantly sent troops in to enforce the law in Little Rock, Arkansas in 1957.

1961–1963: John F Kennedy (JFK) (Democrat)

- In 1960, Senator **John F Kennedy** narrowly defeated Vice-President, **Richard Nixon**. He was the first Roman Catholic President

- He accused the Republicans of letting the US fall behind the Russians in technology and promised to put a man on the moon

- In the Cold War (see Section 2.4) he faced crises over:
  - The building of the **Berlin Wall**
  - Soviet missiles in **Cuba**

- He increased American involvement in Vietnam

- He reluctantly supported the civil rights movement (see Section 5.3)

- He was assassinated in Dallas in November 1963.

1963–1969: Lyndon B Johnson (LBJ) (Democrat)

- As Vice-President, Johnson took over after Kennedy's death

- He supported the civil rights movement (see Section 5.3) and greatly increased help for the disadvantaged (the **Great Society**)

- He hugely increased American involvement in Vietnam (see Section 2.6) This diverted resources away from his social programmes and damaged the American economy (see Section 4.3)

- In 1968, he decided not to contest the election for President.

1969–1974: Richard M Nixon (Republican)

- Nixon saw men land on the moon (see Section 3.3) and slowly ended US involvement in Vietnam

- He encouraged a *détente* with the Soviets by visiting Moscow

- He also recognised the communist government in China and visited Beijing (see Section 2.8)

- He tried to improve the economy by freezing wages and devaluing the dollar
- His support for Israel led the Arab States to impose an **oil embargo** which damaged the economy (see Section 4.1)
- He won re-election in 1974, but during the campaign there was a break-in at the Democratic headquarters in the **Watergate** building in Washington. When he was linked to it, he was forced to resign.

1974 – 1977: Gerard Ford (Republican)

- Vice-President, Gerard Ford took over
- He officially ended the Vietnam war
- He continued the *détente* with the Soviet Union
- He faced economic problems with inflation and high unemployment, but failed to solve them
- His reputation was also damaged when the communists took over in South Vietnam.

1977 – 1981: Jimmy Carter (Democrat)

- He improved the economy but his policies were damaged by a second oil crisis in 1979–1980
- He negotiated a peace between Israel and Egypt at Camp David and negotiated a disarmament treaty with the Soviet Union (see Section 2.8)
- In **Iran**, after the 1979 Islamic Revolution, Americans were held hostage for over a year. Carter's failure to get them out probably cost him the election.

1981 – 1989: Ronald Reagan (Republican)

- Once a film star, then Governor of California, Reagan became President at the age of 69
- His economic policies involved large tax cuts for the rich and increased military spending (see Section 4.1)
- Inflation fell from the mid-1980s and employment increased
- He ended the *détente* with the Soviet Union, calling it an 'evil empire' and proposed building a 'star wars' missile system to protect the US from attack
- When a reformer, **Mikhail Gorbachev**, came to power in the Soviet Union, Reagan negotiated with him, thus contributing to the ending of communist rule in Europe in 1989 (see Section 2.8)
- In spite of many scandals he remained personally popular with the American people and was succeeded by his Vice-President, **George Bush**.

2.1   1945–1949: The Start of the Cold War

Introduction

- In the decades after the second World War, two powerful countries dominated the world – the **United States** and the **Soviet Union (USSR)**. They were known as the **superpowers**
- Rivalry with the Soviet Union was central to American foreign policy from 1945 to 1989. It is called the **Cold War** because the superpowers never actually fought one another directly
- However, they engaged in **indirect conflicts**, sometimes called '*proxy wars*' in **Korea, Vietnam, Afghanistan** and other places
- In the US, the deep fear of communism led to an anti-communist hysteria (**McCarthyism**) in the 1950s
- The Cold War also featured an **arms race** that included the development of nuclear weapons, inter-continental ballistic missiles and the **space race**
- The arms race and the space race produced a range of new technologies such as computers and the internet.

Ideological differences between the superpowers

- Distrust between the USSR and the US went back to the 1917 Russian revolution and was based on the **ideological differences** between them:
  - Lenin and after him, Stalin set up a **Marxist/communist dictatorship** in which all property, land and business belonged to the state
  - The US was a **democracy** that supported **unrestrained capitalism**, with most property, land and business belonging to individuals or private corporations.

1945–1948: The Cold War begins

- Despite the differences between them, the two countries joined together to defeat Hitler in the second World War
- But once peace came, the differences returned. They mainly concerned the fate of Europe once Hitler was beaten
- The US hoped that all countries in Europe would become capitalist democracies, but:
  - Between 1946 and 1948, Stalin imposed **communist dictatorships** on the countries in eastern Europe that his army controlled
  - In **France** and **Italy**, communist parties did well in elections
  - In **Greece**, a civil war broke out between communists and royalists.

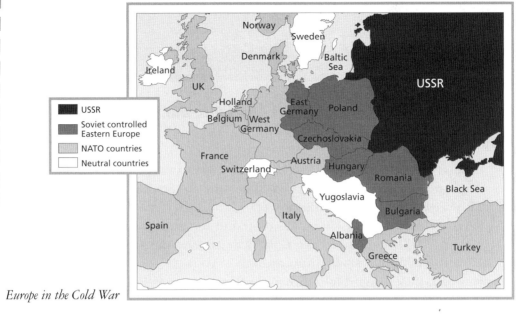

Europe in the Cold War

Containment, the Truman Doctrine and Marshall Aid

- Truman and his advisors thought these developments showed that Stalin planned to take over Europe
- To stop him, they adopted a policy called '**containment**'. That meant **containing** (i.e. keeping) Soviet power **within the area it controlled in 1945** – not letting it expand any further
- They issued the **Truman Doctrine**. It promised American aid to any government fighting a communist take-over
- They then sent military help to the Greek government
- To stop the Soviets taking over the rest of Europe they decided:
  ○ To keep US troops in Europe
  ○ To give billions of dollars in **Marshall Aid** to European governments to rebuild their economies. They hoped this would undermine support for communism.

Europe divided

- Western European governments accepted Marshall Aid and developed their economies along capitalist lines
- Stalin would not let the Eastern European countries he controlled to accept Marshall Aid. He forced them to become communist
- This divided Europe into the **pro-American capitalist West** and the **Soviet-controlled communist East**
- The dividing line between them, known as the **iron curtain**, ran through Germany. This created a number of crises during the Cold War.

Remember...

In 1946, Churchill called the line dividing Stalin's Europe from the rest '**the iron curtain**'.

1948 – 1949: Germany after the second World War

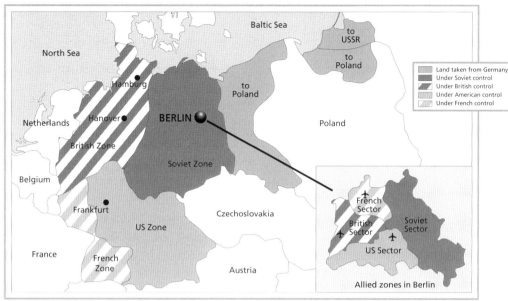

Germany after 1945

- As the war ended in 1945, the allied leaders met in **Yalta** and **Potsdam**
- They agreed to **divide Germany** and its capital **Berlin** into four zones, each run by one of the Allies, the USSR, the US, Britain and France
- In 1948, the three western Allies joined their zones together, accepted Marshall Aid and began to develop a democratic German government
- In 1949, this became **the Federal Republic of Germany (West Germany)**
- Stalin refused to let his zone accept Marshall Aid and imposed a communist dictatorship on it. It became the **German Democratic Republic (East Germany)**.

1948 – 1949: The Berlin Blockade

- Berlin was deep inside the **Soviet zone**. In 1945, it too was divided into four zones. Two million people lived in the zones which the western Allies controlled (**West Berlin**)
- To get to West Berlin, the western Allies had to use road, rail and air transport which crossed Soviet-controlled territory
- In 1948, as tension rose between the two sides, Stalin closed **all land routes** from West Germany to West Berlin. He did not think the western allies could supply Berlin by air alone
- Truman decided to challenge Stalin's blockade. For 11 months, US aircraft carried food, fuel and other supplies to the people of west Berlin (the **Berlin Airlift**)
- In 1949, Stalin gave in and allowed land transport to resume.

1949: The key year in the Cold War

- As well as the Berlin blockade, a number of other developments made 1949 the crucial year in the Cold War
- **China becomes communist**
  - ○ In the second World War the Chinese joined the Allies against Japan which occupied large parts of China
  - ○ When the war ended, Chinese nationalists led by **Chiang Kai-shek** fought a civil war with the Chinese communists, led by **Mao Zedong**
  - ○ In 1949, the communists won. China became a communist State, the **People's Republic of China**
  - ○ Chiang's Chinese nationalists withdrew to the island of **Taiwan** and claimed they were the real government of China
  - ○ The Americans recognised this claim. For many years they refused to let communist China take China's place on the United Nations Security Council
- **Military Alliances: NATO**
  - ○ The Berlin Blockade, Stalin's treatment of Eastern Europe and communist victory in China encouraged the US, Canada and ten democratic countries in Europe to form the **North Atlantic Treaty Organisation (NATO)**
  - ○ It was an American-led military alliance that aimed to stop Soviet expansion in Europe
- **The Soviet Union's atom bomb**
  - ○ From 1945 to 1949, the US was the only country with an **atom bomb**. This gave it an advantage over the USSR
  - ○ But in 1949, Soviet scientists exploded the USSR's **own A-bomb**. This equalised the relationship between them
  - ○ This began **an arms race** between the two superpowers (see Section 3.1).

2.2 McCarthyism and the Cold War inside America

Anti-communist 'witch-hunts' in America

- The start of the Cold War and communist expansion in Europe and Asia led to a '**red scare**' in America
- People saw communist conspiracies everywhere. A **Loyalty Program** was set up to root out government workers suspected of communist sympathies
- In 1947, the House of Representatives set up the **House Un-American Activities Committee (HUAC)**. It searched out '*communist sympathisers*' especially in the film industry

> **Remember...**
>
> **Witch-hunt:** called after a panic in 17th century America when hysterical accusations of witchcraft led to many innocent people being punished.

- Artists and writers were called before it and asked about their involvement in left-wing activities
- The only way to escape censure was to denounce others. Some did; others did not and were **blacklisted**, making it hard for them to find work
- The panic increased in 1949 with the communist victory in China and the Soviet A-Bomb. Many believed that there were communist spies in the US government and several people were tried in sensational spy trials
- Republicans accused the Democrats of being '*soft on communism*' and blamed Truman for '*losing China*'
- This anti-communist hysteria reached its peak between 1950 and 1953, under the leadership of **Senator Joseph McCarthy**. Because of this it is sometimes referred to as **McCarthyism**.

Joseph McCarthy (1908–1957)

- Born in Wisconsin, Joseph McCarthy was first a Democrat, but joined the Republicans after he failed to be chosen as a Democratic candidate. In the war he had a desk job, but he won a Senate seat by lying about his war record
- In 1950, fearing he would not be re-elected, he launched an anti-communist witch-hunt using information leaked to him by journalists and his friend, **J Edgar Hoover**, head of the FBI
- He claimed that 57 people in the State Department (Foreign Ministry) were members of the Communist Party and were passing information to the Soviets. The Truman government, he said, knew this and did nothing
- None of this was accurate, but when Democrats protested he said this proved they were communist sympathisers. Some of those who opposed him lost their seats in the 1950 elections. That made others cautious about challenging him
- As chairman of the **Senate Committee on Government Operations** he was able to call civil servants before him, questioning them about past left-wing sympathies. He made it clear that the only way to show they were loyal to the US was to name others who might have been involved with them in the past
- At first many Americans believed McCarthy. His campaign, which was aimed mainly at Democrats, helped the Republican **Dwight D Eisenhower** win the 1952 election
- Eisenhower disapproved of McCarthy, but dared not oppose him publicly
- In 1953, a TV documentary damaged McCarthy's credibility. Then he attacked the US army, and his investigations were televised. This exposed and discredited his bullying tactics. In 1954, the Senate censured him and ended his brief reign of terror. He died, of alcoholism it is thought, in 1957
- About 10,000 Americans were imprisoned or lost their jobs as a result of the McCarthy's witch-hunts
- McCarthyism damaged America's image as a free country and gave a propaganda victory to the Soviet Union.

2.3 1949–1961: Korea and the Cold War in the 1950s

The Cold War spreads to Asia

- In Asia, the second World War ended when the Americans dropped the atom bomb on two Japanese cities in 1945. The Japanese surrendered and the US army occupied the country
- But after China became communist, the Americans organised a democratic government in Japan, helped them rebuild their economy and made a treaty allowing American bases to stay there
- The Americans also formed alliances with other anti-communist governments in Asia, promising to defend them against a communist attack.

1950–1953: The Korean War

- Before the second World War, **Korea** was a Japanese colony. When the Japanese surrendered, the Soviets occupied the north of Korea, as far south as the **38th parallel**, and the Americans occupied the south
- This partition was meant to be temporary but as the Cold War developed it became permanent. In **North Korea**, Stalin backed a communist dictator **Kim il Sung** while the Americans supported a capitalist dictator in **South Korea**
- In 1950, Kim invaded South Korea, aiming to unite the country under his control
- With the support of the **United Nations**, Truman sent an American-led army to defend South Korea and uphold the policy of containment
- UN forces, led by **General McArthur**, defeated the North Koreans at the **Battle of Inchon** but McArthur then invaded North Korea, against Truman's wishes
- This brought the Chinese into the war and forced the UN forces back to the 38th parallel. When McArthur publicly suggested invading China, Truman sacked him
- In 1953, Stalin died and the new US President, **Eisenhower**, agreed to a truce, with both sides back where they started at the 38th parallel.

Remember…

In 1950, the Soviets had boycotted the UN because the US blocked the admission of communist China, so Truman was able to get his resolution about Korea passed.

The results of the Korean War

- About 2.5 million people died, including over 30,000 American soldiers
- Concern about the war helped Eisenhower become President
- US spending on arms increased greatly
- The Americans became more involved in Asia, setting up another anti-communist alliance, the **South-East Asian Treaty Organisation (SEATO)**

- They also developed the '**domino theory**' which led to their involvement in Vietnam (see Section 2.5).

Eisenhower and Khrushchev

- After Stalin's death, the new Soviet leader **Nikita Khrushchev** said he wanted '**peaceful co-existence**' with the west
- That eased the tension between the Americans and the Soviets
- Khrushchev visited America and met Eisenhower. This began the '**summit conferences**', by which the leaders of the two superpowers kept in touch throughout the Cold War.

Superpower tension in the 1950s

But rivalry between the two sides remained and could sometimes erupt into a crisis.

- **Khrushchev:**
  - ○ He continued the arms race. At first it seemed the Soviets had gained the upper hand when they put up the first man-made earth satellite (**sputnik**) in 1957 and the first man in space (**Yuri Gagarin**) in 1961
  - ○ He also supported independence movements in Asia and Africa, hoping the newly independent countries would adopt communism
  - ○ His biggest *coup* was to get **Fidel Castro** to agree to set up Soviet missiles in **Cuba** (see below).
- **Eisenhower:**
  - ○ He supported anti-communist regimes around the world, even when they were unsavoury dictatorships
  - ○ But when people rebelled against Soviet tyranny in **East Germany** in 1953 and **Hungary** in 1956 he did nothing to help them because they were already under Soviet control
  - ○ To counter Soviet success in space, he set up the **National Aeronautics and Space Administration** (**NASA**) in 1958 and increased military spending
  - ○ He used high-flying **U2 planes** to spy on the USSR. When one was shot down in 1960, on the eve of a summit conference, it damaged relations between the superpowers.

2.4 Kennedy's foreign policy, 1961–1963

John F Kennedy's foreign policy

- In 1960, the Democrat, John F Kennedy, won the Presidential election. He was assassinated in 1963
- Three important foreign events happened while he was President:
  - ○ The building of the Berlin wall
  - ○ The 'Bay of Pigs' and the Cuban Missile Crisis
  - ○ America's growing involvement in Vietnam.

1961: The Berlin Wall

- In the 1950s, West Germany prospered, while East Germany did not. Many East Germans went to Berlin to escape to the West
- To stop them, the East German government, with Khrushchev's backing, **built a wall** on the border between East and West Berlin
- Kennedy went to Berlin soon after. He spoke to the people of the city (*'Ich bin ein Berliner'*), but did nothing about the Wall which remained as a visible symbol of the division of Europe throughout the Cold War.

1963: The Cuban Missile Crisis

- Cuba is a Caribbean island 90 miles south of Florida. Up to 1959, it was ruled by an unpleasant dictator, General Batista, and its economy was dominated by American businesses
- In 1959, **Fidel Castro** overthrew Batista and took over the American companies. The American government then imposed a trade embargo on Cuba and Castro turned for help to the Soviet Union
- When Kennedy became President, he approved a CIA plan to invade Cuba and overthrow Castro. The invasion force landed at the **Bay of Pigs**, but was easily defeated

Remember...

CIA = Central Intelligence Agency, i.e. America's spies.

- After this, Castro agreed to Khrushchev's plan to build missile-launching sites in Cuba. Missiles from there could reach American cities which, until then, had been safe from Soviet attack
- American spy planes photographed the sites. After some hesitation, Kennedy imposed a naval blockade on Cuba to stop Soviet ships arriving with missiles
- War threatened, but Khrushchev backed down. In return for the removal of missiles from Cuba, Kennedy secretly removed US missiles in Turkey.

The results of the Cuban Missile Crisis

- Realising how near they had come to war, a 'hot-line' was installed between the Kremlin and the White House to let the leaders communicate with each other
- In 1964, Khrushchev was replaced as Soviet leader by **Leonid Brezhnev**. He was in favour of *détente* (i.e. reducing the tension between the two sides)
- Disarmament talks began, leading to international treaties which limited the **testing** and **proliferation** (spread) of nuclear weapons (see Section 3.1).

2.5 How America became involved in Vietnam

Vietnam before 1945

- Vietnam was an ancient kingdom in south-east Asia. After resisting the Chinese for centuries, it was taken over by the French in the 19th century, along with the neighbouring kingdoms of **Cambodia** and **Laos**

- In the second World War, the Japanese invaded. Resistance to them was organised by the **Vietminh**, whose leader was **Ho Chi Minh**
- Ho Chi Minh was a nationalist who had spent many years in exile in the United States and Europe. He was influenced by the ideas of **Karl Marx** and **Lenin**
- After Japan was defeated, Ho Chi Minh hoped that the US would back Vietnamese independence. Instead, Truman backed the return of the French because he needed their support in Europe.

War between the Vietminh and the French

- In 1946, the Vietminh began a War of Independence
- By 1950, their army led by the brilliant **General Giap**, had 250,000 men. They got arms from the USSR and from China after the communists took power there in 1949
- Eisenhower supported the French against the Vietminh. By 1954, the US was paying 80% of the cost of the French army
- They did this because:
  - ❍ They believed Ho Chi Minh was a communist allied to Stalin and Mao Tse Tung. If he won, communist power would expand in south-east Asia, thus breaching their policy of containment
  - ❍ They had developed the '**domino theory**'. It said that if one country in Asia fell to the communists, others were bound to fall too (like a row of dominoes)
  - ❍ Republicans accused Truman of '*losing China*' and won the 1952 Presidential election as a result. No later President dared to '*lose*' Vietnam.

1954: Dien Bien Phu and the Geneva Accords

- Giap used guerrilla tactics to wear down the French, and in 1954 he defeated a big French army at **Dien Bien Phu**
- This forced the French to make the **Geneva Accords** which divided Vietnam along the 17th parallel into:
  - ❍ **North Vietnam**, with Hanoi as its capital, under a communist regime headed by **Ho Chi Minh**

○ **South Vietnam**, with Saigon as its capital, under a capitalist regime led by **Ngo Dinh Diem**
○ France also recognised the independence of **Cambodia** and **Laos**.
● The Geneva Accords said there would be elections to unify Vietnam, but Diem refused to hold them, fearing he would lose. The Americans backed this decision.

The war resumes

● From 1954 to 1959, Ho Chi Minh consolidated his grip on North Vietnam. He imposed collectivisation on the peasants (farmers) and brutally suppressed resistance
● In 1957, Ho Chi Minh and Giap began their campaign to re-unite Vietnam. They used South Vietnamese communists (**Vietcong**) and the North Vietnamese Army (**NVA**) to wage a guerrilla war against the South Vietnamese government
● Soldiers and supplies went to South Vietnam through Laos and Cambodia along the route known as the **Ho Chi Minh Trail**.

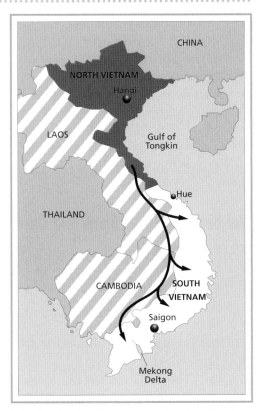

The Ho Chi Minh trail from North to South Vietnam passed through Laos and Cambodia

Direct American involvement begins

● Eisenhower backed Diem's government in South Vietnam, even though it was corrupt and unpopular
● From 1955 to 1961, he spent billions of dollars and sent almost 1,000 'advisers', about half of them military, to support the South Vietnamese.

Kennedy and Vietnam

● The next President, **John F Kennedy**, advised by his Secretary of State, **Dean Rusk**, and his Secretary for Defence, **Robert McNamara**, increased US support for Diem's government

- They did this because:
  - Communists had several successes (Bay of Pigs, Berlin Wall) and they could not let them win in Vietnam too
  - They believed in the domino theory
  - They knew little about Vietnam and did not understand that many South Vietnamese wanted unity and hated Diem
- Kennedy sent large numbers of tanks and aircraft to strengthen the South Vietnamese army (**ARVN**) and increased the number of US 'advisors' to 16,000
- But US weapons, designed for war in Europe, did not suit a guerrilla war in the mountainous and jungle-covered Vietnamese countryside.

The fall of Diem

- By 1963, Kennedy knew that Diem was a problem:
  - Diem had rounded up peasants and put them in '**strategic hamlets**', i.e. villages fortified against a Vietcong attack. The peasants hated being moved from their lands, so this only increased support for the Vietcong
  - He was a Catholic and favoured the small Catholic minority over the Buddhist majority
  - He appointed Catholics to command the South Vietnamese army (**ARVN**), regardless of their ability. This made it less able to stand up to the Vietcong
  - In 1963, his soldiers fired on a Buddhist march, killing seven. In protest, a 73 year-old-Buddhist priest burned himself to death
- Kennedy became convinced that Diem had to go. In November 1963, the ARVN, with American approval, overthrew and killed him
- From then on, South Vietnam was ruled by a succession of military dictators.

●●●Case study

2.6 Lyndon Johnson and the Vietnam War
President Lyndon B Johnson (1963–1969)

- Shortly after Diem's death, Kennedy was assassinated and his Vice-President, **Lyndon B Johnson (LBJ)** became President
- Johnson promised to continue with Kennedy's policies, including in Vietnam. He did this because:
  - The emotion created by Kennedy's assassination made it difficult to question anything he had done
  - Knowing little about foreign affairs, he kept Rusk and McNamara as his advisers. They encouraged him to believe in the domino theory

- ○ Johnson was strongly anti-communist. He did not want to see them extend their power and as a patriotic American he did not want to admit the US might be defeated
- ○ He feared he and the Democratic Party would lose the 1964 election if he 'lost' Vietnam
- For these reasons Johnson escalated American involvement in Vietnam well beyond anything considered before.

August 1964: The Gulf of Tonkin

- Early in 1964, Ho Chi Minh sent more North Vietnamese soldiers south to support the Vietcong. The Soviets and Chinese also increased their supplies of arms. By March, the communists controlled about half of South Vietnam
- The South Vietnamese asked the Americans for more help
- By then, the US Presidential election campaign was under way, with Republicans accusing Johnson of being '*soft on communism*'
- Rusk and McNamara advised Johnson to increase the number of US troops and begin bombing North Vietnam, but he needed an excuse to convince Congress to back him. He got it in the '**Gulf of Tonkin**' incident
- The Americans claimed that on 2 August, North Vietnamese gunboats made unprovoked attacks on two American ships in the Gulf of Tonkin. It is still not clear whether this really happened or whether the Americans manufactured the incident
- On 7 August, the Senate passed **Gulf of Tonkin Resolution**. It allowed Johnson to 'take any necessary steps' to defend the US and its Allies. Most Americans approved of this decision (according to opinion polls).

The 1964 Presidential election

- Johnson then launched limited bombing missions against North Vietnam. This made him look tough which was important for the election campaign
- However he also reassured opponents of war by promising: '*We are not going to send American boys away from home to do what Asian boys ought to be doing for themselves*'
- Many voters feared his opponent, **Barry Goldwater**, would increase American involvement, so Johnson was re-elected by a large majority
- He believed this gave him a mandate to continue with the war and to increase American involvement.

Winter 1964–1965: What to do about Vietnam?

- After the election, Johnson had to decide what to do about Vietnam. His advisors were divided:
- ○ A minority were '*doves*'. They questioned the domino theory, wondered if Vietnam really was important for America, and even supported the idea of withdrawal

- ○ A majority, including most senior generals, were '**hawks**'. They wanted to increase American involvement, perhaps use nuclear weapons, or even attack China because of its support for North Vietnam
- Over the winter of 1964–1965 the Vietcong attacked American installations in South Vietnam. This showed that the South Vietnamese were not able to resist alone
- Opinion polls showed that 70% of Americans supported the bombing of North Vietnam and opposed withdrawal
- These developments explain why Johnson escalated the war in 1965, though not as much as some 'hawks' wanted.

1965: The war escalates

- In February 1965, Johnson ordered the bombing of North Vietnam to increase. The aim was to
  - ○ Undermine the will of the northerners to go on fighting
  - ○ Destroy North Vietnamese industry
  - ○ Stop the flow of arms and soldiers along the Ho Chi Minh trail
- Called '*Operation Rolling Thunder*', it was supposed to end after eight weeks, but went on for three years
- In March, **General Westmoreland**, the US commander in South Vietnam, asked for more ground troops, and by April, Johnson had sent over 20,000
- The numbers continued to rise through the rest of 1965, reaching 500,000 by 1966
- In all, about 2.7 million American soldiers served in Vietnam.

How the war was fought

- The Vietcong used **guerrilla tactics**. They staged ambushes, booby-trapped houses and villages, dressed as peasants to launch surprise attacks and used the jungle for cover
- Westmoreland sent his soldiers on '*search and destroy*' missions to root out the Vietcong. They measured their success in '*body counts*'. Every body was counted as a Vietcong
- But as they could not tell which Vietnamese were Vietcong and which were not, they killed many innocent civilians
- The US air force bombed towns and villages. They dropped cluster bombs that scattered hundreds of smaller bombs and **napalm** which burned into the skin
- The Vietnamese dug tunnels as escape routes and bomb shelters, retreating into them when the bombers came
- To make it easier to see its enemies, the air force sprayed herbicides (weed killers), mostly **Agent Orange**, over six million acres of trees and crops
- This killed many Vietnamese people. The herbicides also affected pregnant women, leading to birth defects

- Americans de-personalised the Vietnamese, calling them 'gooks'. That made it easier to ignore the suffering they were causing.

The collapse of American morale

- Many soldiers serving in Vietnam were **conscripts** (i.e. they were forced to fight). In theory, all young men could be drafted to serve in the army, but in practice well off boys could easily '*dodge the draft*' by going to university
- As a result, most soldiers came from poor white or black families. They felt the draft was unfair
- This lowered the morale of American troops. Over a third took drugs, many deserted and some killed unpopular officers
- To survive, many soldiers tried to avoid any contact with the enemy. Others behaved savagely towards the Vietnamese. The most notorious case was the **My Lai Massacre** in 1968, when troops killed 347 men, women and children in one village.

Opposition to the war in America

- As the war dragged on and the number of deaths rose, many Americans began to wonder if they should be in Vietnam
- Newspaper reports and TV images showing how American actions affected the Vietnamese strengthened these doubts
- Opposition to the war first developed among students, many of whom faced the possibility of conscription. From the mid-1960s, there were marches and demonstrations protesting at the war
- The number of 'doves' in the Democratic Party grew, with Congressmen and Senators coming out against the war
- Respected black leaders, like Martin Luther King and Muhammad Ali, began to oppose it, claiming that black men were fighting a white man's war.

The 1968 Tet Offensive and its result

- Up to 1968, Americans could still believe they were winning, but the **Tet Offensive** shattered this view
- The North Vietnamese chose the Tet holiday for a surprise attack. They entered the US embassy in Saigon and briefly captured the ancient city of Hué
- They hoped the South Vietnamese would support them, but they did not. The South Vietnamese army fought well and after a few weeks they had regained control
- Tet was a military victory for the US, but a political defeat. Images of North Vietnamese in their embassy profoundly shocked Americans. Support for the war fell further

Remember...

Tet = Vietnamese New Year holiday

- Because of this Johnson decided not to contest the 1968 election, which was won by the Republican candidate **Richard Nixon**.

Assessing Johnson's role in the Vietnam war

- Johnson's involvement in the Vietnam war overshadowed his achievements in other areas like civil rights and social welfare
- The war diverted resources from these projects and made them less effective
- He refused to raise taxes to pay for the war and this created inflation which undermined the US economy in the 1970s
- His inability to either win or leave destroyed his career and forced him to retire early.

2.7 America leaves Vietnam
Nixon and the Vietnam war

- President Nixon wanted to get out of Vietnam. He proposed '*Vietnamisation*', i.e. letting the South Vietnamese do most of the fighting. He also extended the bombing into Cambodia to destroy the Ho Chi Minh Trail
- Between 1969 and 1972, he gradually reduced the number of troops from over 500,000 to under 70,000
- This undermined the anti-war movement, but protests continued. The most notable was at **Kent State University** in May 1970, when National Guardsmen killed four students
- The leaking of the *Pentagon Papers*, which showed that Johnson had lied about the progress of the war, also increased support for a pull-out.

1973: The war ends

- Nixon hoped to talk to the North Vietnamese, and when they refused he launched **Operation Linebacker** to bomb North Vietnamese cities. As a result, the North agreed to peace negotiations
- In January 1973, an agreement was reached with the North Vietnamese:
  - They agreed to a ceasefire and to return all US prisoners
  - The US agreed to leave within 60 days
- The Americans left Vietnam in **March 1973**
- War continued between North and South Vietnam. In 1975, the North invaded and the South collapsed. Saigon fell on 30 April, and was renamed **Ho Chi Minh city**.

The results of the Vietnam war

- It was America's longest war in which 58,000 US soldiers died, as well as about 2.3 million Vietnamese
- The war cost the Americans about $110 billion and damaged the American economy in the 1970s
- In 1975, Vietnam was re-united under communist rule and communists gained control of neighbouring Laos and Cambodia
- The war divided Americans more deeply than at any time since the Civil War in the 1860s. Americans began to distrust their governments and support for the Democratic Party fell.

2.8 1973 – 1989: Nixon, Reagan and the last years of the Cold War

Détente 1962 – 1979

- The Cuban Missile Crisis in 1962 showed the superpowers that they could destroy each other and the world. This led to a period of *détente*
- *Détente* also happened because:
  - The Americans were caught up in Vietnam
  - The Soviet leader **Leonid Brezhnev** was in dispute with China and wanted to reduce tension with the US
  - Nixon's Secretary of State **Henry Kissinger** argued that the Soviets were not a threat and that the US could weaken them by taking advantage of their quarrel with China

> **Remember…**
>
> *Détente* = an easing of tension

  - Nixon accepted China's membership of the United Nations and made a State visit to China
- *Détente* led to a number of agreements which reduced the threat of a nuclear war:
  - The **Test Ban Treaty** (1963) ended above-ground testing
  - The **Nuclear non-Proliferation Treaty** (1968) limited the spread of nuclear weapons
  - **Strategic Arms Limitation Talks (SALT)** began in 1969 leading to agreement to restrict the numbers of missiles each side had
  - A second round of talks (**SALT II**) led to the **Helsinki Final Act** in 1975. Thirty five countries accepted the boundaries of Europe set after the second World War, and agreed to monitor how governments respected the civil rights of their people
  - In 1975, the two superpowers co-operated in a joint space programme, the **Apollo-Soyuz Project**
  - In 1979, the **SALT II Agreement** further limited the numbers of nuclear weapons.

The end of Détente

- *Détente* ended in 1979 when:
  - ○ President Carter's concern about human rights in the Soviet Union angered the Russians
  - ○ Republicans attacked SALT II as weakening America. To appease them, Carter approved a new missile system and increased military spending
  - ○ The Russians invaded Afghanistan
  - ○ Carter then imposed trade sanctions on the USSR, stopped the ratification (i.e implementing) of SALT II, and announced a US boycott of the Moscow Olympic Games in 1980.

Ronald Reagan and the end of Détente

- Reagan, a former film star, saw the Cold War as a conflict between good and evil and was not interested in diplomacy
- He abandoned SALT II and constantly criticised the Soviet record on human rights
- He helped Islamic militants who were fighting the Soviets in Afghanistan and supported various right-wing dictatorships in South America
- He increased military spending by 50%, and in 1983, announced the **Strategic Defence Initiative** (nicknamed 'Star Wars') to build a counter-missile system
- The Soviets saw this as a return to the arms race, but realised they could not match US spending. They thought Reagan was a war-monger and they seriously feared a US attack.

Mikhail Gorbachev and the end of the Cold War

- In 1985, a younger man, **Mikhail Gorbachev**, became the leader of the Soviet Union. He wanted economic and political reform, but to do so he needed to improve relations with the US
- Meetings between Reagan and Gorbachev led to the **Intermediate Range Nuclear Forces Treaty** in 1987. Both sides eliminated many missiles
- Gorbachev's reforms in the USSR encouraged people in the communist countries of Eastern Europe to demand democracy
- In 1989, Gorbachev made it clear that the Soviets would not send in tanks to support the communist governments there
- Starting in Hungary, one communist government after another collapsed. In November 1989, the East Germans opened the **Berlin Wall**, thus symbolically ending the Cold War
- In 1991 the Soviet Union itself collapsed.

3.1 The arms race and the Cold War

The arms race and the Cold War

- During the second World War the United States spent vast sums of money on developing new weapons. Their main achievement was the **atom bomb**, which they used against Japan in 1945
- During the Cold War, the two superpowers also competed to produce more deadly weapons and the means to deliver them. This is called the **arms race**
- This arms race also led to the invention and development of new technologies, such as computers and the internet, which were of value to civilian society.

The Military-Industrial Complex

- The arms race poured huge sums of money into large American firms like Boeing and IBM to develop new weapons systems
- This link between the army and business is often called the **Military-Industrial Complex**. Some American political leaders fear that it had a bad effect on American democracy.

Developing bigger bombs

- In 1949, the Soviet Union exploded its own atom bomb. This encouraged the US to produce a **hydrogen bomb** in 1952. It was over 1,000 times more powerful than the first A-bomb
- In the early 1960s, a **neutron bomb** was developed. It was designed to kill people, while leaving the buildings standing
- Tests of these bombs were carried on in the open, leading to contamination by radiation. This ended with the **Test Ban Treaty** in 1963.

Developing delivery systems

- **Planes**: After the second World War the **jet engine** appeared. The US first used jet planes in Korea. Supersonic planes appeared in the 1950s. In the 1980s, **stealth** technology produced planes which could avoid detection by enemy radar
- The US also produced huge **air-craft carriers**, nuclear powered from the 1980s, which could carry American air-power to any part of the world
- **Missiles**: The **Minuteman**, developed in 1962, could be fired at short notice from underground bunkers and carry nuclear war-heads into the

Soviet Union. Later, missiles like the **Peacekeeper**, were developed – it had the ability to break into several war-heads, each carrying a bomb to a separate target

- **Nuclear-powered submarines** were developed in the 1960s. Able to cruise for long periods under the sea, they were armed with **Polaris**, and later **Trident**, missiles carrying nuclear bombs. Americans believed that the Soviets would be **deterred** from attacking by the knowledge that the submarines could retaliate, even if the US was destroyed.

Spying on the enemy

- The US wanted to watch what the Soviet Union was doing. At first, they used high-flying planes like the U-2 which could fly at 70,000 feet
- Later, they developed spy-satellites which orbited the earth, taking photographs and listening in on radio communications. These then developed into **Global Positioning Systems (GPS)**, which allowed soldiers to identify targets on the battlefield.

The theory of deterrence

- By the 1970s, each side had enough weapons to destroy the other (and the earth) many times over
- Some historians think that may have **deterred** (stopped) the superpowers from going to war because they feared 'mutually assured destruction' (**MAD**) (i.e. everyone would be destroyed).

3.2 Developments in Information Technology

Early computers

- Weapons systems and space exploration depended on **powerful computers**
- The first computers were built in England to help break secret German codes. The American military took them over and produced the first general computer in 1946. Weighing 19 tonnes, it was used in nuclear research
- The first commercial computer, the **Universal Automatic Computer (UNIVAC)** appeared in 1951. Using punch cards to input information, it cost over $1 million, occupied a lot of space and its memory could only hold 1,000 words
- The invention of the **transistor** changed computing. Computers from the 1960s, most of them made by IBM, were cheaper and easier to programme, but they still occupied a separate room. Most were used by banks and universities.

Personal computers

- To do more complex calculations several transistors were combined on a piece of silicon. These **integrated circuits** or **microchips** allowed computers to become smaller and faster
- In the 1970s, the development of the **micro-processor** led to the personal computer with a small screen. Operators no longer needed cards but could type information in directly
- **Apple** developed the first personal computer in 1976. They were affordable and easy to use. The **Apple Macintosh** (1984) was the first to use a mouse and a drop-down menu
- Through the 1980s, computers got smaller, more powerful and cheaper. The number of home computers rocketed. The **Microsoft** company came to dominate the market
- The spread of personal computers led to computer games, such as **Nintendo** and **Game Boy**.

The Internet

- The US military worried about what would happen if a Soviet bomb blew up their central control. To avoid that they created a network of computers (**ARPANET**) loosely linked together (i.e sharing information), which could survive an attack. This formed the basis of the modern **internet**
- At first, this just linked universities, but around 1990 it took off with ordinary people buying computers and linking up
- Developments in **fibre optics** in the 1990s allowed vast quantities of information to be carried along a phone line to a computer with a modem.

●●●Case study

3.3 The space race and the Moon Landing

1945-1961: Competing rocket technologies

- The most spectacular aspect of the arms race was the moon landing. It grew out of the competition between the superpowers to develop bigger and better rockets to carry their weapons into the enemy's territory
- During the second World War, the Nazis developed the **V1** and **V2** rockets. In 1945, the Soviets and Americans competed to capture German rocket scientists. The US got **Werner Von Braun**, head of the German research team
- The US did little about rocket technology until the Russians launched the first **Inter-Continental Ballistic Missile (ICBM)**, and the first man-made earth satellite, **sputnik**, in 1957
- This created panic in America: could the Soviets launch a rocket attack from space? Was there a '*missile gap*'? Spending on missile technology grew rapidly

- Late in 1957, the Americans launched their first ICBM, the **Atlas rocket**. In 1958, they sent up their first earth satellite and Eisenhower established the **National Aeronautics and Space Administration (NASA)** to encourage space exploration
- But the Soviets were still ahead. In 1960, their **Luna II** rocket hit the moon and in 1961 their astronaut, **Yuri Gagarin** became the first man in space
- These developments spurred President Kennedy to promise in 1961 that the US would put a man on the moon by the end of the 1960s.

The first steps

- To land men on the moon, NASA first had to find out if they could survive in space and be safely returned to earth
- The **Mercury Programme** (1959–1963) flew six manned test flights. As part of the programme, **John Glen** became the first American to orbit the earth in 1962
- In the **Gemini Project** (1963–1966), ten space flights tested and improved ways of controlling craft in space and linking one space craft to another (**docking**)
- The 1965, **Gemini** 4 saw the first American 'space walk' when an astronaut left the craft and returned safely
- In 1967, **Gemini** 7 spent two weeks in space showing that men could survive a long period of weightlessness and **Gemini 8** successfully docked two space craft.

The Apollo Programme (1961–1972)

- The **Apollo Programme** was to carry out the moon landing
- It used the **Saturn V**, the most powerful rocket ever built. It was designed by Werner von Braun. Holding one million gallons of fuel, it was divided into three stages. After blast off, stages dropped away one by one to save weight
- The Saturn rocket carried:
  - A **Command Module** (**Columbia**), where the astronauts lived. Designed to orbit the moon and return to earth, it was enclosed in special tiles which could withstand high temperatures on re-entry to the earth's atmosphere
  - A **Lunar Module** (nicknamed the **Eagle**) which was to break away from the Command Module and land on the moon. It had two stages. The **lower** contained exploration equipment and rockets to slow down the descent onto the moon. It was to be left behind on the moon. The **upper** would carry the astronauts back to the Command Module
- To test each step, there were ten Apollo missions before the moon landing. NASA used the lessons learned from each mission to improve the design of its rockets and modules

- In December 1968, **Apollo 8** carried three men into orbit around the moon and returned them safely to earth
- In 1969, **Apollo 10** took another three to within nine miles of the moon's surface and returned safely
- By July 1969, everything was in place for the final attempt.

16 – 19 July: The journey to the moon

- At 9.32 am on 16 July, **Apollo 11** lifted off from the Kennedy Space Centre in Florida. It carried three men, **Neil Armstrong, Buzz Aldrin** and **Michael Collins** – who had been chosen from 20 trained astronauts, to go to the moon
- After orbiting the earth, thruster rockets sent the Command Module, **Columbia**, towards the moon at 25,000 mph
- The journey took three days. Conditions in Columbia were cramped. The men had to adapt to weightlessness. They had to squeeze food into their mouths and tie themselves into their bunks to sleep
- On 19 July, Columbia went into orbit 69 miles above the surface of the moon. It circled the moon every two hours.

20 July: Landing on the moon

- Collins remained in Columbia, while Armstrong and Aldrin transferred to the Lunar Module
- It separated from Columbia and headed for the moon's surface, at all times being under the control of computers at Mission Control in Florida
- As they approached the surface, they saw the chosen landing site was covered with rocks. Armstrong took the controls and guided the Module to a flat area in the **Sea of Tranquillity**
- Cheering broke out in Mission Control when they heard him report: "*The Eagle has landed*"
- The astronauts checked the equipment and then put on their space suits. Armstrong went first, setting off a TV camera to record the moment. He said: "*That's one small step for man – one giant leap for mankind*"
- The moment was watched by an estimated 600 million people back on earth
- The two men planted the American flag, collected about 60 pounds of moon rock, took many pictures and set up a number of scientific experiments.

The journey home

- After that, Armstrong and Aldrin returned to the Lunar Module. They left unnecessary equipment behind and blasted off for the waiting Columbia. After docking with it, they abandoned the Lunar Module too

- Columbia reached earth again on 24 July. Parachutes slowed its descent into the Pacific
- Navy divers helped the astronauts out and they transferred to an aircraft carrier where President Nixon greeted them
- The return was watched by millions of television viewers around the world. But reports of this American success were not broadcast in the USSR or China.

Later Apollo flights and the end of the space race

- There were five more moon landings between 1969 and 1972
- **Apollo 13** almost turned into a disaster when an oxygen tank exploded. As the world watched with bated breath, the astronauts got home safely, crammed into the Lunar Module
- The 1972 Apollo mission was the last. Interest in manned space exploration had declined since the first moon landing
- It had cost $27 billion to put men on the moon and many Americans did not see why they should go on with this hugely expensive operation once they had achieved their aim
- The US economy declined in the 1970s, so less money was available and the *détente* with the Soviet Union reduced the need to compete with it
- The US turned to other, less expensive, forms of space exploration, sending unmanned probes to nearby planets, like Mars and Venus, to take photographs and make scientific observations
- It also tried with limited success to develop a re-usable 'space shuttle'.

Why did the US win the space race?

- By putting men on the moon the US won the space race, but although this was a huge propaganda victory, it made little difference to the cold war
- The Americans won because all Presidents after Kennedy were prepared to pour money into the project
- The Soviet Union was not willing to devote such large resources to getting to the moon and concentrated instead on developing a space station which orbited the earth.

Questions

For Examination questions on Later Modern History of Europe and the Wider World, Topic 6 see page 279.

4.1 American economy 1945–1989: affluence and recession

The Age of Affluence: 1940–1968

- In the 1930s, America had suffered from the Great Depression when unemployment and poverty were widespread
- The Depression ended when the government invested heavily in armaments during the second World War
- From then until the early 1970s, the US was a wealthy society in which jobs were plentiful and wages good
- For the first time in history a majority of people could afford a decent house, lots of luxury goods and holidays. For that reason, this period is often referred to as the **age of affluence**.

Why the US economy did well after the second World War

- When the second World War ended in 1945, the US was the world's wealthiest economy. It had escaped war damage, and the rest of the world wanted to buy what it produced
- America was rich in natural resources such as coal and oil which provided cheap fuel for its factories
- After 1945, the government continued to invest in the economy
  - The 1944 **GI Bill** gave grants to returning soldiers to buy houses, start businesses or continue their education
  - The number of people working for the government increased rapidly
  - The **Cold War** and the arms race with the Soviet Union, together with the **Korean** and **Vietnam wars** kept government spending on arms high
  - In 1956, the **Federal-Aid Highway Act** gave Federal grants to build a network of motorways across the US
  - The Federal and some State governments spent more on education and welfare than before. The biggest increase came in the 1960s with President Johnson's **Great Society** programme
- This investment caused an economic boom which lasted for 25 years.

The consumer society

- The emergence of '**the consumer society**' also helped to keep the economy booming
- During the war, Americans had earned good wages, but there were few consumer goods to buy. Their savings grew and when the war ended they

rushed to buy the furniture, cars, washing machines and refrigerators they could not get before

- After the war unemployment remained low, averaging about 4% between 1945 and 1968. Plentiful jobs pushed the average income up from $3,000 to $8,000

- For the first time in history a majority of people had money to spend on luxuries, such as TVs or holidays, as well as on necessities, like food and shelter (housing)

- This created a demand for a big range of consumer goods and services. New industries sprang up to meet the demand

- Consumer credit expanded to enable people to buy more goods without having to save for them in advance.

The creation of giant corporations

- Before the war many Americans were self-employed or worked for small companies but after 1945 more of them worked for the government or for large corporations

- In the 1950s and 1960s, US companies began to grow bigger through **mergers** (two or more companies joining together) and **acquisitions** (one company taking over another). For example, Ford and General Motors swallowed up smaller car manufacturers, and Boeing took over smaller aircraft companies.

Multinational corporations and globalisation

- Mergers and acquisitions spread outside the US as American corporations took over foreign companies. This created giant **multinational corporations**, like IBM or Exxon which had factories and offices in many countries

- Some US companies also set up overseas branches to take advantage of low wages or lower taxes in other countries

- Until the 1990s, most overseas investment was in Canada and Western Europe because other areas were either under communist control or politically unstable

- The American government supported overseas expansion. Believing America would benefit from freer trade, it backed plans to remove tariffs (import taxes) around the world through the **General Agreement on Tariff and Trade (GATT)** and the **World Bank**

- These developments led to **globalisation**, i.e. the closer integration of the world's economies. This process got a huge boost from the fall of communism in 1991.

243

The end of affluence: the economy after 1968

- From the end of the 1960s, the American economy experienced many difficulties
- International competition increased particularly from Germany and Japan. American's share of world trade fell from 25% in 1947 to 10% by 1975
- Americans bought more foreign goods like cars. This created a **trade deficit** and hit jobs
- By the 1970s, the US had to import much of the oil it used from the Arab States. Following wars between the Arabs and Israel, the **Organisation of Oil Exporting Countries (OPEC)** forced up the price of oil in 1973 and 1979. This damaged the economy further
- The cost of the Vietnam war and Johnson's **Great Society** welfare programme created **a budget deficit**. To avoid raising taxes, the government borrowed to fill the gap. That caused **inflation**
- By 1980, America suffered from economic stagnation and high inflation (often called **stagflation**).

> **Remember...**
>
> Trade deficit = a country importing more than it exports.
> Budget deficit = a government spending more than it gets in taxes.
> Inflation = prices rising

Ronald Reagan and 'reagonomics'

- Ronald Reagan was elected in 1980, in the middle of America's worst economic depression since the 1930s. Unemployment was 10% and inflation was 13%
- Reagan cut welfare programmes and personal taxes, arguing this would encourage people to work harder
- He also greatly increased government spending on arms, announcing plans for a defence system against Soviet missiles, known by its critics as 'Star Wars'
- The economy recovered slowly and in 1986 began to grow again
- In the Reagan years, new jobs were created, many of them in the new areas of electronics and computing
- Other jobs emerged in the services sector. Many of them were poorly paid and the government removed many of the protections which poorly paid employees had enjoyed
- The number of very wealthy people grew rapidly while the amount they paid in taxes fell. The gap between rich and poor Americans increased significantly.

4.2 Changes in American society 1945–1989

Demographic change – the expanding population

- The population of America grew steadily after the war

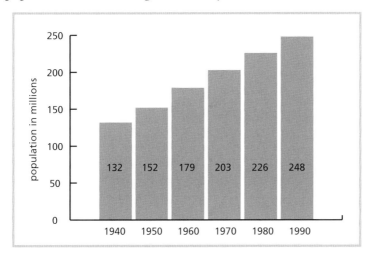

- This growth was partly due to a big increase in the number of births (the **'baby boom'**) between 1945 and 1960
- The children born at that time, known as the 'baby boomers', were better fed, better educated and demanded more of their society than their parents (see Section 6.2)
- From the 1960s contraception became easily available and the number of births declined
- Immigration was not a huge contributor to the population growth until the 1970s, when the number of people admitted to the country grew rapidly
- Before the second World War most Americans lived in the north where the industries were located. But from the 1960s, many companies set up in California and the southern 'sun belt' States. The population grew faster in these areas than elsewhere.

Changing patterns of work

- The work Americans did changed greatly between 1945 and 1990
- In 1945, more than half of American men worked in **heavy industry**, such as mining, steel milling, car making, etc
- Referred to as **'blue-collar'** workers, most were unskilled or semi-skilled, with a limited education
- From the 1960s, the number of blue-collar workers declined because **automation** and competition from overseas reduced the demand for unskilled or semi-skilled workers. This forced their wages down, and made their jobs less attractive
- At the same time the number of jobs in the 'service industries', such as banks, shops, teaching, medicine, etc, grew. Workers in these industries had to be skilled and educated.

- Often called '**white-collar workers**' because they went to work in a suit, not in overalls, they had a higher status than blue-collar workers, even though they were not always better paid
- During the 1950s and 1960s, white-collar workers replaced blue-collar workers as the biggest group in American society. This was due to:
  - ○ The spread of higher education encouraged by the GI Bill and the growing demand for skilled labour
  - ○ The decline in the number of low skill jobs in farming and heavy industry
- Farmers did not share the prosperity of the post-war years. Between 1945 and 1960 the price of food fell, cutting their incomes by 25%. Many small farmers sold up and went to work in towns where they could earn more
- By 1980, 75% of Americans lived in urban areas and much of America's farm land was owned by large corporations which farmed it using machines rather than people.

The growth of suburbs

- In the 1930s, many blue-collar workers dreamed of moving out of rented flats in the crowded city centres and buying a house in a pleasant suburb
- The post-war prosperity made this dream a reality for millions. From the 1950s, **suburbs** expanded around most US cities
- Usually suburbs were pleasant places with shops, schools and churches
- But women who stayed at home to rear their children often found life in the suburbs lonely and boring

The Organization Man

- In 1956, in a book called *The Organization Man*, William H Whyte described the life of a typical suburban white collar worker
- Usually a former soldier, he was the first member of his family to have gone to college, thanks to the GI Bill
- He worked at the middle levels of a government department or a multinational corporation and his main aim was to move up a few steps on the corporate ladder
- Totally loyal to his organisation, he worked long hours, moved wherever they sent him and behaved in the way they thought he should behave
- In return, he expected to have job security and a pension
- At home, he lived in one of the new suburbs where his neighbours were just like him. Each morning, neatly dressed in shirt and tie, they drove or caught the train to the office
- Their wives all stayed at home to mind the children, cook, wash and welcome the weary bread winner home in the evening.
- Apart from unpaid work for the church or school, they did not work outside the home
- Whyte criticised *The Organization Man*, claiming that he was losing the old American values of independence, hard work and risk-taking.

- Suburbs also made cars essential, so that people could get to work. This led to congestion and traffic jams
- Many industries, especially new clean industries like electronics, moved out to the suburbs from the late-1950s.

4.3 Troubled affluence: urban poverty, crime and drugs

The decay of the city centres

- Not all Americans gained from the post-war economic boom. By 1960, almost one American in five still lived in poverty. While some were farmers, most of the poor lived in the inner cities
- The centres of American cities decayed as the suburbs grew. By 1960, only people too old, too poor or too unskilled to escape still lived there
- Many were housed in government '*projects*', huge soulless tower blocks built to house the poor who had previously lived in slums
- Since most people in the inner cities were in poorly paid jobs or on welfare they did not pay much in taxes. This left city governments with less money to spend on schools, hospitals and sanitation
- Poor quality schools made it harder for young people to get the education they needed to escape the **poverty trap**.

Inner city ghettos

- About 25% of the population of the biggest cities were black people who moved from the South hoping to find work
- Racial discrimination and their own lack of education and skills meant that these hopes were often disappointed
- Black women could get low-paid jobs as waitresses or cleaners, but black men found it harder to get work, especially as, from the 1950s, many industries began to move out of the cities
- These conditions led to the formation of '**black ghettos**' – whole areas of a city where most inhabitants were black.

Crime and drugs

- Crime flourished in the inner cities. Young men joined gangs and having no work, could make money in criminal activities, such as robbing banks, etc
- Crime was accompanied by violence. Police were armed and criminals could get guns easily because the US Constitution guaranteed the right to carry arms
- In the 1960s, criminal gangs began dealing in drugs which were smuggled into the US

- Drugs added to the violence as addicts robbed to feed their habit, and drug gangs fought to control their territories
- By the 1970s, crime in US cities was far higher than anywhere else in the world
- 'Law and order' became a political slogan, especially for Republicans. Harsher sentences were imposed and more prisons built. The death penalty, which had almost disappeared, was revived in many States.

Johnson's Great Society and the 'war on poverty'

- In the 1960s, poverty became a political issue. In 1964, President Lyndon Johnson declared a 'war on poverty' with his **Great Society** programme
- Johnson got Congress to pass the **Economic Opportunity Act** which provided a fund of $1 billion to fight poverty. It set up the **Office of Economic Opportunity** which organised:
  - **Head Start** to provide pre-school education, meals and health checks for poor inner-city children
  - A **Jobs Corp** to provide skills training for young school leavers
  - A training programme for unemployed adults
  - A system of cheap loans to small businesses
- In 1965, Johnson set aside billions of dollars to provide rent and food subsidies and health care for the poor and elderly (**Medicaid** and **Medicare**).

The end of the Great Society programme

- These programmes reduced the numbers living in poverty, but middle-class tax payers resented the cost
- Critics said millions were wasted on bureaucracy and that the poor resented the 'do-gooders' who interfered in their lives
- These criticisms were re-enforced when race riots broke out in many cities in the late-1960s and 1970s. The first major riot was in the **Watts** district of Los Angles in 1965
- By 1970, the rising cost of the Vietnam war and the decline in the American economy reduced spending on poverty
- President Nixon kept Johnson's programmes in place, but from 1980 President Reagan cut Federal spending on the poor. He hoped private charities would step in instead. They did not and the poverty of the inner cities remained as bad as ever.

Questions

For Examination questions on Later Modern History of Europe and the Wider World, Topic 6 see page 279.

5.1 Black life after slavery: the promise betrayed

A brief promise of freedom

Legend:
- The South
- Border States
- The North and West

- From 1619, Africans were brought to America and sold as slaves. Most of them lived in the Southern United States where slavery was legal
- In 1861, a civil war broke out between the Southern and Northern States. One of the issues between them was slavery
- The North won, and as a result the **13th, 14th** and **15th Amendments to the United States Constitution** ended slavery, promised equal protection of the law to both black and white people and granted black men the right to vote
- Congress also passed **civil rights laws** which recognised African Americans as citizens, prohibited racial violence and ended discrimination in transport and public places.

The promise betrayed

- But this promise of equal treatment was soon broken. In law black people remained full citizens with the right to vote, but the Federal government left it to the States to enforce this right

- In the former slave States of the South the white majority quickly found ways to stop black men (and later women) from voting:
  - ○ Voters had to pay a **poll tax** in cash. It was collected at a time when poor farmers (white as well as black) had not yet sold their crops and so had no cash
  - ○ Voters had to pass **literacy tests** (i.e. show they were able to read). But white officials set the tests. They made them impossibly hard for blacks and very easy for whites
  - ○ Terrorist gangs, like the **Ku Klux Klan**, intimidated black people who tried to put their names on the voters' register
- As a result, by 1900, only 3% of black men were registered to vote across the South.

The failure of the Supreme Court

- The function of the **US Supreme Court** is to see that the Constitution is observed, but for many years it did little to protect black people:
  - ○ In 1883, it said that discrimination in private housing and transport was legal
  - ○ In 1893, it decreed that local government could provide '*separate but equal*' facilities for blacks and whites
- These decisions opened the way for **racial segregation** and the reduction in the quality of services given to racial minorities.

The Jim Crow Laws

- From the 1890s to the 1960s, States passed over 400 laws (known as **Jim Crow laws**) that legalised segregation and discrimination based on race
- They divided schools, cinemas, parks, beaches, trains, etc, into 'whites only' and 'coloureds only' areas. Inevitably, the 'coloureds only' part was far from equal in quality and standard to the 'whites only' one

> **Remember...**
>
> Racial discrimination = favouring one race above another.
> Racial segregation = keeping the races apart.

- In some places, blacks were forbidden to work in the same room as whites. This limited the jobs they could get
- Laws also banned marriage between Europeans and people of other races (this was called **miscegenation**)
- The Southern States passed 80% of the Jim Crow laws, while some Northern and Western States had similar laws, often aimed at Chinese people or Native Americans
- By 1949, only 15 States, all in the North, did not discriminate in some way against racial minorities.

Life under Jim Crow

- Every day, black people suffered small humiliations as a result of the Jim Crow laws
- The *'separate but equal'* rule meant:
  - That black people could order food in a restaurant, but had to collect it at the back door and eat it outside
  - In cinemas they could only sit on the balcony; in buses, they had to sit at the back
  - They were not allowed to use many public facilities, like toilets, libraries, parks or beaches
  - 'White' ambulances would not pick up injured black people, nor would 'white' hospitals receive them
- Black men knew they must never look directly at or touch a white woman, even by accident. **Lynching** – killing someone without a trial, often by hanging – was the common punishment for breaking this rule.

Terrorising black people

- Whites used intimidation and terrorism to control black people. Anyone who tried to assert their rights could be evicted from their farms, sacked from their jobs or even lynched by white mobs
- Between 1882 and 1968, almost 5,000 lynchings were reported in the press, but many more went unreported
- Lynch-mobs subjected their black victims to sadistic tortures that included burning, dismemberment or being dragged behind cars
- Some Southern newspapers reported lynchings with approval and the participants, including children, often posed for photographs in front of their victim's body
- The all-white State police seldom intervened, but if they did, all-white juries would always find white people innocent.

Racial stereotyping

- Whites claimed discrimination was justified because black people were **mentally, culturally** and **morally inferior** to whites
- This view was reinforced by **constant stereotyping** in the press, on radio, in theatre, films and advertising
- Black people appeared in the media either as evil or as lazy and stupid:
  - The first full-length American movie, *The Birth of a Nation* (1915), showed black men as dangerous rapists and the Ku Klux Klan as heroes
  - Films showing slavery, like the very popular *Gone with the Wind* (1939), suggested that slaves were happy with their lot and felt lost and bewildered when freed.

Poverty and lack of education

- In reality, poverty and lack of education made it difficult for Southern black people to show what they could do
- Up to the 1920s, most were poor 'share-croppers'. They farmed land belonging to white men and paid for it with a share (up to 66%) of the crops they grew
- Primary schools for black children lacked basic facilities, like books or blackboards and black teachers were paid half as much as whites
- Until the 1940s, there were hardly any High (secondary) Schools for black students and they were not admitted to State-run universities
- From the 1920s, many black people moved into Southern cities or went North to look for work, but discrimination and poor education limited their opportunities
- Black women worked mainly as cooks or maids. Black men only got jobs white men did not want. Blacks were paid less than whites for the same work.

African Americans develop their own culture

- Most African-Americans turned away from white society. They set up their own churches, businesses and clubs
- They founded their own colleges which produced the lawyers, teachers and doctors who led the campaign for civil rights
- They developed black music such as **jazz** and **rhythm and blues**, and black artists like **Billie Holiday** and **Paul Robeson**, won the interest and respect of the wider white community outside the South.

The Role of the Black Churches

- Black churches, mostly Baptist and Methodist, played an important part in black life
- Most churches were self-governing, so in them black people could take on leadership roles and earn public respect in ways not available in the wider community
- Ministers were often spokesmen for their communities
- Southern Ministers usually did not attack discrimination directly because it was too dangerous to do so. But in the North, Ministers could be much more outspoken in condemning racial discrimination.

The National Association for the Advancement of Coloured People (NAACP)

- Some African Americans campaigned against discrimination though at first they got little support from the white community, the Federal government or the courts
- In 1909, the **National Association for the Advancement of Coloured**

People (**NAACP**) was set up. It was a multi-racial organisation which hoped to resist Jim Crow laws by:
- ❍ Publicising lynching and other injustices
- ❍ Getting blacks to register to vote, starting in the North
- ❍ Urging the Federal government to outlaw discrimination
- ❍ Taking States and cities to court on issues like school conditions, all white juries and voting rights
- These campaigns began to pay off in the 1930s and 1940s.

Gradual improvement

- During the second World War, **President Roosevelt** yielded to black pressure and forbade racial discrimination in war industries
- As a result, over two million blacks got well-paid jobs in arms factories, mainly in the North. Another million black people joined the American forces though they remained segregated
- At the end of the war, many black servicemen took advantage of the **GI Bill** which gave government funds to soldiers who wanted to go to college. This significantly raised the educational level of the black community
- To win the support of black voters in the North, **Harry Truman** ended segregation in the armed forces, prohibited job discrimination by the Federal government and gave government backing to NAACP court cases
- By 1950, the NAACP had won important legal victories. The Supreme Court said that literacy tests, poll taxes and other tricks to stop blacks voting were illegal. It also outlawed segregation in juries, in housing and in transport between the States.

Why change came

- Northern States accepted these rulings. By 1950, legal segregation had largely disappeared there, though economic discrimination remained
- But in border and Southern States, a large majority of whites supported segregation and voted for **segregationist politicians**. They would not change the Jim Crow laws unless the Federal government forced them to do so

> **Remember...**
>
> EDCO REVISE WISE POINTS TO NOTE
>
> White supremacists/ segregationists: People who wanted to keep Jim Crow laws.

- By 1950, a number of developments made it likely that this would happen:
- ❍ There were now educated black leaders who were able to make the case for equality
- ❍ Due to the work of the NAACP more black people could vote so politicians became interested in helping them
- ❍ Nazi racist policies in the second World War led to a revulsion against racism everywhere

- Discrimination against black people was bad for America's image as 'leader of the free world' during the Cold War
- TV images of lynchings made a bigger impact on Northern voters than newspaper or radio reports.

5.2 The Civil Rights campaign begins
The start of the civil rights campaign

- In the mid-1950s, a campaign began to win full civil rights for black people
- Three events marked the start of this campaign:
  - The Supreme Court's judgement in the **Brown Case**
  - The lynching of **Emmett Till**
  - The **Montgomery Bus Boycott**.

May 1954: The Brown Judgement

- The NAACP won court cases that forced school districts to observe the '*separate but equal*' rule. They must pay black teachers the same as white and raise standards in black-only schools
- In 1952, they backed a case that attacked the '*separate but equal*' rule itself
- **Linda Brown** was an eight year-old from Kansas. She lived beside a white school, but had to walk and take a bus to get to her black school. Her father took a case to end segregation
- In court, lawyers for the NAACP claimed that segregated schools made black children feel inferior and made it difficult for them to learn
- The Supreme Court accepted this argument. It ruled that school segregation must end with '*all deliberate speed*'
- The *Brown Judgement* caused outrage in the South, where whites feared that mixed schools would lead to their greatest fear – mixed marriages.

August 1955: The lynching of Emmett Till

- Racial tension rose in Mississippi after the *Brown Judgement*. The Ku Klux Klan revived and several black men were murdered for trying to get black people to register as voters
- In August 1955, Emmett Till, a 14-year-old black boy from Chicago, went to visit relatives in Mississippi. After he whistled at a white woman, her husband and a friend brutally murdered him
- Surprisingly, they were arrested and put on trial, but the all-white jury quickly found them not guilty
- Because Emmett Till was so young and came from Chicago, the case attracted media attention throughout America. The verdict brought home to other Americans what life was like for black citizens in the Deep South.

5.3 The Montgomery bus boycott

Montgomery, Alabama

- Montgomery in Alabama was a typical Southern city. Jim Crow laws kept the races rigidly separate in school and work
- City council services, like fire brigades and rubbish collection, were worse in black neighbourhoods than in white
- Segregated schools gave black pupils a second-rate education which limited the job opportunities open to them. On average black people earned half of what whites earned
- As in most Southern cities, public transport was segregated. All bus drivers were white, though 75% of passengers were poor black workers who could not afford cars
- Black passengers paid the driver at the front door of the bus, then had to go to the **back door** to get on. They could only sit at the back, but if the front became too crowded, they had to give up their seats to white passengers.

Resistance in Montgomery

- Some **black activists** wanted black people to protest at their treatment. They included **E D Nixon**, local head of the NAACP, and several ministers, including **Ralph Abernathy** and **Martin Luther King**
- The *Brown Judgement* encouraged resistance. On the buses protests at bullying by white drivers became more common. The drivers retaliated by carrying guns and calling in the police to arrested any protester
- The NAACP was hoping to find a case around which they could rally the black community. **Rosa Parks** provided it for them.

Rosa Parks

- Rosa Parks was a quiet, 42 year-old black woman and an active member of the NAACP. Though educated, she could only find a poorly paid sewing job
- On **Thursday 1 December, 1955**, weary after work, she boarded a bus and sat with three other blacks in the first of the 'black' seats behind the 'white' section
- After a few stops, the 'white' section filled up and a white man was left standing. The driver ordered the four blacks to give up their seats. Three moved, but Parks refused. The police came and arrested her.

5 December, 1955: The boycott begins

- Parks was just the kind of respectable, unthreatening person the NAACP needed to symbolise black oppression. Nixon got her to agree to a one-day boycott of buses on Monday, the day of her trial

- Martin Luther King wrote later that he would have considered a 60% boycott a success. In fact, it was over 90%
- That night the organisers formed the **Montgomery Improvement Association (MIA)**, with King as president. At a mass meeting they proposed continuing the boycott until:
  - ○ Seats were given on a first come, first served basis
  - ○ Bus drivers agreed to treat blacks with courtesy
  - ○ The bus company hired black drivers
- King spoke movingly at the meeting: *'We are here tonight to say to those who have mistreated us so long, that we are tired – tired of being segregated and humiliated, tired of being kicked about by the brutal feet of oppression'*. All present agreed the boycott would take place.

The boycott continues

- Whites were sure the boycott would collapse quickly. Montgomery's mayor predicted: *'Come the first rainy day and the Negroes will be back on the buses'*
- But that did not happen. Blacks walked or cycled to work, or got lifts from friends with cars. Some organised taxi services, charging 10 cents for a ride, the same fare as the buses
- The city then revived an old law that forbade taxis to charge less than 45 cents, more than most blacks could afford
- In response, King set up a private taxi service. Donations to pay for it came from black and white sympathisers across America. Local churches ran the service with military-like precision.

Whites counter-attack

- White leaders tried a variety of tactics to break the boycott
- Activists, including Rosa Parks, were sacked from their jobs
- Local insurance companies refused to cover the black taxi service, but an agent got cover from Lloyds of London
- Police harassed black drivers, penalising them for every tiny breach of the road traffic laws
- White drivers flung stones and rotten eggs at black pedestrians. Sometimes snipers fired on them. Bombers blew up black taxis and churches.

Attacking Martin Luther King

- As the leader of the MIA, Martin Luther King was especially targeted
- Whites tried to discredit him by spreading rumours that he was embezzling funds
- He was arrested for breaching Alabama's anti-boycotting laws, found guilty and fined $500
- His home was bombed while his wife and baby were in it. When a black crowd demanded revenge, King told them to put their guns away and *'love*

our white brothers no matter what they do to us'. His father begged him to give up but he refused.

Legal victory

- When it became clear that no compromise was possible, the NAACP took a case against bus segregation. They won when the Supreme Court declared that it was unconstitutional
- After 382 days the boycott had achieved its aims. On **21 December 1956**, Parks, King, Nixon and other black people rode in the front seats of the first integrated bus
- But their victory changed little. Whites stopped using buses and the Ku Klux Klan beat up black passengers. The homes and churches of King and Abernathy were bombed. Segregation continued in other areas of life.

Why the Montgomery bus boycott was important

- Although the bus boycott did not end violence or segregation in Montgomery, it achieved other important results
- It undermined the smug Southern white idea that blacks were 'happy' with their status as second-class citizens
- The tenacity and courage of ordinary black people, and the skill with which they organised the boycott, showed that white claims about black inferiority were untrue
- It produced a new black leader in Martin Luther King
- The tactics used – local boycott, non-violent protest and legal action – became the model for successful civil rights campaigns in many parts of the South over the next ten years
- Media coverage, and especially TV images, made many white Americans aware of the deprivation and indignities suffered by Southern blacks and the violence and harassment that followed every attempt to demand equality.

5.4 The end of the Civil Rights movement

1956 – 1965: The campaign continues

Over the next ten years the campaign to win full citizenship for black people continued through a series of confrontations with white Southern authorities.

- **1957: School integration in Little Rock, Arkansas:**
  - When nine black students entered Little Rock's all-white Central High School, white mobs attacked them in front of TV cameras. After the world watched white supremacists shrieking 'lynch her' at a terrified 15 year-old girl, a reluctant President Eisenhower sent in Federal troops to protect the students

- 1960: 'sit-ins':
  - ○ At Woolworth's store in Greensboro, North Carolina black people could buy food in the café but not eat it there. On **1 February 1960**, four black students bought food, quietly sat down to eat and refused to leave until they had finished
  - ○ 'Sit-ins' spread across the South. Over 70,000 people, mostly students entered segregated toilets, cinemas, parks, etc. Following non-violent principles, they allowed themselves to be beaten and imprisoned without retaliation
  - ○ In October, Martin Luther King joined a sit-in in Atlanta. He was arrested and sentenced to hard labour. This pushed the race issue into the Presidential campaign
  - ○ The Republican candidate, Richard Nixon ignored it, but the Democrat, John F Kennedy supported King. A majority of blacks voted for Kennedy, helping him to win
- 1961: the Freedom Ride:
  - ○ The Supreme Court had outlawed segregation on inter-State trains and buses, but Southern States had ignored the ruling. To force the Federal government to act, an inter-racial group of students set out on a two-week 'Freedom Ride' across the South
  - ○ White supremacists met them with horrifying violence, which left two dead. Most State police either ignored violence of white mobs or joined in
  - ○ Media coverage and international embarrassment forced Kennedy to send Federal marshals to protect the students and end segregation on inter-State transport
- 1962: the battle at Mississippi State University:
  - ○ No black student ever attended Mississippi State University before **James Meredith** applied. After Federal courts ordered the university to admit him, Kennedy sent Federal Marshals to protect him. A mob of 3,000 white racists attacked them and Kennedy sent in 13,000 troops to restore order
  - ○ All this violence sickened many Southern whites and businessmen realised that the riots damaged the South's image. Support for segregation began to collapse.

1963: Birmingham and the March on Washington

- In Birmingham, Alabama blacks were excluded from many jobs, the Ku Klux Klan was active and police chief, **Bull Connor**, was famous for his mindless brutality
- Knowing this, King agreed to a march protesting at the lack of black jobs. When Bull Connor turned police dogs on peaceful black marchers, more protests broke out and Kennedy had to propose a **Civil Rights Act**

- To put pressure on Congress to pass it, black activists organised a **March on Washington**. Over 250,000 people turned up and King electrified them with his famous *'I have a dream….'* speech
- After Kennedy was assassinated, President **Lyndon Johnson** used his considerable political skills to get the Civil Rights Act through Congress.

1964: Freedom Summer

- In Mississippi white supremacists, aided by the State police, shot, beat up or killed anyone who tried to get blacks to register to vote
- To draw attention to this, civil rights activists organised a **'Freedom Summer'**. Volunteers from the North, many of them white students, set up schools for black kids and encouraged their parents to register

Remember…

The film, *Mississippi Burning*, is based on this episode.

- Violence flared when white supremacists beat up volunteers. In June two white students and one black were brutally killed
- The death of white students shocked the country. The FBI identified the killers, but Mississippi State officials refused to try them for murder.

1965: Selma and the Voter Registration Act

- When Alabama State troopers attacked a peaceful march in Selma, a black second World War veteran exclaimed *'the Germans were never as inhuman as the troopers of Alabama'*
- King went to Selma to complete the interrupted march. They were under constant attack and a black minister was murdered
- President Johnson went on TV to say that *'it is wrong – deadly wrong – to deny any of your fellow Americans the right to vote in this country'*. By then many members of Congress, even conservatives, had come to the same conclusion
- In 1965, Congress passed the **Voter Registration Act**. Literacy tests and other tricks which stopped blacks from registering were declared illegal, and the Federal government took on responsibility for implementing the rules.

Racial issues in the North

- The civil rights campaign focussed on the South and did little for black people in the North
- Most of them lived in **ghettos** in big cities (see Section 4.3). Poor education and high unemployment meant that they missed out on the affluence that other Americans enjoyed in the 1960s
- They were harassed by white police and suffered from gang violence and drug abuse

- In 1965, their anger exploded into fierce riots in the **Watts** area of Los Angeles. Thirty-four people died and property worth $40 million was destroyed
- President Johnson set up an enquiry and some cities tried to improve conditions in the ghettos
- Martin Luther King went to **Chicago** where howling mobs of Poles, Italians and Irish stopped a protest march
- Lack of support from local black leaders and the Chicago city government forced him to withdraw.

Divisions in the movement

- Divisions now appeared in the civil rights movement as some black leaders lost faith in non-violence:
  - ○ '**Black power**' and '**Black Pride**' groups emphasised the ethnic heritage of African-Americans by wearing African dress and adopting African names
  - ○ '**Black nationalists**' wanted blacks to have their own State, funded by compensation from white Americans for the wrong of slavery. Some also advocated violence
  - ○ The '**Black Panthers**' a tiny group with links to crime and drugs, talked of killing whites
- These extremist groups alienated white supporters from the civil rights movement.

The assassination of Martin Luther King

- After Chicago, King recognised that civil rights were not enough. He opposed the Vietnam war, noting that far more was spent killing Vietnamese than improving living conditions for the poor
- He began a campaign for government funds to develop depressed areas
- In April 1968, he went to **Memphis**, Tennessee to help a strike by sanitation workers
- The protest turned violent and a depressed King returned to his hotel. The next morning he was assassinated
- In over 100 cities across America, his death was marked by violent riots in which 46 people died.

The results of the civil rights campaign

- For many of those involved, King's death marked the end of the civil rights campaign. The results were mixed
- Black people with money or education could now get jobs that had previously been closed to them

- Black people could register to vote and some got elected to office. In 1967, the first black mayor was elected and, in 1989, the first black governor
- Legal segregation disappeared though that did not mean that the races mixed a great deal
- In theory schools were no longer segregated, but in practice they continued to be. In cities, North and South, whites moved into white suburbs and sent their children to local, mainly white schools or to private schools. Older State schools in the city centres became, in practice, mostly black
- To deal with this inequality, the Supreme Court ordered that children be 'bussed' from one school district to another, but this was not successful and was later reversed
- After Ronald Reagan became President in 1980, the Federal government reduced the help it gave to poor (mostly black) communities and largely ceased the pursuit social justice.

Martin Luther King (1929–1968)

Early life

- Born in Atlanta, Georgia, the son and grandson of well-known Baptist ministers, **Martin Luther King** got his early education in segregated schools and colleges in the South but later studied in integrated universities in the North
- He joined the **NAACP** and was elected to its executive council. In 1954 he became pastor of the Dexter Avenue Baptist Church in Montgomery, Alabama.
- He was elected President of the **Montgomery Improvement Association** (MIA) which led the bus boycott and took a successful case to the Supreme Court
- In 1957 he formed the **Southern Christian Leadership Conference** (SCLC) to mobilise the moral authority and leadership of black churches behind the non-violent campaign for civil rights

Ideas and tactics:

- King was influenced by the German theologian, **Reinhold Niebuhr** who said that evil could not be overcome by reason but must be confronted. The non-violent campaign of **Gandhi** against British rule in India also inspired him
- King and the SCLC wanted to bring the deprivation and indignities suffered by Southern blacks to the notice of white Americans. They used the violent reaction of Southern authorities to publicise the situation and strengthen their demands for justice

King and the Civil Rights campaign

- King's skilful rhetoric, moderate goals, great personal courage and insistence on non-violence built a powerful coalition of poor and prosperous blacks with liberal white sympathisers, including Christian and Jewish leaders
- The movement successfully forced a reluctant Federal government to enact Civil Rights legislation and to enforce it in the South
- The coalition broke up after 1965 due to the passing of the Civil Rights Acts, the explosion of black violence in northern cities, divisions among black leaders and King's growing opposition to the war in Vietnam
- Martin Luther King was murdered in Memphis by a Nazi sympathiser, James Earl Ray on 4 April 1968.

5.5 The campaign for women's rights

Although American women had gained the right to vote in 1919, they still suffered from discrimination into the 1960s. The campaign for civil rights for black people made women more aware of their situation and encouraged them to demand equal treatment with men.

Housewives and mothers: 1945-1965

- Before 1940, few married women worked outside the home, but when war came, they replaced men in the arms factories and produced the weapons needed for victory

- When the war ended the men returned to their jobs and women were expected to return to being housewives and mothers. This view of women's role continued up to the 1960s

- In books and films, the stereotypical girl was frivolous and empty-headed. Her main aim was to marry a strong, handsome man who would take care of her for the rest of her life

- This stereotype had an impact on women's career opportunities:
  - The number of women going to university declined in the 1950s
  - Women found it hard to get jobs in government, business or the media except as secretaries or cleaners
  - Able, well qualified women were usually paid less than their male colleagues for the same work and did not get promotion
  - Most women gave up paid work when they married (usually around 20) and depended on their husbands' income. Divorce was rare among ordinary Americans
  - There were few women in politics.

The changing role of women

- By the end of the 1950s the lives of American housewives were starting to change. There were several reasons for this:
  - Life in the new suburbs could be lonely for a wife, separated from family and friends
  - It could also be boring as labour saving devices like dishwashers reduced the amount of work to be done around the house
  - Women who were well educated felt they were wasting their education on housework and childminding
  - Full employment meant that there was a demand for more workers so women easily found jobs outside the home
  - Depending on a husband for money was humiliating so even poorly paid part-time work gave a woman some independence.

Marilyn Monroe (1926-1962)

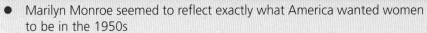

- Marilyn Monroe seemed to reflect exactly what America wanted women to be in the 1950s
- Born Norma Jeane Mortenson, she had a troubled childhood, being moved around between her natural mother, foster parents and an orphanage
- Married at 16, she went to work in a factory while her husband served in the army. Spotted by a photographer, she became a fashion model
- After her picture appeared in several magazines, the film studio, **Twentieth Century Fox** gave her a contract in 1946. Shortly after, she dyed her hair blonde and changed her name to **Marilyn Monroe**
- After playing minor parts, she had her first starring role in 1953 in the film *Niagara*. This led to a string of hit films, like *Gentlemen Prefer Blondes* (1953), *The Seven Year Itch* (1955), and the ever-popular *Some Like it Hot* (1959)
- In these and other films she was typecast as a sex-symbol, the stereotypical brainless 'dumb blonde'
- Monroe herself longed to be taken seriously as an actress, but she was not given the roles which would let her show her talent
- Her private life was unhappy. Her first marriage failed, as did her second to the sports star, Joe DiMaggio. She then married **Arthur Miller**, one of America's most respected playwrights and supported him when he was accused of communist sympathies during the McCarthy period
- He wrote the script for her last film, *The Misfits*, but their marriage too ended in divorce. Unhappiness led to drug use and she became difficult to work with
- She was found dead of a drugs overdose in August 1962. Because she was reported to have had affairs with several rich and famous Americans, including President Kennedy, rumours still surround the circumstances of her death.

Campaigning for women's rights

- Early in the 1960s, inspired by the black civil rights movement, women too began to demand their rights
- One of the leaders of the campaign was **Betty Friedan**.

The achievements of the women's movement

- The women's movement had considerable success
- The **1964 Civil Rights Act** outlawed discrimination on the grounds of gender as well as race
- The Federal government insisted that companies applying for government contracts must employ women and men on equal terms
- More women went to university and major universities, like Yale and Princeton admitted women for the first time
- More women got high-profile jobs in the media, became involved in politics and were elected to office
- Some States legalised abortion, and in a case (**Roe v Wade**) in 1973, the US Supreme Court upheld a woman's right to have one
- But the top jobs in politics and business remained closed to women and the Equal Rights Amendment failed to pass.

Betty Friedan (1921–2006)

- From a prosperous Jewish family, **Betty Goldstein** took a degree in psychology, but gave up work after marrying Carl Friedan and having children
- She found life as a wife and mother in the suburbs frustrating and lonely. She sent a questionnaire to women who had been in university with her and found most of them shared her feelings
- This formed the basis of her book, *The Feminine Mystique*, which appeared in 1963
- Based on interviews with thousands of housewives, Friedan claimed that the happy suburban housewife was a myth. This myth, which she called '*the feminine mystique*', kept women passive and childlike and stopped them using their talents and education to find fulfilment in work
- Freidan argued that there was a gap between what society expected of women and what women wanted for themselves. She called this '*the problem that has no name*'
- Her book influenced many women to change their way of life
- In 1966, she helped to found the **National Organisation of Women** (**NOW**). It campaigned for equal pay for women, access to contraception and abortion and equal opportunities in all walks of life
- She also helped to found the **National Women's Caucus**. It campaigned for more women in political life and for an **Equal Rights Amendment** (**ERA**) to the Constitution
- Friedan organised rallies and made speeches in support of these causes, but she rejected the arguments of more radical feminists who blamed men. In 1963, she said: '*Some people think I'm saying: "women of the world unite; you have nothing to lose but your men". It's not true. "You have nothing to lose but your vacuum cleaners"*'.

Divisions

- The women's movement split in the 1970s. Some extremists blamed men for all the ills of society and wanted to live without them
- These views were rejected by Friedan and the majority of women, but they strengthened the position of people who rejected feminist arguments and still accepted the idea that a woman's place was in the home.

Questions

For Examination questions on Later Modern History of Europe and the Wider World, Topic 6 see page 279.

CHAPTER 6
Culture and religion

6.1   Culture in the age of consensus

The Age of Consensus

The 20 years after the second World War are sometimes called '*the Age of Consensus*'. During them, many Americans agreed in being proud of their country, happy with economic and social conditions and optimistic about the future.

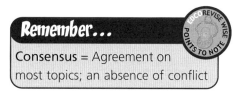

Remember...

Consensus = Agreement on most topics; an absence of conflict

- This consensus was due to:
  - ○ The economic prosperity that followed the hardships of Depression in the 1930s, and war in the early 1940s
  - ○ Pride in America's success as 'defender of the free world' in the second World War and the Cold War
  - ○ The 'red scare' and McCarthyism of the 1950s made it difficult to publicly criticise America without being accused either of sympathising with communism or of being unpatriotic
- In these years it seemed as if '*the American Dream*', – that anyone who worked hard could succeed – was true
- The consensus was reinforced by books, films and TV programmes where the good guys always won and the endings were always happy.

The growth of leisure

- The post-war economic boom gave the majority of Americans a higher income and more free time than ever before
- The average working week fell from over 50 hours in 1914 to 40 by 1960, and the Federal government introduced laws which guaranteed all workers an annual holiday
- Money and leisure allowed many ordinary people to enjoy activities that once only the wealthy could afford
- A leisure industry emerged to supply their needs:
  - ○ Companies sprang up to organise package holidays
  - ○ People took cruises or went on over-seas holidays
  - ○ Firms like Disney branched out from making films to creating theme parks and other holiday activities
- A popular leisure activity was shopping and large shopping malls were opened to take advantage of this.

Films and TV

- Before the war people went to the cinema several times a week and Hollywood stars were admired and copied
- After the war the film industry suffered a double blow:
  - ○ The arrival of TV cut into its audiences
  - ○ The McCarthy witch-hunt (see Section 2.2) targeted leading writers and undermined trust in the industry
- TV was invented before the war, but TV broadcasting in America did not begin until the 1940s
- Early TV sets were very expensive, but prices fell sharply in the 1950s, and by 1960 most homes had one. At first the pictures were black and white, but colour was widespread by 1970
- TV changed family life. The TV set became the focal point of the living room. Families gathered around it during meals, often eating pre-cooked 'TV dinners'
- From the start, TV programmes were sponsored, with up to ten minutes of advertising every hour. Sponsors had a big influence on the programmes that were put out. Many were 'soap operas', but sport was also hugely popular
- The novelty of having entertainment at home tempted people away from the cinemas. Hollywood fought back with colour spectaculars, lavish musicals and special effects which were best enjoyed on a big screen. In the 1980s films like *Star Wars* and *ET* won back audiences from TV.

Sport

- Money and more leisure time allowed more people to enjoy tennis, cycling and golf than ever before. Sports centres and an interest in fitness also encouraged people to swim and run
- But far more people watched sport on TV than ever played a game. Once advertisers realised this they poured millions of dollars into spectator sports
- The main American sports – **baseball** and **American football** – became multi-million dollar businesses. Teams turned professional and star players became famous and wealthy
- Big national competitions, like the **Super Bowl**, attracted millions of viewers and huge advertising revenue for TV channels
- Minority sports, like tennis and golf, also attracted large audiences. The number of tournaments increased rapidly and the leading players made fortunes
- Racial segregation existed in most sports. It was 1947 before a black man was selected for a major baseball team, and it was not until the 1970s that a black manager was appointed. Most golf and tennis clubs practiced racial segregation
- Boxing was one sport where black men fought white men on an even footing. The most famous sportsman of the 1960s was the boxer, **Muhammad Ali**.

Muhammad Ali (1942–)

- Born into a poor family in Kentucky, **Cassius Clay** took up boxing at 12 and won a gold medal in the 1960 Olympics
- He turned professional in 1960, and won all 19 of the fights that followed
- In 1964, he fought the world champion **Sonny Liston**. Before the fight he boasted that he would *'float like a butterfly and sting like a bee'*, but his victory over Liston took everyone by surprise
- Between 1964 and 1967, he defended his title nine times
- In 1964, Clay surprised the world by joining the **Nation of Islam** which rejected Christianity as the religion that enslaved black people. Claiming that Clay was a 'slave name' given to his ancestors by their white masters, he now called himself **Muhammad Ali**
- The Nation of Islam wanted a separate black nation and not the integration of black and white that Martin Luther King hoped for. This made Ali a controversial figure among Americans, both black and white
- He also courted controversy by opposing the Vietnam war. He refused to join the US army, remarking *"I ain't got no quarrel with those Vietcong"*
- In 1967, he was stripped of his title, which meant he could not fight and was also sentenced to jail for refusing to be conscripted
- After three years his sentence was reversed and he was allowed to fight again. In 1971, he met the undefeated **Joe Frazier** in the 'fight of the century'. After a tough fight, Frazier won
- In 1974, he fought the white boxer **George Foreman** in Zaire in Africa. The so-called *'rumble in the jungle'* came to symbolise the racial struggle between black and white Americans. Against expectations, Ali won
- He remained world champion until 1978, when he was defeated by **Leon Spinks**. In 1979, he recovered it when he defeated Spinks again
- Muhammad Ali retired from boxing in 1981 after winning 56 bouts and losing five. Many people consider him the greatest heavyweight boxer of all time.

Literature

- Reading remained a popular activity. Cheap paperback books appeared during the war and helped to encourage an interest in literature, as did the greater leisure time and the general increase in higher education from the 1950s
- The number of publishers increased. Books were sold in supermarkets as well as in traditional bookshops, and lists of 'best-sellers' encouraged people to read the current popular hit
- Most best-sellers were light reading, such as Edna Ferber's *Giant* (1952) or Leon Uris's *Exodus* (1958)
- But towards the end of the 1950s and early 1960s there was a growing interest in more challenging works
- The **Beat** writers, such as the poet **Allen Ginsberg** and the novelist **Jack Kerouac**, experimented with freer forms of writing and discussed drugs and sexuality in ways which were considered shocking at the time
- In *Catch 22* (1961) **Joseph Heller**, satirised the horrors of war and the

ability of modern society, especially bureaucratic institutions, to destroy the human spirit

- One of the most controversial of these new writers was the novelist and journalist, **Norman Mailer**.

Norman Mailer (1923–2007)

- Born into a Jewish family in New Jersey, Mailer grew up in New York and studied aeronautical engineering at Harvard. During the second World War he served with the United States Army in South East Asia
- His first novel, *The Naked and the Dead* (1948) was based on his war-time experiences. Controversial for its strong language, it was published when he was 25 and made him famous
- In the conservative 1950s, he had difficulty getting his next two novels published because of their frank treatment of sex. This led to problems with drink, drugs and violence, culminating in the stabbing of his wife during a drinking bout in 1961. He got away with a suspended sentence when she refused to press charges
- From the late 1950s, he lived in Greenwich Village, New York. He turned more to journalism and became involved in left-wing politics
- At this time he developed a new writing form – the **non-fiction novel**. It used the techniques and insights of novel writing to illuminate factual subjects
- Throughout the 1960s and 1970s, he reported on the Democratic and Republican Conventions, on the civil rights movement and on the protests against the war in Vietnam
- Arrested for his part in an anti-war demonstration, he wrote about the experience in his book, *Armies of the Night* which won the Pulitzer Prize for non-fiction in 1968
- He also used this technique in *Of a Fire on the Moon* (1970) to explore the moon landing and in *The Fight* (1974) which reported on the boxing match between Muhammad Ali and George Foreman in Zaire in 1974. His 1979 book, *The Executioner's Song*, about the convicted killer, Gary Gilmore, was a major popular success
- Mailer was married six times, and had nine children by his various wives
- In 1971, he clashed with the women's movement after suggesting in *The Prisoner of Sex*, that gender may shape how a person perceives reality. This made him a hate figure among some feminists who pointed to the preoccupation with violence in his writing
- Mailer wrote over 40 books, including biographies of Muhammad Ali, Marilyn Monroe and Pablo Picasso. He also wrote many film scripts, essays and journalistic pieces.

6.2 The collapse of consensus

Consensus ends

- In the 1960s, the post-war consensus collapsed because:
  - ❍ Young people challenged the values of their parents
  - ❍ The civil rights and women's movements and the Vietnam war divided Americans

- ○ The revelation of inner city poverty and the race riots undermined faith in the American Dream
- ○ The 1970s recession, which increased poverty and unemployment, further undermined this faith. It also made tax-payers more reluctant to help their poorer fellow Americans.

Youth culture

- The children born after the war (the 'baby boomers') were entering their teens from the late-1950s. The first 'teenagers', they were better educated than their parents, with no memory of economic depression or war
- They could easily get part-time jobs and with money to spend they developed a distinctive youth culture
- A whole industry grew up to supply them with magazines, films, records, make-up and books
- Many of them rejected the consensus of the 1950s and wanted to follow their own tastes and opinions
- This created a '**generation gap**' between young people and their parents.

Music

- Music played a key part of youth culture
- In the late-1950s, musicians like **Chuck Berry** and **Elvis Presley**, with their Rock 'n Roll rhythms ('devil's music' according to many of the older generation) and open sexuality, appealed to teenagers but outraged parents
- In the 1960s, young people admired pop groups like the **Beatles** and the **Rolling Stones**, copied their dress and hairstyles and listened to their views on drugs, race and war.

The sexual revolution

- Young people in the 1960s had a more permissive attitude to sex than their parents because the contraceptive pill reduced the fear of pregnancy
- This in turn undermined support for the censorship of books and films and encouraged the open discussion of issues like pornography, homosexuality and abortion, which before had been almost totally hidden.

Counter-culture

- A minority of young people turned their backs on the consumer society and the American Dream
- Many were students who were active in the civil rights or women's movement or in opposing the Vietnam war
- Others went further. Known as '**hippies**', they wore colourful old clothes, and long hair, used drugs and practiced 'free love'. Some went to live in **communes** where all property was held in common

- A few advocated an all-out attack on the capitalist society, using violence and terror
- The counter-cultural movement fizzled out in the 1970s because:
  - The decline in the economy reduced the amount of money available and forced students to work harder
  - Reasons for protest disappeared when the civil rights movement and the Vietnam war ended and the bans on abortion and homosexuality were removed
  - The spread of sexually transmitted diseases in the 1970s, and especially HIV/AIDS in the 1980s, made casual sex dangerous.

Multiculturalism

- Part of the 'American Dream' was the idea that the US was a 'melting pot' where all races blended and could live together harmoniously
- The civil rights campaign showed this was a myth, at least where black people were concerned
- In the 1970s, some black people began to seek their roots in Africa
- They also pointed out that they and their achievements had been written out of American history and culture. For example, there had been many black cowboys, but they were not mentioned in books or films
- This led to demands that schools and universities teach African-American studies
- Others groups followed their example. American Indians renamed themselves **Native Americans**. They dug up old treaties that the US government had made with their ancestors and demanded that it keep the terms. They also began to revive their ancient cultures and languages
- Women pointed out that women's experiences were also written out of American history. Universities began to offer courses in 'women's studies'
- After that Irish, Jewish, Polish and many other racial groups became interested in the experience of their immigrant ancestors and tried to construct the stories of their people's experience in America
- Until the 1960s, most immigrants to America were from Europe, but that changed in 1965. America now accepted immigrants from around the world on the basis of the skills they had to offer
- This produced a flood of newcomers, many from Asia and Latin America. These people brought their languages and culture with them
- This created a debate on whether multiculturalism was a good policy or whether the US should demand that all new-comers learn English and conform to American values.

6.3 Religion in American society

Religion in the American Constitution

The American Constitution says '*Congress shall make no law respecting the establishment of religion or the prohibiting the free exercise thereof*'. This guarantees American people freedom to practice their religion and prevents the government favouring one religion above another.

The various churches

- America is mainly a Christian country with a small minority of Jews and Muslims
- Over half of all Americans belong to one of the many **Protestant Churches**, such as Presbyterians, Methodists and Baptists. All Presidents have been Protestants, apart from Kennedy who was Catholic
- Many Methodists and Baptists (also called '**evangelicals**') are **fundamentalists**. They believe that the Bible is the word of God and that every word in it is true. Many fundamentalists live in the South and south-west
- Because of the Constitution, anyone can start a new Church, and a number of new religions, such as the **Mormons** and the **Jehovah's Witnesses** began in America in the last 150 years
- About a quarter of Americans are **Roman Catholics**. Their leader is the Pope in Rome, though many American Catholics disagreed with him on issues like birth control and divorce
- **Jews**, divided into Reform, Conservative and Orthodox, are the third biggest religious grouping in the US
- There were few Muslims registered in the US until the 1980s.

Race and religion

- In the American South, white people refused to sit in church with black people, so racially separate churches sprang up
- Black churches helped black people to survive discrimination and black clergymen like Martin Luther King played a leading role in the struggle for civil rights (see ch. 5)
- In the 1960s, some black people, like the boxer **Muhammad Ali**, rejected Christianity as the religion of their oppressors and converted to the **Muslim faith**.

Religion in the 1950s

- During the Cold War the leaders of the churches backed their government in the fight against 'godless communism'
- Few people questioned this. Many considered the US was '*God's own country*'

271

and believed God was on their side in the Cold War. In 1956 *'In God we Trust'* was put on coins and notes as the national motto)

- Protestant evangelicals also organised crusades to persuade people to give up drinking, swearing and gambling and to turn to Christ. One of the most important of these was **Billy Graham**

Billy Graham (1918–   )

- William Franklin (Billy) Graham was born into a Presbyterian family but joined the **Southern Baptist Church** in 1934. He was ordained a minister in 1939
- Graham became a **fundamentalist** and preached at 'Youth for Christ' rallies across the US and Europe in the 1940s. With his sincerity and vitality, he attracted many converts, urging them to read the bible and develop a personal relationship with Jesus
- From 1950, he began to organise his own evangelical crusades through the **Billy Graham Evangelistic Association**
- Arriving in a city, Graham's people would take over a stadium for a week of nightly sermons accompanied by a choir of thousands. The Association made Graham a wealthy man
- Graham consistently supported right-wing causes. In the 1950s, he joined McCarthy's anti-communist campaign, in the 1960s he backed US involvement in the Vietnam war, and in the 1970s he was a friend and adviser to Richard Nixon
- Over the years he never challenged the organisation of American society or called for help for the poor
- These views won him the support of newspapers and magazines like *Time* which called him *'the Protestant Pope'*. He became America's best known clergyman and all Presidents after Truman, felt it necessary to be seen consulting him.

- In 1960, a Catholic, John F Kennedy, was elected President. This worried many Protestants who feared the Pope would be the real ruler of America. Kennedy tried to reassure them by consulting Billy Graham.

Religion in the 1960s

- Religion became less important in US society during the 1960s
- Censorship of films and books declined and people were open to a wider range of influences
- Young people with a better education than their parents demanded the right to make up their own minds on issues of sexual morality like divorce and contraception. Many stopped going to church
- The civil rights movement and the women's movement challenged old (often biblically-based) attitudes to race and gender
- A number Supreme Court judgements limited the government's right to impose religious views on society. They forbade prayers in State-funded public schools and allowed a woman to choose an abortion

- The war in Vietnam also undermined the belief of many Americans that their country always fought for just causes. Many clergy were actively involved in campaigning against it.

The Moral Majority of the 1980s

- The victories for a more open society produced a backlash
- In the 1980s, right-wing Christian groups appeared calling themselves the '**Moral Majority**'. They opposed abortion, wanted prayers in public schools and tax-free status for private religious-run schools
- Most of them were evangelical Protestants, though many Catholics supported them on abortion
- Although they called themselves 'the Moral Majority', opinion polls showed that most Americans did not support their views
- The 'Moral Majority' had the backing of a number of powerful 'televangelists' who used TV to preach not just on Christianity, but on political issues too
- They were influential in the election of Ronald Reagan in 1980, but many mainstream Christian leaders, including Billy Graham, were uneasy at this open linking of religion and politics
- The 'Moral Majority' campaign ended when a number of televangelists were involved in financial and sexual scandals
- But fundamentalist Christians remained a powerful group in America over the last four decades – one which all political leaders have had to pay attention to.

Questions

For Examination questions on Later Modern History of Europe and the Wider World, Topic 6 see page 279.

Your revision notes

Later Modern Ireland, Topic 5: Politics and Society in Northern Ireland 1949–1993

2009 HL (100 marks per question)

1. Who was the more effective leader of Northern Ireland, Brookeborough or O'Neill? Argue your case, referring to both.
2. To what extent were the activities of the Apprentice Boys of Derry and/or the choice of Coleraine as the site of Northern Ireland's second university divisive?
3. What were the social and economic effects of the "Troubles"?
4. What was the importance of one or more of the following: the Sunningdale Agreement, 1973; the Anglo-Irish Agreement, 1985; the Downing Street Declaration, 1993?

2009 OL

B   Write a short paragraph on one of the following (30 marks)

1. The welfare state in Northern Ireland.
2. Seamus Heaney.
3. The impact of the "Troubles" on everyday life in Northern Ireland.
4. Ian Paisley.

C   Answer one of the following: (40 marks)

1. Why were the activities of the Apprentice Boys a source of tension in Derry?
2. What part did John Hume play in the affairs of Northern Ireland?
3. As British Prime Minister, what policies did Margaret Thatcher follow with regard to Northern Ireland?
4. What was proposed by one or more of the following: the Sunningdale Agreement, 1973; the Anglo-Irish Agreement, 1985; the Downing Street Declaration, 1993?

Later Modern Ireland, Topic 3: The pursuit of sovereignty and the impact of partition, 1912–1949

2009 HL (100 marks per question)

1. Why were the Anglo-Irish Treaty negotiations controversial?
2. What were the main social and economic challenges facing Northern Ireland, 1920–1945?
3. During the period 1932–1945, which did Éamon de Valera manage better, the economy or Anglo-Irish relations? Argue your case, referring to both.
4. What attempts were made to promote cultural identity, North and South, during the period, 1912–1945?

2008 HL (100 marks per question)

1. To what extent was the Anglo-Irish Treaty, 1921, responsible for the Irish Civil War?
2. What steps did Irish governments take to consolidate democracy, 1923–1945?
3. What was the significance of the Eucharistic Congress, 1932, for the Irish Free State?
4. How well did the Unionist Party manage the affairs of Northern Ireland, 1920–1939?

2007 HL (100 marks per question)

1. What were the aims and achievements of Patrick Pearse?
2. How did Anglo-Irish relations develop during the period 1923–1949?
3. How was cultural identity promoted in Ireland, North and South, between 1920 and 1949?
4. Following the experience of war, to what extent was the Belfast of 1945 different from that of 1939?

2009 OL

B   Write a short paragraph on one of the following (30 marks)

1. The 1916 Rising.
2. Countess Markievicz.
3. William T. Cosgrave.
4. James J. McElligott.

C   Answer one of the following: (40 marks)

1. What part did Arthur Griffith play in the Treaty negotiations, October–December, 1921 and in later events?

2. What was the importance of the Eucharistic Congress, 1932?

3. As Prime Minister, what part did James Craig play in the affairs of Northern Ireland?

4. What part did Éamon de Valera play in Anglo-Irish relations between 1932 and 1945?

2008 OL

B   Write a short paragraph on one of the following (30 marks)

1. Why Sinn Féin won the 1918 general election.
2. The War of Independence, 1919–1921.
3. Richard Dawson Bates.
4. Evie Hone.

C   Answer one of the following: (40 marks)

1. What part did Countess Markievicz play in Irish affairs between 1913 and 1922?

2. Following the Treaty negotiations, what were the main terms of the Anglo-Irish Treaty signed in London on 6 December 1921?

3. In what ways did the Eucharistic Congress 1932 help to promote the Catholic cultural identity of the Irish Free State?

4. What was the impact of World War II on life in Belfast between 1939 and 1945?

2007 OL

B   Write a short paragraph on one of the following (30 marks)

1. The Third Home Rule Bill, 1912.
2. The Easter Rising, 1916.
3. How partition affected Ireland.
4. William T. Cosgrave.

C   Answer one of the following: (40 marks)

1. What role did Arthur Griffith play in Irish affairs?
2. In what ways was the Eucharistic Congress, 1932, a memorable event?
3. What part did Éamon de Valera play in Anglo-Irish relations between 1932 and 1945?
4. How did World War II impact on the city of Belfast?

Later Modern History of Europe and the Wider World, Topic 3: Dictatorship and Democracy in Europe, 1920–1945

2009 HL (100 marks per question)

1. Why was France unstable during the period, 1920–1940?
2. How did dictators use propaganda and/or terror to maintain their power?
3. What were the main social and economic challenges facing Britain, 1920–1945?
4. What did you learn about World War II from your study of one or more of the following: wartime alliances; collaboration/resistance; technology of warfare?

2008 HL (100 marks per question)

1. What did Lenin and Stalin contribute to communism in Russia?
2. Which had the greater social and economic problems during the inter-war years, Britain or Germany? Argue your case, referring to both countries.
3. What contribution did Joseph Goebbels and/or Leni Riefenstahl make to Nazi propaganda?
4. What was the impact of World War II on the civilian population of Britain and/or France?

2007 HL (100 marks per question)

1. What problems did the Third Republic of France encounter between 1920 and 1940?
2. What were the main characteristics of the Nazi state in Germany between 1933 and 1939?
3. What were the causes and the consequences of the Jarrow March, October, 1936?
4. How significant was the role played by the Soviet Union in World War II?

2009 OL

B Write a short paragraph on one of the following (30 marks)

1. Vladimir Ilyich Lenin.
2. Church-state relations in Germany under Hitler.
3. Winston Churchill.
4. Anti-Semitism and the Holocaust.

C   Answer one of the following: (40 marks)

1. Would you agree that the leadership of Benito Mussolini was a disaster for Italy? Argue your case.

2. How did the Nuremberg Rallies and/or Leni Riefenstahl contribute to the Nazi regime?

3. Why did Stalin set up show trials and did they achieve his desired result?

4. What did Charlie Chaplin and/or Bing Crosby contribute to entertainment?

2008 OL

B   Write a short paragraph on one of the following (30 marks)

1. The growth in radio and cinema, 1920–1945.

2. Church-state relations in Italy under Mussolini.

3. The British economist, J M Keynes.

4. The Vichy state in France, 1940–1945.

C   Answer one of the following: (40 marks)

1. What was the purpose of Stalin's show trials in the 1930s?

2. How did the Nuremberg Rallies help to create propaganda for Hitler and the Nazi regime?

3. What were the economic and social conditions in Britain that led to the Jarrow March in October 1936?

4. How successful was Winston Churchill as a wartime leader between 1940 and 1945?

2007 OL

B   Write a short paragraph on one of the following (30 marks)

1. Vladimir Ilyich Lenin.

2. Economic and social problems in Britain in the 1930s.

3. France during World War II.

4. Winston Churchill.

C   Answer one of the following: (40 marks)

1. What impact did Stalin's show trials have on the Soviet Union?

2. How did Joseph Goebbels and/or Leni Riefenstahl use the German mass media to promote the Nazi movement?

3. How did fascism develop in Italy under Benito Mussolini?

4. How did Bing Crosby and/or Charlie Chaplin become stars of popular culture during the period, 1920–1945?

Later Modern History of Europe and the Wider World, Topic 6: The United States and the World, 1945–1989

2007 HL (100 marks per question)

1. How did McCarthyism and/or the anti-war movement affect US foreign policy, 1945–1972?
2. In what ways did the Montgomery bus boycott, 1956, advance the cause of the civil rights movement?
3. What contribution did Betty Friedan and/or Norman Mailer make to society in the United States?
4. What were the significant developments in US foreign policy, 1973–1989?

2006 HL (100 marks per question)

1. During the period, 1945–1989, what was the impact of one or more of the following on American society: racial conflict; urban poverty; organised crime?
2. Which had the greater impact on the United States: involvement in Korea or involvement in Vietnam? Argue your case, referring to both.
3. What were the successes and failures of the political career of Ronald Reagan?
4. What was the importance of one or more of the following: McCarthyism; the Moon Landing, 1969; developments in information technology?

2007 OL

B   Write a short paragraph on one of the following (30 marks)

1.   Urban poverty, drugs and crime.
2.   The United States and Cuba.
3.   Marilyn Monroe.
4.   The "Organization Man".

C   Answer one of the following (40 marks)

1.   What part did President Truman play in the history of the United States?
2.   How did Senator Joe McCarthy influence the direction of foreign policy in the United States?
3.   What problems did President Johnson encounter in dealing with Vietnam?
4.   How was it possible for the United States to achieve the moon landing in 1969?

2006 OL

B   Write a short paragraph on one of the following (30 marks)

1.   The American multinational corporation.
2.   Betty Friedan and the changing role of women.
3.   Youth culture in modern America.
4.   The Moon landing, 1969.

C   Answer one of the following (40 marks)

1.   Why was the Montgomery bus boycott (1956) so important to the story of the civil rights movement?
2.   What policies did President Johnson follow in relation to the war in Vietnam?
3.   How important were Marilyn Monroe and/or Muhammad Ali in modern American culture?
4.   How and why did Billy Graham become such a popular religious leader in the United States?

Date			
Time			
Section to be revised			

Date			
Time			
Section to be revised			

Date			
Time			
Section to be revised			

Date			
Time			
Section to be revised			

Date			
Time			
Section to be revised			

Date			
Time			
Section to be revised			

Night before exam

Sections to be revised

Date			
Time			
Section to be revised			

Date			
Time			
Section to be revised			

Date			
Time			
Section to be revised			

Date			
Time			
Section to be revised			

Date			
Time			
Section to be revised			

Date			
Time			
Section to be revised			

Night before exam

Sections to be revised

Date

Time

Section to
be revised

Date

Time

Section to
be revised

Date

Time

Section to
be revised

Date

Time

Section to
be revised

Date

Time

Section to
be revised

Date

Time

Section to
be revised

Night before exam

Sections to
be revised

Date				
Time				
Section to be revised				

Date				
Time				
Section to be revised				

Date				
Time				
Section to be revised				

Date				
Time				
Section to be revised				

Date				
Time				
Section to be revised				

Date				
Time				
Section to be revised				

Night before exam

Sections to be revised

Date				
Time				
Section to be revised				

Date				
Time				
Section to be revised				

Date				
Time				
Section to be revised				

Date				
Time				
Section to be revised				

Date				
Time				
Section to be revised				

Date				
Time				
Section to be revised				

Night before exam

Sections to be revised

285

Date			
Time			
Section to be revised			

Date			
Time			
Section to be revised			

Date			
Time			
Section to be revised			

Date			
Time			
Section to be revised			

Date			
Time			
Section to be revised			

Date			
Time			
Section to be revised			

Night before exam

Sections to be revised

Date			
Time			
Section to be revised			

Date			
Time			
Section to be revised			

Date			
Time			
Section to be revised			

Date			
Time			
Section to be revised			

Date			
Time			
Section to be revised			

Date			
Time			
Section to be revised			

Night before exam

Sections to be revised

Francis Frith's
DOWN THE THAMES

PHOTOGRAPHIC MEMORIES

Francis Frith's
DOWN THE THAMES

Martin Andrew

First published in the United Kingdom in 2000 by
Frith Book Company Ltd

Hardback Edition 2000
ISBN 1-85937-121-3

Paperback Edition 2001
ISBN 1-85937-278-3

Hardback Reprinted in 2001

Paperback Reprinted in 2001

British Library Cataloguing in Publication Data

Francis Frith's Down the Thames
Martin Andrew

Frith Book Company Ltd
Frith's Barn, Teffont,
Salisbury, Wiltshire SP3 5QP
Tel: +44 (0) 1722 716 376
Email: info@francisfrith.co.uk
www.francisfrith.co.uk

Printed and bound in Great Britain

AS WITH ANY HISTORICAL DATABASE THE FRITH ARCHIVE IS CONSTANTLY BEING CORRECTED AND IMPROVED
AND THE PUBLISHERS WOULD WELCOME INFORMATION ON OMISSIONS OR INACCURACIES

CONTENTS

FRANCIS FRITH: *Victorian Pioneer*

FRANCIS FRITH, Victorian founder of the world-famous photographic archive, was a complex and multitudinous man. A devout Quaker and a highly successful Victorian businessman, he was both philosophic by nature and pioneering in outlook.

By 1855 Francis Frith had already established a wholesale grocery business in Liverpool, and sold it for the astonishing sum of £200,000, which is the equivalent today of over £15,000,000. Now a multi-millionaire, he was able to indulge his passion for travel. As a child he had pored over travel books written by early explorers, and his fancy and imagination had been stirred by family holidays to the sublime mountain regions of Wales and Scotland. 'What a land of spirit-stirring and enriching scenes and places!' he had written. He was to return to these scenes of grandeur in later years to 'recapture the thousands of vivid and tender memories', but with a different purpose. Now in his thirties, and captivated by the new science of photography, Frith set out on a series of pioneering journeys to the Nile regions that occupied him from 1856 until 1860.

INTRIGUE AND ADVENTURE

He took with him on his travels a specially-designed wicker carriage that acted as both dark-room and sleeping chamber. These far-flung journeys were packed with intrigue and adventure. In his life story, written when he was sixty-three, Frith tells of being held captive by bandits, and of fighting 'an awful midnight battle to the very point of surrender with a deadly pack of hungry, wild dogs'. Sporting flowing Arab costume, Frith arrived at Akaba by camel seventy years before Lawrence, where he encountered 'desert princes and rival sheikhs, blazing with jewel-hilted swords'.

During these extraordinary adventures he was assiduously exploring the desert regions bordering the Nile and patiently recording the antiquities and peoples with his camera. He was the first photographer to venture beyond the sixth cataract. Africa was still the mysterious 'Dark Continent', and Stanley and Livingstone's historic meeting was a decade into the future. The conditions for picture taking confound belief. He laboured for hours in his wicker dark-room in the sweltering heat of the desert, while the volatile chemicals fizzed dangerously in their trays. Often he was forced to work in remote tombs and caves where conditions were cooler. Back in London he exhibited his photographs and was 'rapturously cheered' by members of the Royal Society. His reputation as a photographer was made overnight. An eminent modern historian has likened their impact on the population of the time to that on our own generation of the first photographs taken on the surface of the moon.

VENTURE OF A LIFE-TIME

Characteristically, Frith quickly spotted the opportunity to create a new business as a specialist publisher of photographs. He lived in an era of immense and sometimes violent change. For the poor in the early part of Victoria's reign work was a drudge and the hours long, and people had precious little free time to enjoy themselves.

Most had no transport other than a cart or gig at their disposal, and had not travelled far beyond the boundaries of their own town or village. However, by the 1870s, the railways had threaded their way across the country, and Bank Holidays and half-day Saturdays had been made obligatory by Act of Parliament. All of a sudden the ordinary working man and his family were able to enjoy days out and see a little more of the world.

With characteristic business acumen, Francis Frith foresaw that these new tourists would enjoy having souvenirs to commemorate their days out. In 1860 he married Mary Ann Rosling and set out with the intention of photographing every city, town and village in Britain. For the next thirty years he travelled the country by train and by pony and trap, producing fine photographs of seaside resorts and beauty spots that were keenly bought by millions of Victorians. These prints were painstakingly pasted into family albums and pored over during the dark nights of winter, rekindling precious memories of summer excursions.

THE RISE OF FRITH & CO

Frith's studio was soon supplying retail shops all over the country. To meet the demand he gathered about him a small team of photographers, and published the work of independent artist-photographers of the calibre of Roger Fenton and Francis Bedford. In order to gain some understanding of the scale of Frith's business one only has to look at the catalogue issued by Frith & Co in 1886: it runs to some 670

court card, but there was little room for illustration. In 1899, a year after Frith's death, a new card measuring 5.5 x 3.5 inches became the standard format, but it was not until 1902 that the divided back came into being, with address and message on one face and a full-size illustration on the other. *Frith & Co* were in the vanguard of postcard development, and Frith's sons Eustace and Cyril continued their father's monumental task, expanding the number of views offered to the public and recording more and more places in Britain, as the coasts and countryside were opened up to mass travel.

Francis Frith died in 1898 at his villa in Cannes, his great project still growing. The archive he created continued in business for another seventy years. By 1970 it contained over a third of a million pictures of 7,000 cities, towns and villages. The massive photographic record Frith has left to us stands as a living monument to a special and very remarkable man.

pages, listing not only many thousands of views of the British Isles but also many photographs of most European countries, and China, Japan, the USA and Canada – note the sample page shown above from the hand-written *Frith & Co* ledgers detailing pictures taken. By 1890 Frith had created the greatest specialist photographic publishing company in the world, with over 2,000 outlets – more than the combined number that Boots and WH Smith have today! The picture on the right shows the *Frith & Co* display board at Ingleton in the Yorkshire Dales. Beautifully constructed with mahogany frame and gilt inserts, it could display up to a dozen local scenes.

POSTCARD BONANZA

◆

The ever-popular holiday postcard we know today took many years to develop. In 1870 the Post Office issued the first plain cards, with a pre-printed stamp on one face. In 1894 they allowed other publishers' cards to be sent through the mail with an attached adhesive halfpenny stamp. Demand grew rapidly, and in 1895 a new size of postcard was permitted called the

Frith's Archive: *A Unique Legacy*

FRANCIS FRITH'S legacy to us today is of immense significance and value, for the magnificent archive of evocative photographs he created provides a unique record of change in 7,000 cities, towns and villages throughout Britain over a century and more. Frith and his fellow studio photographers revisited locations many times down the years to update their views, compiling for us an enthralling and colourful pageant of British life and character.

We tend to think of Frith's sepia views of Britain as nostalgic, for most of us use them to conjure up memories of places in our own lives with which we have family associations. It often makes us forget that to Francis Frith they were records of daily life as it was actually being lived in the cities, towns and villages of his day. The Victorian age was one of great and often bewildering change for ordinary people, and though the pictures evoke an impression of slower times, life was as busy and hectic as it is today.

We are fortunate that Frith was a photographer of the people, dedicated to recording the minutiae of everyday life. For it is this sheer wealth of visual data, the painstaking chronicle of changes in dress, transport, street layouts, buildings, housing, engineering and landscape that captivates us so much today. His remarkable images offer us a powerful link with the past and with the lives of our ancestors.

TODAY'S TECHNOLOGY

Computers have now made it possible for Frith's many thousands of images to be accessed almost instantly. In the Frith archive today, each photograph is carefully 'digitised' then stored on a CD Rom. Frith archivists can locate a single photograph amongst thousands within seconds. Views can be catalogued and sorted under a variety of categories of place and content to the immediate benefit of researchers. Inexpensive reference prints can be created for them at the touch of a mouse button, and a wide range of books and other printed materials assembled and published for a wider, more general readership - in the next twelve months over a hundred Frith local history titles will be published! The

THE FRANCIS FRITH COLLECTION
Photographic publishers since 1860

HOME | PHOTO SEARCH | BOOKS | PORTFOLIO | GALLERY   MY CART
Products | History | Other Collections | Contact us | Help?

your town,
your village

365,000 photographs of 7,000 towns and villages, taken between 1860 & 1970.

The Frith Archive
The Frith Archive is the remarkable legacy of its energetic and visionary founder. Today, the Frith archive is the only nationally important archive of its kind still in private ownership.

The Collection is world-renowned for the extraordinary quality of its images.

The Gallery
This month The Frith Gallery features images from "Frith's Egypt".

News...
Image update complete. An additional 5,000 images have been added and the quality of all images has been improved.

Sample Chapters avaliable. The first selection of sample chapters from the Frith Book Co.'s extensive range is now available. All are offered in Pdf format for easy downloading and viewing.

explore FRITH
Search thousands of photographs from one of the worlds' great archives.

Town search
[   ] GO

County search
[Select a county ▾] GO

the FRITHgallery

See Frith at www.francisfrith.co.uk

day-to-day workings of the archive are very different from how they were in Francis Frith's time: imagine the herculean task of sorting through eleven tons of glass negatives as Frith had to do to locate a particular sequence of pictures! Yet the archive still prides itself on maintaining the same high standards of excellence laid down by Francis Frith, including the painstaking cataloguing and indexing of every view.

It is curious to reflect on how the internet now allows researchers in America and elsewhere greater instant access to the archive than Frith himself ever enjoyed. Many thousands of individual views can be called up on screen within seconds on one of the Frith internet sites, enabling people living continents away to revisit the streets of their ancestral home town, or view places in Britain where they have enjoyed holidays. Many overseas researchers welcome the chance to view special theme selections, such as transport, sports, costume and ancient monuments.

We are certain that Francis Frith would have heartily approved of these modern developments, for he himself was always working at the very limits of Victorian photographic technology.

THE VALUE OF THE ARCHIVE TODAY

Because of the benefits brought by the computer, Frith's images are increasingly studied by social historians, by researchers into genealogy and ancestry, by architects, town planners, and by teachers and schoolchildren involved in local history projects. In addition, the archive offers every one of us a unique opportunity to examine the places where we and our families have lived and worked down the years. Immensely successful in Frith's own era, the archive is now, a century and more on, entering a new phase of popularity.

THE PAST IN TUNE WITH THE FUTURE

Historians consider the Francis Frith Collection to be of prime national importance. It is the only archive of its kind remaining in private ownership and has been valued at a million pounds. However, this figure is now rapidly increasing as digital technology enables more and more people around the world to enjoy its benefits.

Francis Frith's archive is now housed in an historic timber barn in the beautiful village of Teffont in Wiltshire. Its founder would not recognize the archive office as it is today. In place of the many thousands of dusty boxes containing glass plate negatives and an all-pervading odour of photographic chemicals, there are now ranks of computer screens. He would be amazed to watch his images travelling round the world at unimaginable speeds through network and internet lines.

The archive's future is both bright and exciting. Francis Frith, with his unshakeable belief in making photographs available to the greatest number of people, would undoubtedly approve of what is being done today with his lifetime's work. His photographs, depicting our shared past, are now bringing pleasure and enlightenment to millions around the world a century and more after his death.

DOWN THE THAMES – *An Introduction*

'Sweet Thames, run softly....' Edmund Spenser

THIS BOOK TAKES the form of an imaginary journey down the River Thames from near its source a few miles south of Cirencester in Gloucestershire down through Oxford, Reading and London into the mud-flat lands of the wide Thames Estuary as far as Shoeburyness, or Sheerness, where it in effect debouches into the North Sea. This is a total journey of about 215 miles, making the Thames the longest river wholly in England. We shall see it change from a stream through a rural village, powering the occasional water-mill, to a mighty trade highway teeming with towed barges and navigated via pound locks, which by-pass the treacherous weirs, into the calmer waters that flow through the great city of London and onwards to the sea.

What is seen on the banks and near the river has changed greatly in some places, and remarkably little in others; this book spans about three quarters of a century in its head-long progress through time and space. Old Father Thames just keeps on flowing ... It has seen the mighty London docks rise to become the busiest and wealthiest in human history, a vast entrepot for the world's goods and products flowing through a great industrial city. These vast docks, excavated on the north and south banks, and lined by cranes, derricks and railways besides millions of square feet of warehouses, flourished from 1799 until finally closing in 1981. Their trade moved further east to the container port of Tilbury. To some extent, we are all blinded by the Industrial Revolution in the North of England to the vast amount of manufacturing and processing that took place in London. Indeed, until about 1800 there were more steam engines in London than in Lancashire, and until the mid 19th century London's manufacturing output was unmatched anywhere in England, let alone the world. Since that time the emphasis has gradually shifted elsewhere; now London's polluting industries have largely been transformed into service industries and offices, always a major element. The docks are now Dockland, a vast complex of offices, houses and flats interspersed with the water of some of the retained docks, which have become ornamental lakes and marinas for the inhabitants. The major benefit for the Thames is the greater cleanliness of the water: it was once described as 110% effluent as it passed the Houses of Parliament in the 1840s, assisting King Cholera and King Typhoid in their deadly work. Salmon have now returned since their disappearance late in the 18th century.

The river's primary function, even down past the Pool of London, is pleasure. Boating became immensely popular with all social classes in the later 19th century. No view of the river on a Sunday was complete without a scrum of skiffs, punts, sailing boats, canoes, steam launches and all kinds of pleasure craft jostling for the water and converging to cram the locks that by-passed the all-too-frequent weirs. All this is superbly described in that comic masterpiece by Jerome K Jerome,

'Three Men in a Boat', published in 1889; it gives a splendid picture of messing about in boats between Kingston and Oxford. Arrayed in their bright striped blazers and straw boaters, flannels, deck shoes, ladies' white dresses and parasols, the new mobile middle and lower middle classes, now with more leisure and disposable income, began the transformation of the river from trade artery to leisure facility. This new role was necessitated by the railway age, which supplanted canals and rivers as the main means of shipping goods.

It was as well that Jerome and his friends took to the water, for without them, and the need for flood control, water conservation and processing the river would not have been maintained as it has: witness the dereliction of many canals, until leisure use and enthusiasts stimulated their gradual restoration in recent years. The main areas having trade as a main

element now lie east of London, with the main container port to the west of Tilbury on the Essex bank, out in the estuarine Thames.

In this book there are two main themes beloved of the Frith photographers: the Thames crossings - that is, bridges - and the locks and weirs. The latter cope with its total descent of 250 feet from the first lock, St

were a normal feature of most weirs until well into the 19th century, and the censuses of 1841, 1861 and 1881 list fishermen among the working-class populations of towns such as Henley and Marlow. Other river-dependent occupations included brewers, brewery workers, mill workers, bargees and wharfingers. Many industries took their power source from

John's Lock at Lechlade, to the last, Richmond Lock and Half-Tide Weir, involving a total of 45 locks. Below Richmond the river is little above sea level and wholly tidal, although Teddington above Richmond is generally regarded as the limit of the tidal Thames - a fact allegedly known by every schoolboy, at least in my young day in the 1950s.

The river had been a trade route of supreme importance from early times, and navigational problems and weirs were constant causes of friction with fishermen and riparian owners. Those earlier fishermen were not leisure anglers, but people dependent on fish for their livelihood. Eel traps

the river by means of water-wheels, and many of the mill buildings survive, although not normally as mills but as offices, flats and other uses. The river's waterwheels provided the power for flour, paper and gunpowder making, leather and tanning, and any industrial process needing power or large amounts of water. Even now, huge quantities of Thames water are extracted, and usually partly returned to the river, from the millions of gallons a day diverted into Didcot Power Station to much lesser quantities for processing plants along the river. Some mills remain as important riverside buildings, providing valuable links with the past, such as Hambleden Mill, now flats, Mapledurham Mill, or

Cricklade Mill, now a house, while others have vanished utterly, including those in Marlow and Reading or Shiplake.

The current locks, which range from the modest ones on the upper Thames to the giant at Teddington (650 feet long and capable of handling eight barges and their tug in one go), emerged during the late 18th century. These are the 'pound locks': the boats are empounded while the water level is equalised to that of the way the boats wish to go by means of sluices, which fill or empty the lock as required.

For many hundreds of years the predecessor of the pound lock was the 'flash' lock, which had only one pair of gates. It is hair-raising to describe how they worked downstream. The gates would be opened in or beside a weir, and the river water thundered through, sweeping or 'flashing' the barge or boat through. The gates would then be closed, usually by means of a series of 'paddles', rectangular sluice planks attached to long poles, and the river would return to its previous level until a further boat or barge arrived and the perilous process would begin again. If a boat wished to come upstream, the paddles would be removed and the boat would be hauled through the gap in the weir by men hauling on stout ropes or by means of a heavy capstan winch. The last surviving capstan, on the north bank below Wittington, west of Marlow, has recently been restored to working condition by Wycombe District Council. The process was a hazardous one; over the years many bargees were drowned when boats were capsized or foundered.

The pound lock was a major advance, not only in safety. It was also more welcome to fishermen and water mill owners, for a busy day through the flash locks could seriously lower the overall river level to reduce water-wheel efficiency, particularly in summer when water levels are particularly low; also, all the fish could be washed downstream. Pound locks replaced flash locks in a remarkably gradual programme. Many were changed from 1771 to about 1810, but ownership problems left many in place. It took the Thames Navigation Act of 1866 to give greater powers to the Thames Commissioners to secure the removal of the last few flash locks in the midst of weirs - these rendered water management a nightmare until the 1930s, despite the locks nearby. The pound locks themselves have mostly been rebuilt several times, and currently a massive programme of lock and weir reconstruction is just coming to an end. This is not surprising: river scour, the enormous power of water, and the frequent use of the gates and machinery necessitate frequent repair and overhaul, particularly as the first locks mostly had turf side walls.

The Thames was indeed a major trade route, with vast tonnages of goods and raw materials being laboriously hauled by ropes up and down stream by gangs of men until the 19th century, when horses put the bargees out of work; goods also travelled by sail and oar in favourable conditions. Sailing barges, once a familiar sight on the lower Thames and in the Estuary, are now transmogrified into leisure craft, and are the preserve of restorers, rather than hauliers. A remarkable view of late 17th-century barges on the river can be seen in oil paintings of the river in Henley and its environs by the Dutch artist Jan Siberechts. Grain, malt, bricks, wool, cloth, coal, flints, limestone, timber and a hundred other products and raw materials made their way up and down the Thames and its tributaries. Canals, such as the Kennet and Avon, opened in 1810, and the Thames and Severn, opened in 1789, all helped maintain the river's supremacy in supplying and trading with London.

To jump a couple of centuries, the leisure boom was captured in a famous painting of Boulters Lock, near Maidenhead, by Edward Gregory, first exhibited in 1897. The pressure on lock mechanisms became enormous, with hundreds of boats passing each way on a Saturday afternoon and a Sunday. To reduce the problem, and speed small craft on their way, boat elevators, ramps with rollers, were installed at some of the busiest locks to reduce congestion. Those at Boulters, Teddington and Richmond Locks are shown in this book, as well as a very narrow lock at Teddington, the Skiff Lock, another leisure adjustment on the river system.

The river as far as Staines had been granted to the City of London by Richard the Lion Heart in 1197, but coherent management of the whole river only started in the 18th century with the appointment of Thames Navigational Commissioners in a 1751 act of parliament. Proving somewhat ineffectual, the Thames Act of 1770 laid the foundations for modern management of the whole river; it resulted in the replacement of many of the flash locks by pound locks, a technical device borrowed from canal design. However, things were still not ideal, particularly as in the earlier 19th century traffic increased vastly with leisure boating and with the advent of steam power for both commerce and passenger carrying. The commissioners were responsible not only for the locks, weirs and the state of the river banks, but also for the towing paths alongside.

In 1857 the Thames Conservancy was

formed; their coat of arms, and that of the City of London, can be seen on the date plaques of many lock-keeper's cottages. The Port of London Authority was set up in 1908 to be responsible for the port of London and all aspects of the river in and to the east of London.

And all the time the Thames passes beneath many bridges of outstanding quality, from the massive ironwork of Hammersmith Bridge, the elegance of Marlow's suspension bridge, or the glorious stonework of Richmond Bridge (1770s), Staines Bridge (1830) or Maidenhead Bridge (1770s) - and, of course, that symbol of London, Tower Bridge. There are also less wonderful bridges, such as the woeful Walton on Thames Bridge (1860s). This book also includes some of the best 'lost' bridges, Waterloo (1810s) and London (1820s) - not that their replacements are unsuccessful. Certainly the bridges across the river have fascinating histories, including the smaller ones such as Lechlade's Ha'penny toll bridge (1790s) or the Whitchurch toll bridge (late 19th century).

This book has its photographs divided into five chapters. The first starts below Thames Head and follows it down as far as Wallingford via Lechlade and Oxford, where, it seems, an 18th-century affectation with no historical basis termed the Thames above Dorchester 'the Isis'. Chapter two follows the river from Streatley through the Goring Gap to pass Reading and Henley to Marlow: real 'Three Men in a Boat' territory. Chapter three takes us as far as Richmond and the last of the river's weirs and locks, while the fourth chapter leads us into the metropolis to finish at Tower Bridge. The last chapter heads into the Thames Estuary past the wonderful Thames Barrier at Woolwich, built to defend the city from flood surges from the North Sea, and passes below the Queen Elizabeth Bridge to head for where the Estuary merges with the North Sea near Shoeburyness. It is a mighty river, passing through wonderful countryside in Oxfordshire, Gloucestershire, Buckinghamshire and Berkshire, ranging from the meadows around Lechlade to the tree-clad river cliffs below Cliveden. Then there are the towns and villages near to or on the river, the mellow golden Cotswold limestones of Lechlade or Ashton Keynes, the stone-built colleges of Oxford, the splendid towns of Henley and Marlow, the shattered husks of Maidenhead and Staines, and then one of the greatest cities in the world: London.

This introduction, I hope, conveys the fascination and excitement of this great river; I hope, too, that the selection of photographs goes some way to capturing the character of the river in its various moods and the very different landscapes through which it flows, now cleaner than it has been for a couple of hundred years. As a parting shot I commend you to read or re-read Jerome K Jerome's 'Three Men in a Boat', an affectionate and amusing snapshot of the river in 1889, close to the date of most of the oldest views in the book and highly evocative. My own memories from part of my boyhood in Ealing in the 1950s Include the irridescent flash of a kingfisher in a muddy Brentford creek and trains of lumbering barges hauled by dirty ancient tugs along a brown and unappetising looking river. All that has changed: the barges have gone, and coxed fours and pleasure boats now ply along a clean and healthy river.

ASHTON KEYNES, CHURCH WALK WITH MILL HOUSE AND THE RIVER THAMES c1955 A144305
Our photographic tour starts some four or five miles from the traditional source of the Thames in this delightful Cotswold stone village, through which the young river flows as little more than a vigorous stream. It formerly powered a watermill with the Mill House on the right and its mill-leet to its left.

ASHTON KEYNES, HIGH ROAD c1955 A144301
This Wiltshire village is known locally as the village of four crosses, all medieval. This view looks along High Road with Church Walk on the left past the cross shaft, and the young Thames just out of picture on the left. Cocks House, in the distance at the junction with Back Street, is unchanged.

CRICKLADE
St Mary's Church c1955
Cricklade, ten miles from the Thames source, is an ancient town with evidence of Anglo-Saxon town walls as well as of Roman occupation. It has two medieval churches, the splendidly towered St Sampson behind the High Street, and the less grand St Mary's at the north end of the High Street, which has this fine complete 14th-century churchyard cross.

◆

CRICKLADE
High Street c1955
This small Wiltshire market town has a long, roughly north-south High Street, seen here looking north from the junction with Bath Road. The houses on the right were demolished to improve the junction with Calcutt Road, but little else has changed. The 1897 Diamond Jubilee clock tower survives outside The Vale pub.

CRICKLADE, ST MARY'S CHURCH C1955   C300002

CRICKLADE, HIGH STREET C1955   C300003

INGLESHAM, LITTLE HOLME YHA c1955 I26001
Moving downstream, it is no use the hopeful walker knocking on the door of this early 19th-century farmhouse, Littleholme, in Upper Inglesham, hoping for a bed: it is no longer, as it was in the 1950s, a Youth Hostel. Next to it, however, is the Inglesham Forge Restaurant, so at least the walker could eat.

LECHLADE, THE RIVER c1955 L147045
About twenty-five miles downstream from its source we reach the stone-built town of Lechlade on the Gloucestershire bank of the Thames. The Ha'penny Bridge was built in 1792 to replace a ferry. It is an elegant single arch with a tall, pyramid-roofed tollhouse, and so named because of the original crossing toll.

LECHLADE, THE CHURCH FROM THE RIVER C1955 L147057

Looking north from roughly the same viewpoint on the south bank of the Thames, the Perpendicular Gothic parish church with its tall spire, one of Gloucestershire's fine 'wool' churches, dominates the view. The willows have gone or been replaced, and there is more building in the plots behind the High Street on the left, but the scene is still just as tranquil.

LECHLADE, RIVERSIDE TEA GARDENS c1955 L147049

The warehouse on the right is now the Riverside Free House, but it and the dock reflect the commerce that made Lechlade a prosperous medieval town, where wool and cheese were loaded onto barges for shipment down river. Nowadays the fields to the far left are a leisure yacht park - yachts are the river's modern traffic - and the tea garden in the middle distance has long gone.

LECHLADE, THE SQUARE c1955 L147041

The focus of the town is the triangular medieval market place, with the best buildings on its south side: the Old Vicarage of 1805 with its Venetian ground floor windows, mansard roof and battlemented porch, Maple House beyond with its battlemented parapet and, of course, the superb St Lawrence's parish church's tower and spire.

LECHLADE, THE SQUARE c1955 L147063

This view looks north out of the Market Place, past the corner of St John Street, with the Old Vicarage on the right. This is Burford Street, with stone houses of all shapes and sizes from cottages to the Swan Hotel on the left, a part-Tudor building, and the urbane Georgian of Ryton House on the right with its four brick chimneystacks.

LECHLADE, THE MILL AND WATERFALL c1955 L147037

Lechlade Mill, a mile east of the town, was powered by the River Leach which reached the Thames just below St John's Lock. The mill buildings on the left are now converted into a house with further extensions, but well designed, and in a very pretty location.

OXFORD, THE EIGHTS 1922 72063
The Thames, or Isis, plays an important role in
Oxford University life. Here, seen from the tow path
along the west bank, looking north towards
Christchurch Meadow, the annual Eights Week is in
full swing at the end of May when the college boats
race each other. Spectators in up-to-the-minute 1922
fashions look on from the shore and from punts.

OXFORD, THE EIGHTS 1906 53695

This view, taken from Folly Bridge at the south end of St Aldate's Street, is of an earlier Eights Week with the Christchurch Meadow bank lined with the College Barges. Each college had its own ornate barge: you can see one moored at the Swan Hotel in Streatley further downstream.

OXFORD, ON THE RIVER 1922 72053

It is still Eights Week, but this time in 1922 and during a lull in the racing; this view is taken from just beyond where the River Cherwell meets the Thames. The water seethes with punts, and one of the college barges is in the distance. Many of the latter had a balustraded upper deck and a large flagpole for the college colours.

OXFORD, VIEW ON THE CHERWELL 1906 53704
Punting is and was a very popular pastime, and anyone, not only students, can hire a punt. The River Cherwell is quieter than the Thames; a popular run on a summer evening is up for a drink to the Victoria and Albert pub at Old Marston, whose garden runs down to the river.

OXFORD, FROM MAGDALEN TOWER 1890 26802

From the vantage point of Magdalen College belfry we look westwards along the High Street towards some of the wondrous 'dreaming spires', including the 14th-century spire of St Mary's Church; to its right is the dome of the sublime Radcliffe Camera, built in the 1740s by James Gibbs. To the left is Jackson's splendid Jacobethan Examination Schools, completed only eight years before this view was taken.

OXFORD, HIGH STREET 1922 71992

This view looks past Queen's College with its early 18th-century Baroque frontage to the High, the pedimented wings framing a gatehouse surmounted by a delicate domed tempietto. Beyond is St Mary's, with its superb spire bursting forth from a scrum of pinnacles. Can a city present a more sublime mellow stone townscape?

OXFORD
Carfax Tower 1922 71997
Things fall off a bit when the High reaches Carfax, at the corner of St Aldate's Street and Cornmarket Street. The medieval Carfax Tower belongs to St Martin's Church, the rest of which was demolished in 1896. Boffin's was replaced in 1931 by a Martin's Bank, now the Abbey National. Beyond, on the left of Queen Street, all has since been replaced.

OXFORD, CORNMARKET STREET 1922 71996
As we turn right along Cornmarket Street, the most striking
building amid the shops is the rough-hewn late Anglo-Saxon
tower of St Michael's Church, with its two tiers of paired
belfry windows. To the right, the tall gabled building of 1915
is still occupied by W H Smith, but there have been some
losses on the left side of the street, now partly pedestrianised.

ABINGDON, THE LOCK FROM BELOW 1890 26990

ABINGDON
The Lock from Below 1890

Downstream, you reach the market town of Abingdon, once noted for its important medieval abbey, dissolved in 1538. The monks appear to have diverted the Thames closer to their abbey; much later, Abingdon Lock was formed at the east end of Abbey Meadows in 1790. Since this view was taken, the lock has been reconstructed; the lock-keeper's cottage was rebuilt in 1928 by the Thames Conservancy.

ABINGDON
Abbey Mill 1890

Abingdon Abbey was founded in 675 AD, and the town grew up at its gates. However, nothing remains of its great monastic church. Along Thames Street, east of the town's medieval river bridge, abbey buildings remain. Note the gabled 13th-century chimney stack to The Chequer. The mill, functioning in 1890, is now a house, and the weatherboarded bag-hoist house has gone.

ABINGDON, ABBEY MILL 1890 26992

ABINGDON, THE BOAT HOUSE 1890 26987
We are looking upstream from the centre of the 14th-century stone bridge across the Thames where it crosses Nag's Head Island. The landing stage to the Crown and Thistle, a hotel some way away on Bridge Street, now belongs to The Mill House, the pub on the island. The weatherboarded outbuilding has since been demolished.

ABINGDON, VIEW FROM THE ELMS 1890 26988x
Downstream, this view looks back to the town from the east bank with Nag's Head Island separating the two river channels .The octagonal building on the left is the former gaol, now the Old Gaol Leisure Centre, an austere building of 1805-1811.

ABINGDON, STERT STREET 1893 31693

Rather unkindly, Jerome K Jerome of 'Three Men in a Boat' fame, and our constant companion along the river from Oxford to Kingston, described Abingdon as 'quiet, eminently respectable, clean and desperately dull'. This view looks along Stert Street towards the tower of St Nicholas Church which faces the Market Place; the street still retains much of its character, apart from the traffic.

ABINGDON, MARKET PLACE 1890 26994

This is very much an archive photograph, for only the bank on the left survives from 1890: Queen Victoria's statue, commemorating her Golden Jubilee of 1887, was moved to the abbey park in 1946, while the gutless Corn Exchange of 1886 and the Queen's Hotel of 1864 were swept away for the awful 1960s Bury Street shopping street.

CULHAM, THE COLLEGE 1900 45208

South-east of Abingdon, on the A415 and a mile west of the Culham Science Centre, the former Culham College is a large and austere Victorian Gothic building based on an Oxford collegiate layout with a quad. It was founded in 1852 by Bishop Samuel Wilberforce as an early teacher training college; it is now the European School, minus the creeper.

SUTTON COURTENAY, THE VILLAGE 1890 27001

This remarkable village has three medieval stone houses, as well as the Norman church whose tower we see in this view. The Swan pub dates from the 1870s and, apart from the loss of the boundary wall and railings, remains, as do the cottages. The green now has more lime trees along its edge and an unusual World War I memorial.

CLIFTON HAMPDEN, THE VILLAGE AND THE CHURCH 1890 27006

This photograph, taken from the east bank of the river, south of the Barley Mow pub, manages to exclude George Gilbert Scott's rather fine 1864 seven-arched brick bridge over the river. At the right, on the ridge, is St Michael and All Angels Church, which owes its picturesqueness to Scott rather than the middle ages.

CLIFTON HAMPDEN, THE BARLEY MOW INN 1890 27010

On the east bank, beyond the bridge, this medieval inn is noted for its 'cruck' construction, the large curved timbers in the gable wall, and for the fact that Jerome K Jerome commends it in 'Three Men in a Boat'. The timbers are now painted black rather than being (correctly) limewashed as in this view. A house is now built behind.

DORCHESTER, THE VILLAGE 1924 76211

Our progress down-river reaches Dorchester. It was a Roman town and the seat of an Anglo-Saxon bishopric, and is now dominated by its great late 11th-century Abbey church. Nowadays the by-passed winding High Street is again peaceful. The cottage on the left has been demolished but the others remain, including the rather fine White Hart Hotel, dated 1691 but in fact earlier, a former coaching inn.

SHILLINGFORD, THE SWAN HOTEL 1890 27018

Now known as the Shillingford Bridge Hotel, and with a large and rather poor extension replacing the clapboarded building to the right, this Georgian inn is situated on the south bank by the elegant bridge of 1826, which was a toll bridge until 1874. The bridge replaced others which in their turn had replaced a ferry.

WALLINGFORD, THE BRIDGE BOAT HOUSE 1899 42988
A little further downstream we reach historic
Wallingford, an Anglo-Saxon borough, much of whose
9th-century earthen ramparts remain. There are the
earthworks also of the Norman castle in the north-east
quarter of the town. Here the old town landing-stage
is north of the bridge; the quay is much altered, with
the boathouse now the Mill House pub.

WALLINGFORD, MARKET PLACE 1893 31712

In Wallingford's town centre is a fine Market Place. The railed enclosure with the lamp post has gone, but the 1885 drinking fountain and canopy, to the right of the 'growler' cab, remain, or rather were reinstated in 1979. The buildings on the left have gone, their replacements dull to awful.

WALLINGFORD, THE CHURCH AND THE BRIDGE 1899 42986

Back on the river, this view looks north-east from the Crowmarsh Gifford bank to Bridge House, with the remarkable spire of St Peter's Church beyond. Designed by the normally staid Sir Robert Taylor, the church is inventive and free Gothic, but of 1777. The bridge is remarkable too, and long, with seventeen arches, three of them medieval, three of 1809 and the rest of 1751.

STREATLEY, FROM STREATLEY DOWNS 1890 27052
Downstream from Wallingford, the Thames cuts the Goring Gap between the Chilterns and the Berkshire Downs. Brunel's Great Western Railway also took advantage of the gap for his route from Paddington to Bristol. In this view from the Downs, we look north over Streatley, which was then in Berkshire: its parish church is on the left, with Goring on the right, across the river.

STREATLEY, THE VILLAGE 1904 52933
Streatley lies at the junction of several major routes as they converge on the Goring Gap. This is now the busy A329, and the B4009 Newbury road is between the Bull at Streatley pub on the left, where the Three Men in a Boat lunched, and the Georgian Elm House beyond. The 'Wells' grocer's sign survives, but the shop is now a living room.

STREATLEY, THE SWAN HOTEL 1899 42994
Now The Swan Diplomat Hotel, the main building is
much extended to the right out of picture, to the left
and to the front. The thatched room is now tiled, and
the outbuilding to the left converted to hotel rooms.
To the right is now moored one of the Oxford College
Barges seen in earlier views.

STREATLEY, THE LOCK AND WEIR c1955 S221004

Seen from the road bridge, its balustrades recently brutalised by the Oxfordshire County Engineer, the lock, rebuilt in 1922, is little changed, although the Victorian former lock-keeper's cottage is now painted white. The weir has been rebuilt recently.

GORING, THE LOCK 1896 38313

Further along the bridge we look into the backwater with the lock island on the left and the old lock-keeper's cottage beyond the tree. Goring collected a number of late Victorian and Edwardian riverside houses and boathouses between the river and the village proper. The now tiled boathouse on the right is today a doctor's surgery.

GORING, THE VILLAGE 1899 42991

Opposite the well-known Miller of Mansfield hotel and pub, mainly Georgian with older parts, is the Goring Free Church, dated 1893, on the corner of Manor Road, still looking pretty fresh in this view only six years later. Little has changed in this view over the last century, apart from the traffic levels.

PANGBOURNE, WHITCHURCH BRIDGE 1890 27066

The Thames emerges from the Goring Gap at Pangbourne, and the valley widens out again. This view looks downstream from the riverside garden of Waterside House towards Whitchurch Bridge. This late Victorian iron bridge renewed a timber bridge erected in 1792 to replace a ferry, and is one of few surviving toll bridges (cars 10p).

PANGBOURNE, THE SWAN HOTEL 1890 27060
Frith's photographer swivelled his camera, while crossing the little River Pang which reaches the Thames here, and walked a few yards along the bank to capture this view back upstream towards the recently rebuilt weir. The Swan Inn, whose outbuilding close to the weir survives, claims to date back to 1642.

PANGBOURNE, WHITCHURCH LOCK c1955 P5039
The lock is only accessible by water, for it is cut off from Whitchurch by a backwater and house gardens: even the Thames Path misses the river here, only going through the churchyard. This view looks from the lock-keeper's cottage garden eastwards into the lock. The chestnut palings are now a smart well-trimmed beech hedge.

PANGBOURNE, THE VILLAGE 1893 31719

We are in the centre of the village; this view looks north along Church Street with the churchyard wall on the left. Sad to relate, the pines have now gone, and there are pavements to protect pedestrians from the surging traffic. The Cross Keys remains, but the two houses in the distance on either side of the High Street junction are now estate agents.

MAPLEDURHAM, THE LOCK 1890 27089

Moving downstream towards Reading we reach Mapledurham Lock. Although since this view was taken the lock, the footbridge, and the lock-keeper's cottage have all been rebuilt, it is still a tranquil stretch; the steam launch entering the lock may be similar to the one that towed the Three Men in a Boat through on their way upstream to Pangbourne.

MAPLEDURHAM, THE MILL 1890 27091

Mapledurham's old part-Tudor watermill survives; its waterwheel can be seen in this view. Apart from a lean-to added to the front, the building is remarkably unchanged; a lane leads into the superb village with its great Elizabethan mansion.

CAVERSHAM, THE BRIDGE 1904 52027

The Thames flows past Reading. The town centre is closer to the River Kennet, on its way to merge with the main river. Here from the Reading bank we look towards the 1869 iron Caversham bridge; it was demolished in 1924 to be replaced in 1926 by the present concrete one.

CAVERSHAM, THE CHURCH 1913 65923
This view shows the tower of St Peter's Church from the now much-municipalised Reading bank. The church tower was rebuilt in 1878. The mansion to the right amid the trees is Caversham Court, which was demolished in 1933; its 17th-century stable block remains, and the grounds are a most attractive public park.

CAVERSHAM, BRIDGE STREET 1908 59962
The Thames Valley Hotel on the left was built in 1891
and is now flats, while the Crown Hotel on the right was
rebuilt when the present bridge was constructed. The
1869 bridge seen here replaced an odd 18th-century
one: it was made of timber on the Berkshire south side
and stone on the Oxfordshire or Caversham side, owing
to a cross border disagreement.

CAVERSHAM, THE LOCK 1890 27105

Much in this view has changed since 1890: the mid 19th-century lock-keeper's cottage was rebuilt by the Thames Conservancy in 1931 and the area to the left has been built up with industrial buildings and boat repairers, while the lock itself has been substantially altered. To the right across a stream, fine plane trees planted in King's Meadow park now overhang the towpath.

SONNING, THE LOCK 1890 27159

About three miles downstream we reach Sonning Lock, seen here on a tranquil late summer's day. The lock has since been entirely reconstructed, and the lock-keeper's cottage, seen peeping from the trees, was rebuilt in 1916. Note the tall ladder leaning in the apple tree. To the right are the grounds of the Reading Blue Coat School which moved here in 1946.

SONNING, THE BRIDGE 1904 52035
Seen from the footbridge to the Oxfordshire bank, the eleven-arch bridge is an 18th-century one that carries a vast amount of traffic, for Sonning is in effect Reading's eastern by-pass. The Great House Hotel on the left is now much extended, and the church tower is largely concealed by more mature trees.

SONNING, THE VILLAGE 1904 52040
South of Thames Street the through traffic can be avoided. In this view we look down Pearson Street, with the High Street off to the left beyond the cart. The best house in this view is the one with the diagonal chimneystacks, The Grove: it is Tudor, with an 18th-century pink-washed facade and a superb Queen Anne door hood.

SHIPLAKE, THE MILL AND LOCK 1890 27167

As we reach Shiplake Lock, only the lock, albeit entirely reconstructed, survives in this view looking upstream to the lock. The large weatherboarded watermill was demolished around 1900 and only the mill house remained, just off the picture to the right. The waterwheel housing can be seen on the left wall of the mill.

WARGRAVE, FROM NEAR THE FERRY 1890 27173

The ferry has long gone, but this view from the Oxfordshire bank looking north-east captures the river's character well. To the right is the ferry slipway behind the St George and Dragon pub. The central trees hide Wargrave Manor with its parkland; further along the bank there are now a number of larger Edwardian and later houses.

WARGRAVE, THE VILLAGE 1890 27177
The photographer has captured a sleepy Thames-side village just on the point of modernising to meet new demands from the middle classes, who were building along the river and around the villages. A brand new terrace of shops on the left replace some cottages, and soon after 1890 the Greyhound and Burgis' stores were rebuilt more grandly.

HENLEY-ON-THAMES, THE REGATTA 1890 27203
The Henley Royal Regatta has become one of the key social occasions of the year, on a par with Royal Ascot and Wimbledon. Here, seen from near Poplar Point on the Berkshire bank, the eights race past the houseboats which lined the opposite bank to provide elegant floating grandstands for hospitality and shelter from the rain.

HENLEY-ON-THAMES, THE REGATTA 1890 27200

It all started when the Oxford and Cambridge Boat Race was held here in 1829, but the first Regatta proper was held in June 1839. This scene shows the 1890 crowds lining the course, which started at Temple Island in the distance. The Firs on the left, with its oriel window, is at the end of Riverside, now private parking for the hotel.

HENLEY-ON-THAMES, REGATTA DAY 1899 43017

Looking from Henley's superb river bridge of 1786 with keystones carved by Anne Seymour Damer with the heads of Isis and Thames, we see the boathouses at the east end of Riverside, which are still in use, and the houseboat grandstands. There are now two grandstands in the middle distance instead.

HENLEY-ON-THAMES, HART STREET 1893 31733

The photographer walked away from the river bridge up Hart Street towards the Town Hall in Market Place and turned back by the Bell Street junction to take this view towards the church with its dominating earlier 16th-century tower. All the buildings survive today, except for a tall half-timbered Barclays Bank of 1910 inserted on the right hand side.

MARLOW
From the Lock 1890

This view, taken from Lock Island, looks towards the beautiful suspension bridge and the 1832 parish church which replaced the medieval one. This old church had been regularly flooded, particularly after the pound lock was built in 1773, and it partly collapsed in 1831. Here we see the old spire of 1832, a curiously knobbly affair with gigantic crockets.

◆

MARLOW
The Weir 1901

Ten years after photograph No 23672, the church has its brand new spire, completed in 1899. This was designed by John Oldrid Scott, second son of the great Victorian architect, George Gilbert Scott, who built Clifton Hampden's bridge over the Thames further upstream, as well as St Pancras station and the Foreign Office in London.

MARLOW, FROM THE LOCK 1890 23672

MARLOW, THE WEIR 1901 47129

MARLOW, FROM THE LOCK 1901 47125
Marlow, and Henley further up river, were important inland ports
handling mainly the corn, malt and timber of the Chiltern Hills
behind them. Both are now prosperous middle-class towns, and the
ripe language of the former bargees, fishermen and wharfinger
inhabitants would not be welcome. This view has been a very popular
one with photographers and painters over the years.

MARLOW, THE EMBANKMENT c1955 M35024

Nowadays the bank is more formalised and the trees are fewer than in this view, which looks along the river bank north-east to the suspension bridge. This bridge, by William Tierney Clark, and opened in 1832, so impressed a visiting Hungarian nobleman that Clark was commissioned to built a larger one over the Danube to link Buda and Pest.

MARLOW, THE FISHERMAN'S RETREAT 1890 23690

We end this chapter in St Peter Street, which originally led to the old wooden bridge replaced by the present one further west. The tumbledown cottages, now long gone, were occupied by bargees, wharfingers, brewery labourers and others, while the Fisherman's Retreat, the house with the blinds, was popular with anglers and pleasure boaters, including Jerome K Jerome, who often stayed here.

COOKHAM, ODNEY COMMON 1925 77588

Downstream beyond Marlow the Thames reaches Cookham, where it blunders about and divides into three channels before turning south by chalk cliffs. This view is from Odney Common, an island along the north side of one of the channels, here named Lulle Brook. This view south is little changed, apart from a footbridge in the middle distance.

COOKHAM, THE MILL STREAM 1899 43029

As we look back towards Cookham from near the viewpoint of photograph No 77588 towards the bridge onto Odney, since rebuilt, the Thames is beyond the trees with its two channels. The northern one meanders past Hedsor Wharf, cut off by the Lock Cut of 1830. The Lulle Brook in the view is the third and southernmost channel.

COOKHAM, HIGH STREET 1925 77584

The village main street is little changed, although Bel and the Dragon on the right is no longer also a garage. To the left, just out of view, is the Stanley Spencer Gallery in the old Methodist chapel of 1846. This quirky artist is Cookham's famous son, being born at Fernlea further down the High Street in 1891 and buried in the churchyard.

MAIDENHEAD, THE FERRY AND THE COTTAGE 1906 54103

Past Cliveden is one of the most beautiful stretches of the Thames with its tree-clad river cliffs. Here, a little south of Cookham, is the My Lady Ferry with the lock-keeper's cottage on the far bank. Now defunct, it originally carried barge-towing horses to the opposite towpath; later it became more of a leisure ferry to Cliveden House on the plateau above.

MAIDENHEAD, BOULTERS LOCK BRIDGE 1906 54082

The artist Edward Gregory's famous painting 'Boulters Lock, Sunday Afternoon' superbly captured the cheerful, crowded chaos of a summer weekend, even featuring himself lounging in a boat. Starting it in 1882, he finished it only in 1897. He lived his last few years in Marlow, further upstream, and is buried in its churchyard.

MAIDENHEAD, BOULTERS LOCK 1906 54083

This Edwardian view at one of the Thames' most famous locks captures well the increasing affluence of the middle and lower middle classes; they flocked out of London in their thousands onto the river at weekends, hiring punts, skiffs, rowing boats, sailing boats and steam launches by the score. On Ascot Sunday 1888 over 800 boats and 72 steam launches passed through the lock.

MAIDENHEAD, BOULTERS LOCK 1913 65542
A little later, the year before the First World War started, the great boating craze of the later Victorian and Edwardian years is still in full swing. According to Jerome K Jerome, the oarsmen and punters loathed the steam launches and went out of their way to annoy them: this would mean an uneasy truce in the confines of the lock.

MAIDENHEAD, BOULTERS LOCK 1913 65543

The lock, first built in 1830 to cope with the six foot fall in the river, was rebuilt in 1912, the year before this view was taken. It has subsequently been rebuilt again, but the more elaborate balustered bridge of 1912 remains, replacing the one featured in Gregory's painting. The lock-keeper's cottage was partly rebuilt in 2000.

MAIDENHEAD, BOULTERS LOCK, THE ELEVATOR 1913 65545

These elevators were installed at a number of busy locks to cope with the vast numbers of small leisure boats spawned by the boating craze these views capture. The wooden elevator ramps have now long gone, but their concrete runways remain. The bridge has been rebuilt; on the right is the Boulters Lock Hotel, which is still thriving.

MAIDENHEAD, BRIDGE STREET 1890 23633

Poor old Maidenhead: a rather good Georgian coaching town on the old London to Bath road, it was overlaid by Victorian development after the railway arrived in 1841, and has really suffered from ring road and redevelopment mania in the 1960s. Here, looking towards the town centre, very little survives. The pub on the right, now Anthonia's Bistro, is one of few surviving reference points.

MAIDENHEAD, HIGH STREET 1911 63797

Here we see the flat-fronted Georgian buildings interspersed with Victorian and Edwardian ones that gave Maidenhead a distinctive character. The turreted and lead domed building of 1903, now Dorothy Perkins, survives, but the left hand one was replaced by a nine-storey monster office block, Berkshire House, and others were swept away in the vandalistic 1960s.

MAIDENHEAD, THE BRIDGE 1906 54099
Half a mile downstream the river passes through Sir Robert Taylor's supremely
graceful and beautiful sandstone bridge of the 1770s that still carries the busy A4
London to Bath road. For once, the balustraded parapets have not been interfered
with by over-zealous highway engineers, as at Staines. The buildings on the right
have been replaced by 1990s blocks of flats.

MAIDENHEAD, KING STREET 1904 52372

The north end of King Street has changed dramatically since 1904: the right hand side is mostly occupied by the backside of Tesco's, and on the left only The Rose pub, with the tall chimney, and the Methodist Church of 1859 beyond remain. This once busy road led to the Great Western Railway station further south.

WINDSOR, THE CASTLE FROM THE RIVER 1895 35368A

Frith's photographer could not resist one of the most photographed views along the Thames: Windsor Castle on its cliff-top towering above the town and river. The largest continuously inhabited medieval castle in the world, it covers thirteen acres. However, much of what we see now owes more to the 1820s; at that time George IV expended the then fabulous sum of £1,000,000.

WINDSOR, CASTLE HILL 1914 66981
Queen Victoria's Golden Jubilee statue of 1887 replaced a market cross, and emphasises the 'company town' nature of Royal Windsor, for the castle has been a royal residence since 1075. The keep (with the flagpole) was raised to three storeys and the outer walls and towers refaced in the 1820s: the walls still look remarkably fresh in 2000.

ETON, COLLEGE BARNES POOL 1923 74801
On the Buckinghamshire bank (since 1974 in Berkshire) Henry VI's great foundation, Eton College, has rendered this another 'company town'. Behind the hipped roofs of Corner House loom the pinnacles of Eton College chapel, built between 1449 and 1483. The morning-coated and top-hatted scholars stroll past Barnes Pool, rebuilt in 1930 in Neo-Georgian style.

ETON, FOURTH OF JUNE PROCESSION OF BOATS 1906 53724
Back at the river, this view shows the crowds watching the Procession of
College Boats, held every year on 4 June to commemorate George III's
birthday. The king took a keen interest in the College, and often crossed
the bridge to talk to scholars. The Etonians and their guests here throng
the Eton bank: toppers, Eton collars and ladies' floral hats aplenty.

WINDSOR, RIVERSIDE GARDENS 1906 53721

On the Windsor bank the non-Etonian spectators watch the Procession of College Boats. In the distance, lined with spectators, is the bridge, nowadays pedestrianised. There was a timber bridge here by 1172, but the present one with cast-iron spans dates from 1821. These Riverside Gardens have been reduced to a narrow stone walled strip to accommodate a widened Barry Avenue.

WINDSOR, ROMNEY LOCK 1906 53722

A little further downstream, Romney Lock gives excellent views of Eton College across the river. The lock has since been reconstructed and the lock-keeper's cottage was rebuilt in 1919. The Thames Path reaches the lock from Windsor via Romney Walk, sandwiched between the river and the railway which arrived at Windsor as a branch line in 1850.

STAINES, BELL WEIR LOCK 1907 58000

Below Old Windsor, the river reaches Runnymede, where in 1215 on an island now named Magna Carta Island, King John signed the great charter, widely regarded as the foundation of English liberty. Past it is Bell Weir Lock, now reconstructed, as is the weir on the right: it used to have a pitched roof structure to protect the weir machinery.

STAINES, THE BRIDGE 1907 57990

This view looks downstream from the Egham bank. The refined and somewhat austere rusticated three-arch bridge of 1829-32 by John Rennie, the architect of old Waterloo Bridge, has been marred by a widening in 1958 in which footways were cantilevered from each side and Rennie's simple solid parapets replaced by skinny railings. The ABC cinema now fills the skyline above the left hand arch.

STAINES, VIEW FROM THE BRIDGE 1907 57991

As we pass beneath the bridge, still on the Egham bank, the 18th-century Swan Hotel on the right now also occupies the boathouse and garage in front of it, behind the ladies with their parasols. On the left is the roof of Staines' Town Hall, a dull building dated 1880. The chimney and works of William Ridley and Sons has now gone.

STAINES, THE RIVER 1907 57993

A little further downstream, just through the railway bridge, the view down river from the Staines bank has changed; now there is extensive housing development on both banks, much fortunately still hidden by riverside trees. The fences on the left belong to the back gardens of houses in Laleham Road, a Victorian and Edwardian expansion of the town.

STAINES, HIGH STREET 1907 57995

Staines was formerly in Middlesex. It is an ancient town with a medieval layout and a wide gently curving High Street, now mainly pedestrianised. Most of the right hand side has been rebuilt, but The Angel on the left survives (albeit with fake timber-framing), as does the tall twin-gabled building next to it of 1873. Beyond, survival is more patchy.

WALTON-ON-THAMES, THE ANGLERS 1908 60037

As Jerome K Jerome observed, 'only the tiniest corner of it (Walton on Thames) comes down to the river'. Here, as we look downstream by the former ferry and towpath, working barges mingle with leisure rowing boats for hire. Beyond is the Swan's garden, then boathouses (now the Boathouse Gallery); the sheds have been replaced by The Anglers pub, probably built about 1910.

WALTON-ON-THAMES, THE BOATHOUSE 1899　43040

WALTON-ON-THAMES
The Boathouse 1899
Downstream, past Weybridge, the Desborough Cut of 1935 by-passes a winding loop, to reach Walton-on-Thames. Beyond Walton Bridge is this boathouse and its harbour inlet off the river, here charmingly informal. It is now Walton Marina, with an emphasis on cabin cruisers rather than punts. The building survives, clad in plastic weatherboarding, but the banks have been sheet-piled and denuded of trees.

TEDDINGTON
The Bridge 1899
As every schoolchild knows (or used to), the tidal Thames finishes at Teddington. The main river is crossed by this spindly-looking suspension bridge of 1888, seen here from the lock island. To the left of The Anglers, out of view, are the famous Teddington TV Studios, while the boathouse to the right is the home of the British Motor Yacht Club.

TEDDINGTON, THE BRIDGE 1899　43051

TEDDINGTON, THE LOCK AND THE ROLLERS 1899 43054

Seen from the north end of the lock island are the boat rollers, now disused, then the narrow skiff lock, nicknamed 'The Coffin', and then a further two locks, both now rebuilt. The main lock is vast, 650 feet long, and designed to accommodate eight Thames barges and a steam tug. A footbridge carries pedestrians across the lock.

TWICKENHAM, FROM THE ISLAND BOAT HOUSE 1890 23534

This and photograph No 23535 are taken from Eel Pie Island, apparently named after the famous pies sold at the Island Tavern. Here the photographer looks towards St Mary's 14th-century church tower, with the triangular pediment of the Georgian nave, designed in 1714 by John James, to its right. The church is now more visible, for the house in front has since been demolished.

TWICKENHAM, KING STREET 1909 T91001
This view of King Street looks east towards the grand Portland stone bank at its end. Built as the London and Provincial Bank, this Palladian-style Edwardian building is now a Barclays Bank; it is more visible now, as the right hand buildings were demolished and rebuilt further back to allow King Street to be widened.

TWICKENHAM, THE ISLAND 1890 23535

This view, from the footbridge onto the Island, is a photograph of what has passed - for all to the left of the sash-windowed and pedimented house on the right was cleared away in the 1950s. To get your bearings, the road behind the slipway is Water Lane. It is regrettable that little of coherence or merit has replaced any of it.

RICHMOND, MESSUMS BOATYARD 1899 43741

As we approach Richmond, this view from the west bank looks towards the Petersham Road across to the former Messum's Boatyard. All survives, including the terrace of boathouses and the central building, now reduced to two storeys by the removal of the weatherboarded upper storey; it is now the Richmond Canoe Club. The gabled Three Pigeons to its right is now derelict.

RICHMOND, FROM THE BRIDGE 1899 43739

Beyond the scrum of pleasure boats for hire in this view looking downstream from Richmond Bridge is the three-storeyed White Cross pub. The area between the White Cross and the photographer is now occupied by Richmond Riverside, a splendid collection of 1980s Georgian-style office blocks by Quinlan Terry above a zig-zag of ramped terraces down to the embankment.

RICHMOND, THE BRIDGE 1890 23544
Looking back upstream past the boathouses in front of
the 1830s St Helena Terrace and The White Cross, we
see a fine view of Richmond Bridge, which dates from
the 1770s and is one of the Thames' finest Georgian
bridges. Beyond the bridge the skyline is now
dominated by the vast Neo-Georgian Star and Garter
Home for disabled ex-servicemen, built in 1921.

RICHMOND, THREE BRIDGES 1899 43738

Downstream from the town, the photographer looks back to the Richmond Half-Tide Weir and Footbridge. There are boat rollers by the Isleworth bank on the right, and Richmond Lock is on the left. This and the stylish pedestrian bridge date from 1892-4. Between this and the 1848 railway bridge beyond is now Twickenham Bridge of 1930, in effect the Richmond by-pass.

KEW GARDENS 1899 43757

Between Richmond and Kew, on the Surrey bank, are the three hundred acres of the Royal Botanical Gardens, opened to the public in 1841. Besides the botanical collections there are a number of superb buildings, including Sir William Chambers' Chinese Pagoda of 1761 and Decimus Burton's stupendous Palm House of the 1840s, which is 360 feet long and partly 62 feet high. It is astonishingly simple and pure architecture for its date.

HAMMERSMITH, THE BRIDGE c1965 H387019

The Thames is now flowing into London proper, and we reach Hammersmith, with its monumentally-scaled iron bridge. This replaced William Tierney Clark's suspension bridge of 1827, a smaller version of which survives across the Thames at Marlow. The current one, now painted a tasteful green with architectural ornament picked out in gold, is by Sir Joseph Bazalgette and is dated 1887.

HAMMERSMITH, THE BRIDGE c1965 H387014

We meet Bazalgette later at the Embankment in central London; seen here from the Barnes bank towpath, his suspension bridge has a 420-foot main span, and the towers are finished with French-style pavilion roofs, all in sheet iron. Beyond the left tower are the tower blocks of the Queen Caroline Estate, and to the right the BBC's Riverside Studios.

HAMMERSMITH, THE PIER c1965 H387003

The photographer looks west from Hammersmith Bridge along Lower Mall, a good jumble of 18th-, 19th- and 20th-century building, including the well-known Doves pub. Beyond the pier is Upper Mall where William Morris lived from 1878 to 1896, naming his Georgian terrace house, number 26, Kelmscott House after his country house in Oxfordshire.

LONDON, CHELSEA 1890 L130084
Further along the north bank the Thames passes Chelsea's Cheyne Walk. The pavilion roofs on the right were once Lindsey House of 1684, subsequently owned by the Moravian Sect, who added the French mansard roofs. In 1774 it was subdivided into five houses. Bomb damage removed the buildings left of the white stucco, which were to be replaced by the Cremorne Estate in the 1950s.

LONDON, CHELSEA EMBANKMENT 1890 L130091
This is a much changed view: the working barges have gone, to be replaced by ranks of houseboats. The buildings in the foreground and the far left have gone, although the mansard roof of Lindsey House can be seen beyond the stuccoed M-roof. This area is now part of the Chelsea Embankment, part of which opened in 1874.

LONDON, CHELSEA EMBANKMENT 1890 L130083

LONDON
Chelsea Embankment 1890

This is an evocative view of a long-dead Chelsea, with sailing vessels moored along the Embankment, one apparently with a cargo of hay. These types of boats have now been replaced by the brightly painted houseboats which are so characteristic of the Chelsea scene.

LONDON
The Houses of Parliament c1890

Further down the Thames are the Houses of Parliament - or rather, the Palace of Westminster. This replaced the old palace, which burned down in 1834. The major difference between then and now are the then heaving commercial wharves and warehouses coming right up to the foot of the Victoria Tower: these produced interesting smells in summer, no doubt.

LONDON, THE HOUSES OF PARLIAMENT c1890 L130277

LONDON, THE HOUSES OF PARLIAMENT 1908 L130149
By this time the wharves have been cleared away to create Victoria Embankment Garden, a more fitting context for the Mother of Parliaments, rebuilt in Gothic style between 1839 and 1860 by Pugin and Sir Charles Barry. Beyond Victoria Tower is the great royal abbey, Westminster Abbey, with its pair of west towers and the centrepiece of the medieval palace, along with Westminster Hall.

LONDON, WESTMINSTER BRIDGE, THE DIAMOND JUBILEE PROCESSION 1897 L130219
This remarkable and historic view from high on the Houses of Parliament shows Queen Victoria's open landau leading the procession across Westminster Bridge. All the buildings on the Lambeth side have gone: County Hall, begun in 1912, is now a Marriott Hotel and aquarium, and to the left is the London Eye, the giant ferris wheel for the Millennium.

LONDON, THE HOUSES OF PARLIAMENT 1890 L.130162
From the south bank, near Westminster Bridge, completed in 1862, this view shows the bell tower known universally by its great bell, Big Ben. To the right of the bridge, the steep-roofed buildings have recently been replaced by architecturally exciting MPs offices; to the right is now Norman Shaw's 1890-1906 New Scotland Yard, with its tourelles and brick and stone bands.

LONDON, THAMES EMBANKMENT 1890 L130189

Moving east, this view looks along the Embankment from Charing Cross Bridge to Cleopatra's Needle, an Egyptian obelisk of 1500 BC, given to Britain in 1819 by the Viceroy of Egypt, but only erected here in 1878 following a hair-raising sea voyage. The Savoy Hotel is to its left, which opened the previous year.

LONDON, WATERLOO BRIDGE 1895 L130052

Apart from the wintry ice of a semi-frozen Thames, this view from Savoy Pier shows the old Waterloo Bridge, which was designed by Sir John Rennie and completed in 1817. It was a bridge of great beauty, with pairs of Greek Doric columns to each pier. Unfortunately, in 1936 it was demolished, to be replaced by the present elegant concrete bridge completed in 1942.

LONDON, THE EMBANKMENT FROM TEMPLE PIER 1890 L130077

The Embankment, with its dolphin lampposts dated 1870, is by Bazalgette; in fact it hides the great sewers he built to collect London's effluent and take it further east to rid the city of its appalling cholera epidemics and other diseases - previously the effluent was discharged directly into the Thames. Bazalgette also designed the Temple Pier and its arch of 1868.

LONDON, BLACKFRIARS BRIDGE 1890 L130070

Taken from the Southwark side, this photograph gives a fine view of St Paul's Cathedral, Sir Christopher Wren's Baroque masterpiece (1675-1711) which replaced the medieval cathedral destroyed in the Great Fire of 1666. Nowadays, to the left beyond the cathedral are the tower blocks of the Barbican, completed in 1981. Blackfriars Bridge, dated 1869, screens the now part-demolished railway bridge of 1864.

LONDON, LONDON BRIDGE c1880 L1303429
Further east is yet another bridge by John Rennie, this time father and son. Completed in 1831, it replaced the 12th-century one of nursery rhyme fame, which had only had its houses finally removed in 1762 and lasted for over six centuries. Demolished in 1968, this London Bridge was re-erected in the USA at Lake Huvasu City in Arizona.

LONDON, ST PAUL'S CATHEDRAL 1890 L130126

From the south bank the photographer looks across to Queenhithe dock. Although the river bank is relatively unchanged, all the riverside buildings have gone, the last only in 1996. Beyond is the noble dome of St Paul's Cathedral, while behind the photographer Shakespeare's Globe Theatre has recently been entirely reconstructed, and the massive Bankside Power Station of 1960 is being converted for the Tate Gallery.

LONDON, LONDON BRIDGE 1904 L130178

Here the 1903 widening of the bridge has just been completed, hence the pristine stonework. All to the left on the north bank, apart from the grand pedimented and columned Fishmongers Hall of 1831 near the bridge, has now gone. To the right the tower of Wren's St Magnus the Martyr, and The Monument, erected where the Great Fire of 1666 started, are glimpsed between later office blocks.

LONDON, THE TOWER OF LONDON c1955 L1305022

As we look from Tower Bridge, the dominance of William the Conqueror's White Tower keep, dating from the late 11th century and still the focus of the castle, is now somewhat reduced by office blocks, including the 600 foot high 1970s NatWest Tower and the bizarre 1980s Minster Court. The other tower in this view is the former Port of London Authority building, Edwardian Baroque completed in 1922.

LONDON, THE OPENING OF TOWER BRIDGE 1894 L130019

The bridge was authorised by Act of Parliament in 1885 and opened in 1894. The bascules carrying the roadway are in their fully raised position to allow tall-masted ships and sailing barges to pass through, giving a clearance of 140 feet and a width of 200 feet. The boats dressed overall with signal flags have just passed through.

LONDON, TOWER BRIDGE UNDER CONSTRUCTION 1890 L130050
This murky view looks west from the Pool of London towards what was to become one
of the mechanical wonders of the late 19th century. Here we see the towers - 'steel
skeletons clothed in stone' as described by Sir John Wolfe Barry, the architect - not yet
stone clad, and the upper walkway taking shape.

LONDON, TOWER BRIDGE 1896 L130519

The bustling wharves include Billingsgate on the left, and show why the Tower Bridge design was necessary for masted ships to gain access to this part of the river. Nowadays the biggest ship hereabouts is the light cruiser HMS 'Belfast', a floating World War II museum, moored on the right hand side, while the bridge opens relatively rarely.

LONDON, TOWER BRIDGE 1910 L130058

This photograph was taken from the west. Tower Bridge has become a virtual symbol of London, and it is certainly a very striking and remarkable structure. There are lifts in the towers, for the original idea was for pedestrians to use the high level footways when the bridge was raised by hydraulic machinery. Fascinating technically to civil engineers, the bridge is beautiful to look at for the rest of us.

LONDON, THAMES SHIPBUILDING c1910 L130056

This chapter opens with some views of a long-lost industrial Thames. Here we see workers arriving by boat at one of the ship-building yards that once dotted the eastern banks; these included the great Millwall Yards, which launched among others Brunel's 'Great Eastern' in 1857. In crisis by 1900, the last yards closed a couple of years after this view was taken.

LONDON, OLD FERRY WHARF 1890 L130085

All along the Thames, and described powerfully by Charles Dickens, houses, inns and tenements tottered and decayed in places such as Deptford, Wapping and Shadwell. Those that survive are now very expensive and desirable riverside houses, and a far cry from their squalid past. You can get an idea of a (non-squalid) riverside house by visiting the Prospect of Whitby pub in Wapping.

LONDON, THE DOCKS c1965 L1305174

The port of London held the absolute key to Britain's stupendous 19th-century industrial wealth. From 1799 onwards the docks east of the Tower of London were dug, becoming one of the industrial wonders of the world and a tourist attraction! Here we see the docks near the end of their life; closures started soon after, with the last docks closing in 1981.

LONDON, THAMES WHARF 1910 L130057

Besides the vast acreage of excavated docks, there were numerous riverside wharfs, from the grandeur of Hay's Wharf near London Bridge to this rather less grand one near the west entrance to the Royal Victoria Dock. All contributed to make London the busiest port in the world: this era is long past, for now Docklands is all smart housing, flats and offices, symbolically dominated by the 850-foot-high Canary Wharf office tower.

ERITH, THE THAMES c1955 E58022

Moving into the Thames Estuary, the river passes Erith, a much rebuilt and rather forlorn remnant with its medieval church of St John the Baptist; the town is now joined by development inland to Bexley. Here in the 1950s ships still pass on their way to and from the Port of London; this view is from the William Corey Promenade, as it is now called, close to the High Street.

GRAVESEND, HMS 'GLEANER' 1902 49043

Anchored off Gravesend is the torpedo gunboat HMS 'Gleaner', built at Sheerness Dockyard in 1890 and sold off in 1905; by that time the faster torpedo boat destroyer, later abbreviated to destroyer, had superceded it. Sheerness, founded in 1665, closed in 1960, and Chatham Dockyards, founded in the 16th century, in 1984, finally severing the Royal Navy's connection with the Thames Estuary.

GRAVESEND, THE PARADE 1902 49042
We are keeping to the Kent bank of the Thames Estuary as the river reaches Gravesend, beyond the Queen Elizabeth II Bridge at Dartford. The town is now greatly expanded inland, but the core of this ancient port is still recognisable around the two piers and the Georgian parish church. Here, in a view now much changed, the photographer looks east towards the town piers and jetties.

GRAVESEND, THE FERRY 1902 49044

Gravesend has two Victorian piers: the Royal Terrace Pier of 1843 lies to the east of the slightly later Town Pier we see in this view. Reached via a cobbled yard in front of The Three Saws pub, and visually obstructed by the high sea wall, the pier is somewhat run down, unlike the Royal Terrace Pier. The Wealdway long distance footpath now starts here.

SHEERNESS, THE ESPLANADE AND BEACH c1955 S528048

East of Gravesend, near where the Thames Estuary meets the North Sea, is Sheerness, a port and seaside resort on the north-west corner of the Isle of Sheppey. Here the funfair and amusement park buildings have been replaced by a new Amusement Park and, behind, a Tesco's, while the sea embankment has also been rebuilt and raised.

GRAYS, THE DARTFORD TUNNEL 1963 G85045

We are now on the north or Essex bank of the Thames Estuary. This rather quaint view shows the then 'up to the minute' toll booths of the newly-opened Dartford Tunnel. Since then and the completion of the M25, the twin tunnels are one way; vehicles crossing from the Essex side use the graceful Queen Elizabeth II suspension bridge which soars above the river.

GRAYS, THE RIVER c1955 G85032

This view captures well the character of much of the Thames estuary: a somewhat bleak, flat shoreline and a smudge of distant chalk hills on the Kent side. Shipping in the roads lies off a somewhat forlorn Grays riverside park, complete with a boating pool and, here, a few benches; along all the estuary, high concrete flood barrier walls now obstruct long views.

GRAYS, THE LIGHTSHIP c1955 G85034

Grays is a much re-developed town, but it has a fine Norman church. South of the town, a long-redundant lightship lies on the slipway near Argent Street; its light was hauled up to the masthead on cables. It is remarkable that it still survives, albeit moved a hundred yards west to the other side of the Thurrock Yacht Club, where it continues to moulder gently on the beach.

TILBURY, THE FERRY c1960 T114027

A little further east along the Essex shore our photographer reaches Tilbury and continues his maritime theme; he firmly turned his back on the remarkable 1670s Tilbury Fort, built by a Dutch engineer to defend the Thames against his own countrymen and the French. Here, the Neo-Georgian harbour buildings with their cupola are seen beyond the landing stages.

TILBURY, THE FERRY c1960 T114001
Sir Edwin Cooper designed the landing stage, baggage halls and offices in the late 1920s; the end of them can be seen on the left. The current Gravesend ferry sails from the right quay, and the harbour buildings are now the London International Cruise Terminal; the great modern container port that supplanted the London Docks are to the west.

SOUTHEND, THE BEACH 1898 40912
There are still remnants of Southend's more select era when it became a fashionable seaside resort after 1791: Royal Terrace and the Royal Hotel, for example. The railway arrived in the 1850s, and Southend expanded rapidly. This view captures its earlier atmosphere, including bathing machines; the gigantic, coarse Palace Hotel of 1901 behind the pier had not yet been built.

SOUTHEND, THE PIER 1898 41377

Southend is proud of its pier, which is over a mile long and has its own railway. The pier opened in 1889, but lost these rather elegant buildings in the 1920s for stylised Art Deco ones. The pier is now flanked by large areas of reclaimed land on which sit a brash funfair and amusement park, Peter Pan's Adventure Island.

SOUTHEND, THE BEACH 1898 40911

Much of this view looking west from the pier is now dry land occupied by the west part of Adventure Island, while Never Never Land lies amid the now much thinned trees on the right. Southend was immensely popular with the lower middle and working classes from north and East London: none of the genteel pretensions of an Eastbourne here.

SOUTHEND, THE SEAFRONT 1898   41382

This view looks east from the pier: excursion sailing boats are waiting for trade. Several of the mid and later 19th-century stucco terrace buildings remain, interspersed with garish work like the Electric Avenue 1990s revamp. Further east is The Kursaal of 1902 with a big dome. The foreground is now the east part of Peter Pan's Adventure Island amusement park.

SHOEBURYNESS, WEST BEACH c1955   S275007

East of Southend, the Thames meets the North Sea at Shoeburyness and its long journey ends. Here, on a sunny 1950s summer's day, the shingle West Beach is crowded; in the distance is Southend and its pier. The view is now changed, with 1960s tower blocks of flats on the skyline. Shoeburyness is now the eastern part of a 'Greater Southend'.

Index

Frith Book Co Titles

www.francisfrith.co.uk

The Frith Book Company publishes over 100 new titles each year. A selection of those currently available are listed below. For latest catalogue please contact Frith Book Co.

Town Books 96 pages, approx 100 photos. County and Themed Books 128 pages, approx 150 photos (unless specified). All titles hardback laminated case and jacket except those indicated pb (paperback)

Amersham, Chesham & Rickmansworth (pb)			Derby (pb)	1-85937-367-4	£9.99
	1-85937-340-2	£9.99	Derbyshire (pb)	1-85937-196-5	£9.99
Ancient Monuments & Stone Circles	1-85937-143-4	£17.99	Devon (pb)	1-85937-297-x	£9.99
Aylesbury (pb)	1-85937-227-9	£9.99	Dorset (pb)	1-85937-269-4	£9.99
Bakewell	1-85937-113-2	£12.99	Dorset Churches	1-85937-172-8	£17.99
Barnstaple (pb)	1-85937-300-3	£9.99	Dorset Coast (pb)	1-85937-299-6	£9.99
Bath (pb)	1-85937419-0	£9.99	Dorset Living Memories	1-85937-210-4	£14.99
Bedford (pb)	1-85937-205-8	£9.99	Down the Severn	1-85937-118-3	£14.99
Berkshire (pb)	1-85937-191-4	£9.99	Down the Thames (pb)	1-85937-278-3	£9.99
Berkshire Churches	1-85937-170-1	£17.99	Down the Trent	1-85937-311-9	£14.99
Blackpool (pb)	1-85937-382-8	£9.99	Dublin (pb)	1-85937-231-7	£9.99
Bognor Regis (pb)	1-85937-431-x	£9.99	East Anglia (pb)	1-85937-265-1	£9.99
Bournemouth	1-85937-067-5	£12.99	East London	1-85937-080-2	£14.99
Bradford (pb)	1-85937-204-x	£9.99	East Sussex	1-85937-130-2	£14.99
Brighton & Hove(pb)	1-85937-192-2	£8.99	Eastbourne	1-85937-061-6	£12.99
Bristol (pb)	1-85937-264-3	£9.99	Edinburgh (pb)	1-85937-193-0	£8.99
British Life A Century Ago (pb)	1-85937-213-9	£9.99	England in the 1880s	1-85937-331-3	£17.99
Buckinghamshire (pb)	1-85937-200-7	£9.99	English Castles (pb)	1-85937-434-4	£9.99
Camberley (pb)	1-85937-222-8	£9.99	English Country Houses	1-85937-161-2	£17.99
Cambridge (pb)	1-85937-422-0	£9.99	Essex (pb)	1-85937-270-8	£9.99
Cambridgeshire (pb)	1-85937-420-4	£9.99	Exeter	1-85937-126-4	£12.99
Canals & Waterways (pb)	1-85937-291-0	£9.99	Exmoor	1-85937-132-9	£14.99
Canterbury Cathedral (pb)	1-85937-179-5	£9.99	Falmouth	1-85937-066-7	£12.99
Cardiff (pb)	1-85937-093-4	£9.99	Folkestone (pb)	1-85937-124-8	£9.99
Carmarthenshire	1-85937-216-3	£14.99	Glasgow (pb)	1-85937-190-6	£9.99
Chelmsford (pb)	1-85937-310-0	£9.99	Gloucestershire	1-85937-102-7	£14.99
Cheltenham (pb)	1-85937-095-0	£9.99	Great Yarmouth (pb)	1-85937-426-3	£9.99
Cheshire (pb)	1-85937-271-6	£9.99	Greater Manchester (pb)	1-85937-266-x	£9.99
Chester	1-85937-090-x	£12.99	Guildford (pb)	1-85937-410-7	£9.99
Chesterfield	1-85937-378-x	£9.99	Hampshire (pb)	1-85937-279-1	£9.99
Chichester (pb)	1-85937-228-7	£9.99	Hampshire Churches (pb)	1-85937-207-4	£9.99
Colchester (pb)	1-85937-188-4	£8.99	Harrogate	1-85937-423-9	£9.99
Cornish Coast	1-85937-163-9	£14.99	Hastings & Bexhill (pb)	1-85937-131-0	£9.99
Cornwall (pb)	1-85937-229-5	£9.99	Heart of Lancashire (pb)	1-85937-197-3	£9.99
Cornwall Living Memories	1-85937-248-1	£14.99	Helston (pb)	1-85937-214-7	£9.99
Cotswolds (pb)	1-85937-230-9	£9.99	Hereford (pb)	1-85937-175-2	£9.99
Cotswolds Living Memories	1-85937-255-4	£14.99	Herefordshire	1-85937-174-4	£14.99
County Durham	1-85937-123-x	£14.99	Hertfordshire (pb)	1-85937-247-3	£9.99
Croydon Living Memories	1-85937-162-0	£9.99	Horsham (pb)	1-85937-432-8	£9.99
Cumbria	1-85937-101-9	£14.99	Humberside	1-85937-215-5	£14.99
Dartmoor	1-85937-145-0	£14.99	Hythe, Romney Marsh & Ashford	1-85937-256-2	£9.99

Available from your local bookshop or from the publisher

Frith Book Co Titles (continued)

Title	ISBN	Price	Title	ISBN	Price
Ipswich (pb)	1-85937-424-7	£9.99	St Ives (pb)	1-85937415-8	£9.99
Ireland (pb)	1-85937-181-7	£9.99	Scotland (pb)	1-85937-182-5	£9.99
Isle of Man (pb)	1-85937-268-6	£9.99	Scottish Castles (pb)	1-85937-323-2	£9.99
Isles of Scilly	1-85937-136-1	£14.99	Sevenoaks & Tunbridge	1-85937-057-8	£12.99
Isle of Wight (pb)	1-85937-429-8	£9.99	Sheffield, South Yorks (pb)	1-85937-267-8	£9.99
Isle of Wight Living Memories	1-85937-304-6	£14.99	Shrewsbury (pb)	1-85937-325-9	£9.99
Kent (pb)	1-85937-189-2	£9.99	Shropshire (pb)	1-85937-326-7	£9.99
Kent Living Memories	1-85937-125-6	£14.99	Somerset	1-85937-153-1	£14.99
Lake District (pb)	1-85937-275-9	£9.99	South Devon Coast	1-85937-107-8	£14.99
Lancaster, Morecambe & Heysham (pb)	1-85937-233-3	£9.99	South Devon Living Memories	1-85937-168-x	£14.99
Leeds (pb)	1-85937-202-3	£9.99	South Hams	1-85937-220-1	£14.99
Leicester	1-85937-073-x	£12.99	Southampton (pb)	1-85937-427-1	£9.99
Leicestershire (pb)	1-85937-185-x	£9.99	Southport (pb)	1-85937-425-5	£9.99
Lincolnshire (pb)	1-85937-433-6	£9.99	Staffordshire	1-85937-047-0	£12.99
Liverpool & Merseyside (pb)	1-85937-234-1	£9.99	Stratford upon Avon	1-85937-098-5	£12.99
London (pb)	1-85937-183-3	£9.99	Suffolk (pb)	1-85937-221-x	£9.99
Ludlow (pb)	1-85937-176-0	£9.99	Suffolk Coast	1-85937-259-7	£14.99
Luton (pb)	1-85937-235-x	£9.99	Surrey (pb)	1-85937-240-6	£9.99
Maidstone	1-85937-056-x	£14.99	Sussex (pb)	1-85937-184-1	£9.99
Manchester (pb)	1-85937-198-1	£9.99	Swansea (pb)	1-85937-167-1	£9.99
Middlesex	1-85937-158-2	£14.99	Tees Valley & Cleveland	1-85937-211-2	£14.99
New Forest	1-85937-128-0	£14.99	Thanet (pb)	1-85937-116-7	£9.99
Newark (pb)	1-85937-366-6	£9.99	Tiverton (pb)	1-85937-178-7	£9.99
Newport, Wales (pb)	1-85937-258-9	£9.99	Torbay	1-85937-063-2	£12.99
Newquay (pb)	1-85937-421-2	£9.99	Truro	1-85937-147-7	£12.99
Norfolk (pb)	1-85937-195-7	£9.99	Victorian and Edwardian Cornwall	1-85937-252-x	£14.99
Norfolk Living Memories	1-85937-217-1	£14.99	Victorian & Edwardian Devon	1-85937-253-8	£14.99
Northamptonshire	1-85937-150-7	£14.99	Victorian & Edwardian Kent	1-85937-149-3	£14.99
Northumberland Tyne & Wear (pb)	1-85937-281-3	£9.99	Vic & Ed Maritime Album	1-85937-144-2	£17.99
North Devon Coast	1-85937-146-9	£14.99	Victorian and Edwardian Sussex	1-85937-157-4	£14.99
North Devon Living Memories	1-85937-261-9	£14.99	Victorian & Edwardian Yorkshire	1-85937-154-x	£14.99
North London	1-85937-206-6	£14.99	Victorian Seaside	1-85937-159-0	£17.99
North Wales (pb)	1-85937-298-8	£9.99	Villages of Devon (pb)	1-85937-293-7	£9.99
North Yorkshire (pb)	1-85937-236-8	£9.99	Villages of Kent (pb)	1-85937-294-5	£9.99
Norwich (pb)	1-85937-194-9	£8.99	Villages of Sussex (pb)	1-85937-295-3	£9.99
Nottingham (pb)	1-85937-324-0	£9.99	Warwickshire (pb)	1-85937-203-1	£9.99
Nottinghamshire (pb)	1-85937-187-6	£9.99	Welsh Castles (pb)	1-85937-322-4	£9.99
Oxford (pb)	1-85937-411-5	£9.99	West Midlands (pb)	1-85937-289-9	£9.99
Oxfordshire (pb)	1-85937-430-1	£9.99	West Sussex	1-85937-148-5	£14.99
Peak District (pb)	1-85937-280-5	£9.99	West Yorkshire (pb)	1-85937-201-5	£9.99
Penzance	1-85937-069-1	£12.99	Weymouth (pb)	1-85937-209-0	£9.99
Peterborough (pb)	1-85937-219-8	£9.99	Wiltshire (pb)	1-85937-277-5	£9.99
Piers	1-85937-237-6	£17.99	Wiltshire Churches (pb)	1-85937-171-x	£9.99
Plymouth	1-85937-119-1	£12.99	Wiltshire Living Memories	1-85937-245-7	£14.99
Poole & Sandbanks (pb)	1-85937-251-1	£9.99	Winchester (pb)	1-85937-428-x	£9.99
Preston (pb)	1-85937-212-0	£9.99	Windmills & Watermills	1-85937-242-2	£17.99
Reading (pb)	1-85937-238-4	£9.99	Worcester (pb)	1-85937-165-5	£9.99
Romford (pb)	1-85937-319-4	£9.99	Worcestershire	1-85937-152-3	£14.99
Salisbury (pb)	1-85937-239-2	£9.99	York (pb)	1-85937-199-x	£9.99
Scarborough (pb)	1-85937-379-8	£9.99	Yorkshire (pb)	1-85937-186-8	£9.99
St Albans (pb)	1-85937-341-0	£9.99	Yorkshire Living Memories	1-85937-166-3	£14.99

See Frith books on the internet www.francisfrith.co.uk

FRITH PRODUCTS & SERVICES

Francis Frith would doubtless be pleased to know that the pioneering publishing venture he started in 1860 still continues today. A hundred and forty years later, The Francis Frith Collection continues in the same innovative tradition and is now one of the foremost publishers of vintage photographs in the world. Some of the current activities include:

Interior Decoration

Today Frith's photographs can be seen framed and as giant wall murals in thousands of pubs, restaurants, hotels, banks, retail stores and other public buildings throughout the country. In every case they enhance the unique local atmosphere of the places they depict and provide reminders of gentler days in an increasingly busy and frenetic world.

Product Promotions

Frith products are used by many major companies to promote the sales of their own products or to reinforce their own history and heritage. Frith promotions have been used by Hovis bread, Courage beers, Scots Porage Oats, Colman's mustard, Cadbury's foods, Mellow Birds coffee, Dunhill pipe tobacco, Guinness, and Bulmer's Cider.

Genealogy and Family History

As the interest in family history and roots grows world-wide, more and more people are turning to Frith's photographs of Great Britain for images of the towns, villages and streets where their ancestors lived; and, of course, photographs of the churches and chapels where their ancestors were christened, married and buried are an essential part of every genealogy tree and family album.

Frith Products

All Frith photographs are available Framed or just as Mounted Prints and Posters (size 23 x 16 inches). These may be ordered from the address below. From time to time other products - Address Books, Calendars, Table Mats, etc - are available.

The Internet

Already twenty thousand Frith photographs can be viewed and purchased on the internet through the Frith websites and a myriad of partner sites.

For more detailed information on Frith companies and products, look at these sites:

www.francisfrith.co.uk
www.francisfrith.com
(for North American visitors)

See the complete list of Frith Books at:

www.francisfrith.co.uk

This web site is regularly updated with the latest list of publications from the Frith Book Company. If you wish to buy books relating to another part of the country that your local bookshop does not stock, you may purchase on-line.

For further information, trade, or author enquiries please contact us at the address below:
The Francis Frith Collection, Frith's Barn, Teffont, Salisbury, Wiltshire, England SP3 5QP.
Tel: +44 (0)1722 716 376 Fax: +44 (0)1722 716 881 Email: sales@francisfrith.co.uk

See Frith books on the internet www.francisfrith.co.uk